TARIFF REFO

1860

TARIFF REFORM IN FRANCE 1860–1900

The Politics of Economic Interest

MICHAEL STEPHEN SMITH

CORNELL UNIVERSITY PRESS

ITHACA AND LONDON

Cornell University Press gratefully acknowledges a grant from the Andrew W. Mellon Foundation that aided in bringing this book to publication.

First published 1980 by Cornell University Press.
Published in the United Kingdom by Cornell University Press Ltd.,
2–4 Brook Street, London W1Y 1AA.

International Standard Book Number 0-8014-1257-9
Library of Congress Catalog Card Number 79-25272
Printed in the United States of America
Librarians: Library of Congress cataloging information appears on the last page of the book.

For
Carol

Contents

Preface

The tariff was a major issue among French businessmen, politicians, and civil servants throughout the nineteenth century, and the tariff policies formulated late in the century have had an unquestionable impact on the economic development of modern France (although historians do not agree on whether that impact has been positive or negative).[1] Reflecting its importance, the story of French tariff politics in the years 1860–1900 has been told many times. Unfortunately, most of the accounts have been erroneous or misleading in that they have exaggerated the commitment of French government and business to high protection, have wrongly characterized the free trade policies of the Second Empire as an aberration imposed on an unwilling nation by an autocrat, and have contended that France returned quickly and decisively to protection after the fall of Napoleon III.[2] In contrast,

1. A recent review of the literature is found in Tom Kemp, "Tariff Policy and French Economic Growth, 1815–1914," *Revue internationale d'histoire de la banque,* 12 (1976), 141–155.
2. Standard accounts in English include Arthur L. Dunham, *The Anglo-French Treaty of Commerce of 1860* (Ann Arbor, 1930); Shepard B. Clough, *France: A History of National Economics, 1789–1939* (New York, 1939); Frank A. Haight, *A History of French Commercial Policies* (New York, 1941); and Eugene O. Golob, *The Méline Tariff* (New York, 1944). All of these depend directly or indirectly on the earlier works of Auguste Arnauné, such as *Le commerce extérieur et les tarifs de douane* (Paris, 1911).

this book will show (1) that free trade was supported by a large segment of the French business community in the second half of the nineteenth century; (2) that, given this support, free trade policies were confirmed and extended in the Third Republic's first attempt at tariff reform in 1878–1882; and (3) that the eventual "return to protection" was less severe than is usually thought, with the Méline tariff of 1892 representing not an outright protectionist victory but a compromise between the demands of free traders and protectionists which accommodated all major economic interests.

In addition to presenting a more accurate version of late nineteenth-century French tariff politics, this book seeks to illuminate the business and microeconomic history of modern France. Tariff politics are usually interest politics, and, in nine-teenth-century France, the parties of free trade and protection consisted mainly of commercial and industrial capitalists seeking to obtain tangible benefits for their enterprises through the creation and manipulation of government economic policies. Therefore, in addressing the problem of tariff reform, this book will necessarily address the conditions in various sectors of the economy, explore the business strategies of the entrepreneurs interested in the tariff, and shed light on the overall structure and operation of French commerce and industry in the late nineteenth century.

The examination of tariff politics and economic interests will also shed light on still broader aspects of modern French history. In particular it will illuminate the process by which certain capitalists and their allies—whom Emmanuel Beau de Loménie refers to collectively as "the bourgeois dynasties"—solidified their control of the economy and politics of France in the early decades of the Third Republic and effected a consolidation of the capitalist system which, in turn, established the framework for French political, economic, and social development in the twentieth century.

My efforts to explain the tariff politics of the early Third Republic and to relate them to the larger development of modern France have received assistance and support from many sources.

My initial research, undertaken in France in 1968–1969, was supported in part by an NDEA Title IV Fellowship. Further research at the Harvard Business School was made possible by a Kress Fellowship, and grants from the Institute of International Studies and the Educational Foundation of the University of South Carolina underwrote an additional summer in France. I gratefully acknowledge this financial support and also the cooperation of the staffs of the various libraries and archives I have used: the Olin libraries of Cornell and Washington University (St. Louis); the Bibliothèque Nationale, Archives Nationales, Archives Diplomatiques, and the Chamber of Commerce library in Paris; Harvard's Baker Library (with special thanks to Kenneth Carpenter of the Kress Collection); and the Thomas Cooper Library at the University of South Carolina (particularly the microform and interlibrary loan departments).

Chapters 2 and 5 incorporate passages that first appeared in my article "Free Trade versus Protection in the Early Third Republic: Economic Interests, Tariff Policy, and the Making of the Republican Synthesis," in *French Historical Studies*, 10 (1977). Several passages in Chapter 1 appeared in somewhat different form in "The Free Trade Revolution Reconsidered: Economic Interests and the Making of French Tariff Policy under the Second Empire," *Proceedings*, Western Society for French History, 6 (1978). In both cases, I thank the editors for allowing me to use this material.

On a more personal level, I want to thank all those who have offered counsel and encouragement at various stages of my research and writing. Among these are Sanford Elwitt, L. Pearce Williams, James Riley, Claude Fohlen, David Landes, Louis Bergeron, and François Crouzet. Those who have read all or part of this book in manuscript form and who have offered useful comments and criticisms—without incurring responsibility for the final product—include Richard Kuisel, Rondo Cameron, Glenn Porter, Michael Connolly, and an anonymous reader for Cornell University Press. Edward Whiting Fox not only read and commented on the manuscript; as teacher, dissertation director, and friend, he has been a source of stimulation and good advice for over fourteen years. My debt to him remains incalculable. Finally, to my family—my wife, Carol Reid Smith, my daughter,

Laura Smith, and my parents, Hope and Warren Smith—I owe my deepest gratitude for the love and encouragement that have enabled me to complete this project amid the pressures and distractions peculiar to the academic profession in the 1970s.

MICHAEL STEPHEN SMITH

Columbia, South Carolina

Abbreviations

AN
Annales du commerce extérieur

Archives Nationales
Ministère du commerce, Direction du commerce extérieur, *Annales du commerce extérieur, France, Faits commerciaux.* (Unless otherwise noted, all references are to the subseries, *Situation économique et commerciale, Exposé comparatif.*)

Chamber Tariff Commission,
Procès-verbaux

Chambre des députés, Commission du tarif général des douanes, *Procès-verbaux des séances* (Paris, 1878).

DPF

Adolphe Robert, Edgar Bourloton, and Gaston Cougny, eds., *Dictionnaire des parlementaires français,* 5 vols. (Paris, 1891).

J des ec
Journal officiel

Journal des économistes
Journal officiel de la République française

MAE

Ministère des affaires étrangères, Archives diplomatiques

Sénat, *Enquête*

Sénat, *Procès-verbaux de la Commission d'enquête sur les souffrances du commerce et de l'industrie et sur les moyens d'y porter remède* (Versailles, 1878).

Tableau décennal   Direction générale des douanes, *Tableau décennal du commerce de la France avec ses colonies et les puissances étrangères,* i (1867–1876), ii (1877–1886), iii (1887–1896).

TARIFF REFORM IN FRANCE

1860–1900

Introduction

Controversy over tariffs and trade policies in Europe dates back to the late Middle Ages, when significant interregional commerce first appeared and governments emerged that were willing and able to regulate it. Indeed, as Robert Schnerb once pointed out, as early as the eleventh century "one can discern the coexistence of two tendencies [in Europe], one favoring liberty, the other favoring the restriction of exchange between countries."[1]

In France, however, the controversy really began in the seventeenth century, when the rising centralized monarchy of the Bourbons first instituted a systematic protectionist policy in the form of Colbert's tariff of 1667. That tariff, levied at the kingdom's exterior borders on imported manufactures and exported raw materials, was meant to enhance national economic strength—and thus the power of the Bourbon dynasty—by increasing domestic industrial production. The tariff predictably met with approval from certain manufacturing interests but provoked a hostile response from other interests, especially the landed aristocrats involved in grain export and the port merchants. Once begun, the conflict between these "antimercantilists" and the monarchy and its supporters continued through the

1. *Libre-échange et protectionnisme*, 2d ed. (Paris, 1965), p. 5.

rest of the seventeenth century and throughout the eighteenth, finally culminating on the eve of the Revolution in the scuttling of French protectionist policies by means of the Anglo-French trade treaty of 1786.[2]

But France's first departure from high protection did not last long. The outbreak of war between revolutionary France and monarchical Europe in 1792–1793 led the French government to reestablish prohibitory duties on foreign imports and to launch an experiment in autarky that reached its zenith in Napoleon's Continental System. The simultaneous rise of the British industrial colossus provided more than enough reason to perpetuate, after the coming of peace, the high protection which began as a tactic of economic warfare. Therefore, between 1816 and 1822 the French assembly voted the prohibitions on imported manufactures and the sliding scale duties on grain and other imported foodstuffs that served as the basis of French tariff policy down to 1860.

While fostering renewed protectionism in France, British economic achievement also stimulated free trade sentiments, particularly among merchants seeking to profit from the importation of British goods and among the manufacturers who viewed England as a source of raw materials and as a market for their own products. Consequently, the reimposition of high protection during the Bourbon Restoration was soon followed by growing demands for the liberalization of trade policies under the July Monarchy. This campaign finally bore fruit in Napoleon III's decision to shift France toward freer trade in 1860. This "free trade revolution" in turn set the stage for the climactic struggle between protectionists and free traders in the early years of the Third Republic that is chronicled in this study.

If, as the foregoing sketch demonstrates, the tariff reform of 1860–1900 was part of a long-developing, deeply rooted conflict that had taken on a certain momentum of its own by the nineteenth century, it is equally true that tariff reform was

2. Lionel Rothkrug, *Opposition to Louis XIV: The Political and Social Origins of the French Enlightenment* (Princeton, 1965); W. O. Henderson, "The Anglo-French Treaty of Commerce of 1786," *Economic History Review*, 10 (1957), 104–112.

molded by contemporaneous economic and political developments. On the economic level, the changing fortunes of trade and
production, the structural evolution of the French economy
(especially its increasing integration into the world economy), the
growth and stabilization of capitalist enterprise, and the entrenchment of the capitalist elite all affected the making of tariff
policy in the late nineteenth century. On the political level, tariff
reform was bound up with the achievement and maintenance of
the capitalist bourgeoisie's political and social supremacy in the
early years of the Third Republic.

Nineteenth-century France never experienced what W. W.
Rostow defines as an industrial "take-off," but between 1840 and
the 1870s crucial changes in its economic infrastructure ended
restraints on capitalist enterprise and brought France to the
threshold of the industrial age. The most important of these
changes was the revolution in transport. The building of the
primary and secondary rail networks not only created the truly
national market promised but not realized by the abolition of
internal customs duties during the Revolution, but also helped to
tie this national market into the emerging worldwide system of
exchange, thereby giving French businessmen a doubly expanded
field of activity. At the same time, the revolution in banking—
epitomized in the appearance of new investment banks such as
the Crédit Mobilier and deposit banks such as the Crédit Lyonnais—greatly increased the capital resources available to French
merchants, industrialists, and even agriculturalists. Improvements in credit and transport facilities in turn sustained and
accelerated the growth of French trade and manufacturing (the
value of French special commerce—imports and exports combined—tripled between 1840 and 1860; in the same period the
value of French industrial production rose 50 percent, to over
nine billion francs per year).[3] All of these changes resulted in a
dramatic increase in the size, wealth, and influence of capitalist
enterprise in France in the mid-nineteenth century.

The rapid growth of the 1840s and 1850s slowed in the 1860s

3. Rondo Cameron, *France and the Economic Development of Europe,
1800–1914* (Princeton, 1961), pp. 522–523; T. J. Markovitch, "The Dominant
Sectors of French Industry," in Rondo Cameron, ed., *Essays in French Economic
History* (Homewood, Ill., 1970), p. 242.

and 1870s, and from 1876 to the mid-1890s France experienced a near cessation of growth.[4] As a result, the vigorous expansion of capitalist enterprise and institutions of the midcentury gave way to what Guy Palmade describes as a maturation of the capitalist system bordering on "exhaustion."[5] But the events of this period may perhaps better be described as a process of consolidation and stabilization. This process was marked, particularly in mature industries such as textiles and metallurgy, by an abatement in the continuous rise and fall of enterprises that had characterized the French business scene earlier in the century and by the emergence of a stable hierarchy of relatively large firms by the 1890s. It was also marked by a slowing in the turnover of entrepreneurial personnel—what Jean Lambert-Dansette calls "la rotation patronale"—that had earlier seemed to be the inevitable by-product of industrial growth and by the emergence of a well-established entrepreneurial elite. In the cotton-spinning industry of Lille, for example, in contrast to the influx of new men and the rapid increase in the number of firms (from twenty-seven to forty-three) that characterized the 1850s, production in 1900 was monopolized by just twenty firms, each of which was run by a second- or third-generation spinner.[6]

While the process of consolidation and stabilization proceeded in this manner in particular industries at the turn of the century, the larger business environment was being stabilized by the efforts of firms and their directors to cooperate in managing the economy for their mutual benefit. Within each sector, competitors increasingly joined together in *ententes, comités,* and *comptoirs* to control markets, set prices, regulate production, and even bargain with organized labor.[7] Simultaneously, businessmen from different sectors increasingly worked together in local

4. François Crouzet, "French Economic Growth in the Nineteenth Century Reconsidered," *History*, 59 (1974), 167–179; Maurice Lévy-Leboyer, "La décélération de l'économie française dans la seconde moitié du XIXe siècle," *Revue d'histoire économique et sociale*, 49 (1971), 485–507.

5. *French Capitalism in the Nineteenth Century* (Newton Abbot, 1972), pp. 179–180, 208–210.

6. Jean Lambert-Dansette, *Origine et évolution d'une bourgeoisie: Quelques familles du patronat textile de Lille-Armentières, 1789–1914* (Lille, 1954), p. 186n.

7. In 1890, for example, the *entente des chlorates* was formed to set prices and production quotas and to allocate market shares in the explosives industry.

chambers of commerce and, after 1898, in the National Assembly of Chambers of Commerce and in other national associations to monitor and, in a primitive way, even to plan the overall development of the French economy, often in alliance with government officials. As a result, by the end of the nineteenth century the capitalist system of France had become much more stable and "organized" than it had been a few decades before. Moreover, once established, the stability and organization of the French business system would last well into the twentieth century, in spite of the "destabilizing" effects of the appearance of new entrepreneurs in new industries such as automobiles, electricity, and petroleum.[8]

As this book will show, the making of tariff policy in the late nineteenth century was an integral part of the process of consolidating and stabilizing the French business world. First, the tariff settlement of 1892 established the basis for the organization of capitalism in France by providing in certain cases the necessary degree of protection to allow French producers of a given product to take control of their domestic and colonial markets and to apportion production for those markets among themselves without fear of foreign competition. Second, as a compromise policy, the tariff of 1892 served to mitigate strife among capitalists in different lines or in different sectors by producing an explicit government commitment to a mixed, variegated, and balanced economy in which all major interests could enjoy a certain level of security. In short, it helped to create an economic system dedicated not to prevent growth or change but to controlling growth and change so that neither would occur at the expense of any member of the French capitalist community. In this way, the tariff reform of the late nineteenth century, in addition to its specific short-range effects on commerce, industry, and agriculture, helped to set the overall character of French business enterprise and economic development in the twentieth century.

See Henri Morsel, "Contribution à l'histoire des ententes industrielles," *Revue d'histoire économique et sociale,* 54 (1976), 118–129.

8. H. D. Peiter, "Institutions and Attitudes: The Consolidation of the Business Community in Bourgeois France, 1880–1914," *Journal of Social History,* 9 (1976), 510–525. The concept of "organized capitalism," initially developed with Ger-

In addition to its economic dimension, the tariff reform of the late nineteenth century also had a political dimension. As Emmanuel Beau de Loménie and Jean Lhomme have demonstrated, the political history of France from the Revolution through the Third Republic was largely the story of the bourgeois elite's efforts to gain and maintain control of the state and thereby assure and extend its social and economic supremacy.[9] Not every regime since 1789—or *any* regime, for that matter—was the sole creation or exclusive preserve of the "bourgeois dynasties." But in every regime—regardless of its origins—the grande bourgeoisie (which included the great commercial and industrial capitalists) proved remarkably adroit in occupying positions of authority and influence and in using them for its own advantage. This ability is perhaps most clearly seen in the July Monarchy, wherein Louis-Philippe and his Orleanists formed, in Marx's words, "a joint-stock company for the exploitation of France's national wealth," and in the Second Empire, wherein Napoleon III worked closely with certain "Saint-Simonian" financiers and industrialists to "modernize" the French economy. It is also evident in the formative years of the Third Republic.

As Sanford Elwitt has recently shown, certain members of the capitalist bourgeoisie took the lead in the Republican opposition to the Second Empire in the late 1860s and quickly rallied to the Third Republic after Sedan.[10] Many others still associated Republican government with social revolution and initially withheld their support and maintained their Bonapartist, Orleanist, or even Legitimist allegiances in 1871. Subsequent events, however, soon brought them into the Republican camp. Foremost of these was Louis-Adolphe Thiers's bloody repression of the Paris Commune in May 1871, which finally removed the stigma of

---

many in mind, has been applied more broadly in Heinrich Winkler, ed., *Organisierter Kapitalismus: Voraussetzungen und Anfänge* (Göttingen, 1974). For a critical introduction, see Kenneth D. Barkin, "'Organized Capitalism,'" *Journal of Modern History*, 47 (1975), 125–129.

9. Emmanuel Beau de Loménie, *Les responsabilités des dynasties bourgeoises*, 4 vols. (Paris, 1943–1963), especially vol. I; Jean Lhomme, *La grande bourgeoisie au pouvoir, 1830–1880* (Paris, 1960).

10. Sanford Elwitt, *The Making of the Third Republic: Class and Politics in France, 1868–1884* (Baton Rouge, 1975), pp. 19–52.

radicalism from the Republican system and gave it the imprint of social conservatism. In addition, the specter of a restored monarchy in the hands of the prickly, distinctly antibourgeois Comte de Chambord convinced even those bourgeois with strong monarchist views that there was no alternative to the Third Republic.

Once the bourgeois dynasties had rallied to the Republic and had resolved the conflict among themselves over the locus of power (in the Seize Mai Affair), the Third Republic assumed the political and social character it possessed throughout its subsequent history. With a liberal (that is, constitutional and parliamentary) political structure, power was vested mainly in the Chamber of Deputies (although the Senate served as a sometimes significant check on the Chamber's power). With the members of the Chamber elected by universal manhood suffrage, all social classes were ostensibly in a position to partake of political power and to participate in the shaping of policies. In practice, however, the upper bourgeoisie, along with its middle-class clients (Gambetta's "nouvelles couches sociales"), ran the show with the tacit support of the most numerous class, the peasantry, which had also rallied to the Republic after 1871 in order to preserve the Revolutionary land settlement against the supposed threat of "feudal reaction" posed by the monarchists. As thus defined, the emergent Third Republic was democratic, but also conservative and bourgeois.

The successful setting up of the Republican system in the 1870s did not, by itself, guarantee the continued supremacy of the bourgeois dynasties. The economic troubles of the late 1870s and 1880s quickly eroded their base of support and produced serious challenges to their rule. Specifically, the peasants—whom the bourgeois politicians tended to take for granted—began shifting their allegiance from Republicans to anti-Republicans in the 1880s as they searched for a panacea for the mounting agricultural crisis. At the same time, the workers of the depressed factory towns—who had been relatively docile and apolitical under the watchful eyes of their bourgeois employers—began to threaten the system directly, by going out on strike (1880–1882 witnessed the first major strike wave of the Third Republic), and indirectly, by backing anti-Republican or at least antibourgeois candidates for local and national office. The first electoral manifestation of this rising peasant-worker discontent came in 1885, when both the extreme Right and the extreme Left made major gains in the Chamber of Deputies at the expense of the Republican-bourgeois Middle. A second, more ominous manifestation came in 1888–1889, when General Georges Boulanger, standing in a series of by-elections, staged what was in effect a "serialized plebiscite" against "the system." The challenge continued and deepened in the 1890s as Socialists and syndicalists attacked bourgeois domination from the Left and as nationalists and royalists, using the pretext of the Dreyfus Affair, attacked it from the Right.

It was in the context of this prolonged political crisis for the bourgeois dynasties that tariff reform acquired political importance. Earlier in the century, tariffs had been a political issue only to a limited degree and only at moments when technocratic government officials, seeking to engineer national economic development, clashed with the defenders of narrow economic interests (as occurred to a limited extent in the 1830s and more clearly in the 1850s and 1860s). From 1870, when Napoleon III ended his efforts to dictate tariff policy and turned responsibility for it over to parliament, until the early 1880s, the tariff involved only limited "infraclass" conflict between the free trade commercial-financial bourgeoisie and the protectionist industrial bourgeoisie and thus had little political impact. But then, with the depression of the 1880s, tariffs suddenly became a "mass issue" for the first time, especially for the peasants newly exposed to American agricultural imports because of the building of the third rail network, and tariff reform suddenly took on crucial importance for the grand bourgeoisie's efforts to preserve its political and social supremacy.

The accommodation of interests effected by the Méline tariff served to bolster the political position of the bourgeois dynasties in two ways. First, it eliminated the long-standing split over economic policy between the commercial and industrial wings of the capitalist bourgeoisie and thereby allowed them to close ranks to meet effectively the challenge to "their" Republic emanating from the Left and Right. Second, it restored and perpetuated peasant support for an essentially bourgeois Republic by accommodating the peasants' demand for a return to agricultural protection. Indeed, the accommodation represented by the Méline tariff may be considered a major building block of the "Republican consensus" which, once formed in the 1890s, would continue to support the political, social, and economic preeminence of the capitalist bourgeoisie until the end of the Third Republic.

In the final analysis, then, the tariff reform of the late nineteenth century was bound up with two distinct but related processes: the search for economic order in the wake of the severe dislocations brought on by prolonged depression—a search that involved, above all, the defense of existing capitalist enterprise and the perpetuation of the existing capitalist elite—and the solidification of the capitalist bourgeoisie's political dominance of the Third Republic. This two-sided consolidation of the capitalist system at the turn of the century played an important role in producing many major features of the politics and economics of twentieth-century France, including the longevity, political stability, and social *immobilisme* of the Third Republic; the economic stagnation of the 1920s and 1930s; and even the postwar renewal based on exhortatory economic planning in a free enterprise framework. Thus, to the extent that it illuminates the process of capitalist consolidation, the story of tariff politics and interest accommodation tells us a great deal about the making of modern France.

1

Prelude to Tariff Reform, 1860–1878

The crucial years for the accommodation of interests and for the consolidation of the capitalist system in France came between 1878 and 1892, when the battle between free traders and protectionists was at its height. Accordingly, those years will receive greatest attention in this book. The first chapter, however, necessarily focuses on the two decades before 1878. It examines the creation and subsequent vicissitudes of Napoleon III's free trade policies to show why tariff reform became a national priority in the early years of the Third Republic and how a timetable and agenda for that reform emerged by 1878. It also examines the simultaneous emergence of the free trade and protectionist parties in order to identify the men and interests that later played important roles in tariff politics.

From the 1850s to the late 1870s, French tariff history progressed through four distinct stages, each of which helped to prepare the way for tariff reform under the Third Republic. The first stage, unfolding between 1852 and 1867, involved the liberalization of the French tariff system by Napoleon III. Known as the "free trade revolution," this liberalization produced the policies inherited by the Third Republic which formed the object of later controversy. Indeed, the basic issue of the 1870s and 1880s was whether to keep the policies of the Second Empire intact, to modify them, or to discard them completely. Thus, the free trade revolution created the institutional framework for tariff reform under the Third Republic. It also occasioned the emergence of many of the figures who formed the "party" of free trade and who continued to champion Napoleon III's tariff policies well after the fall of the Second Empire in 1870. By contrast, in the second stage, the protectionist reaction, we meet the political rivals of the free traders and follow their first systematic assault on the commercial policy of the Second Empire. Actually, the protectionist reaction involved two such assaults. The first unfolded in the Corps législatif from 1868 to 1870; the second was embodied in President Louis-Adolphe Thiers's attempt to impose a tax on industrial raw materials and thereby force an upward revision of customs duties on manufactures between 1871 and 1873. Neither succeeded in altering policy permanently, but both were significant in helping to mobilize the protectionist party and in committing the Third Republic, at its outset, to a comprehensive review of the French tariff system.

The third stage in the prelude to tariff reform encompasses the years 1873–1877. In this period the free traders returned to positions of influence, aided by Thiers's fall from power and by a favorable economic climate, and launched, in the name of tariff reform, an effort to perpetuate the free trade policies of the Second Empire. This effort eventually bore fruit in the general tariff law of 1881 and the trade treaties of 1882. In the short run, however, it miscarried in the face of renewed agitation by the protectionists. Indeed, in the crucial twelve-month period 1877–1878, which constitutes the fourth stage in the prelude to tariff reform, the protectionists organized their forces in parliament, blocked the quick enactment of the free traders' reform plan, and prepared an alternate plan of their own. They also formed a pressure group outside parliament, forcing the free traders to respond in kind. By the summer of 1878, both free traders and protectionists had rallied their supporters, entrenched themselves in positions of political power, and delineated their goals. With the issues clearly defined and the rival forces mobilized, the battle over tariff reform began in earnest.

The Free Trade Revolution

The bone of contention in the struggle between free traders and protectionists over tariffs in the early Third Republic was the moderate free trade policy established by Napoleon III. This policy had its beginnings in a series of decrees that, during the 1850s, substantially lowered import duties on key producer goods—coal, iron, machinery, raw wool—and suspended the sliding scale duties on grain. The decisive step in its formation, however, came with the signing of the Anglo-French treaty of commerce on January 23, 1860. This treaty struck down the prohibition, dating from the 1820s, on the importation of certain manufactures and required drastic reduction of import duties on all manufactures. Just as important, it opened the way for the negotiation of similar trade treaties with most other countries of Europe in the next seven years.[1] In addition to opening new markets to French products abroad, these treaties further lowered duties on imported manufactures and made those duties applicable not just to English goods but to goods coming from virtually anywhere in Europe. They were accompanied by a new flurry of executive decrees—thirty-two between 1860 and 1863—that ended or substantially reduced duties on imported foodstuffs, exempted a long list of industrial raw materials from import taxes, and expanded the temporary admissions system whereby semifinished goods to be finished and reexported could enter France duty-free. Finally, in 1866–1867, the new liberal trade system was rounded out by legislation that reduced restrictions on the trade of French colonies, ended the surtax on goods imported in foreign vessels, and abolished the tonnage duty on foreign-built ships.[2]

As a result of these reforms, French trade policy in the late 1860s posed a sharp contrast to the policy of the previous decades.

1. Trade treaties were signed with Belgium (March 1861), the Zollverein (August 1862), Italy (January 1863), Switzerland (June 1864), Sweden and Norway (February 1865), the Hanse (March 1865), Spain (June 1865), the Netherlands (July 1865), the Austrian Empire (December 1866), and Portugal (July 1867).

2. Auguste Devers (Arnauné), "La politique commerciale de la France depuis 1860," *Schriften des Verein für Socialpolitik*, 51 (1892), 127–145; idem, *Le commerce extérieur et les tarifs de douane* (Paris, 1911).

Whereas previously imported raw materials were severely taxed, now most raw materials entered duty-free. Manufactures, whose importation remained prohibited or restricted by high duties under the terms of the old general tariff (which remained on the books and applicable to nontreaty countries), now entered under much lower duties by the terms of the conventional tariff (a composite created by the negotiation of successive treaties and applicable, thanks to the most-favored-nation clause, to all countries linked to France by commercial treaty). For example, foreign cottons and woolens (both cloth and yarn) were prohibited under the general tariff; they entered at duties of only 10 to 15 percent *ad valorem* under the conventional tariff. Likewise, iron and steel entered at duties 50 to 75 percent below previous levels and machinery at duties 80 percent below previous levels.[3] Similarly, imported foodstuffs were taxed at only a fraction of the former rate. In addition, the cost of importation of all commodities was further reduced by the elimination or reduction of the various restrictions and taxes on shipping. In sum, although France did not achieve free trade in an absolute sense or in comparison to the English system in the 1860s, it did experience a dramatic shift away from the protectionism and "prohibitionism" of earlier times toward freer trade. This was unquestionably a shift of revolutionary import for, in conjunction with the ongoing expansion of transport facilities in Europe and worldwide in the 1860s, it curbed the isolation and autarky of the French economy and for the first time exposed French industry, agriculture, and commerce to all the opportunities and hazards posed by the system of international exchange emerging in the nineteenth century.

The free trade revolution in France was primarily an institutional matter, involving a change in economic policy and the resultant rearrangement of France's economic relations with Europe and the world, but it also had a human dimension. It

---

3. The duty on a quintal of steel rails dropped from 37 francs to 9 francs; the duty on spinning machines dropped from 49 francs per 100 kilograms to 10 francs; duties on steam engines from 31F20 per 100 kg to 6F. To compare the duties in the new conventional tariff to those in the general tariff, see Jules Clère, ed., *Les tarifs de douane: Tableaux comparatifs* (Paris, 1880).

involved the rise of a diverse and influential group of men—a sort of "free trade party"—who not only contributed greatly to the making of the free trade system under Napoleon III but remained on the scene after the emperor's fall to work for the preservation and extension of that system. One cannot understand the free trade revolution and why it occurred or appreciate how it helped to set the stage for the battle over tariff policy under the Third Republic without taking into account the emergence of these men.

Who exactly constituted the free trade party under the Second Empire? Surely the most vocal, the most visible, and the best organized of the French free traders at that time were the political economists who had come of age in the 1830s and had thereupon set out to bring government policies into line with the ideas of Adam Smith and his chief French disciple (and their chief mentor), Jean-Baptiste Say. By the 1840s they had assumed a corporate existence through the founding of the Société d'économie politique and had begun to propagate their ideas for policy reform through their own *Journal des économistes* (launched in 1842) as well as through other influential newspapers and periodicals, especially the *Journal des débats* and the *Revue des deux mondes*. By the 1850s they were well entrenched in the University and the *grandes écoles* and had attained positions of political influence. Foremost among them were Louis Wolowski, professor at the Conservatoire des arts et métiers and founder-director of the Crédit foncier; Joseph Garnier, professor of political economy at the Ecole des ponts et chaussées, perpetual secretary of the Société d'économie politique, and longtime editor of the *Journal des économistes*; Louis-Gabriel Léonce de Lavergne, an agricultural economist, collaborator on the *Revue des deux mondes* and *Journal des économistes*, a member of the Institute, and a former (and future) member of parliament; Hippolyte Passy, president of the Société d'économie politique and twice minister of finance under the July Monarchy; and Michel Chevalier, who started his career as a mining engineer and a Saint-Simonian, but moved into the circle of political economists—and into the free trade movement—first as an economic commentator for the *Journal des débats* and later as professor of political economy at the Collège de France (a natural transition since free trade was implicit in the Saint-Simonian dream of binding all parts of the world together through the building of overland railroads and interoceanic canals).[4]

All these political economists worked tirelessly for the liberalization of French tariff policy, first publicly in the unsuccessful campaign for a Franco-Belgian trade treaty in the early 1840s and in the agitation of the Association pour la liberté des échanges in 1846–1848 and then privately during the Second Empire. Ultimately, of course, all these efforts paid off when Michel Chevalier, as a member of the Conseil d'état, won the ear of the emperor and successfully negotiated the Anglo-French treaty of commerce with Richard Cobden in 1860. From that point, the political economists, who had demanded the reform of tariff policy so long and so vociferously, became the staunchest defenders of the status quo.[5]

Although the political economists were an important element in the emerging free trade party in France, they were not the only element. Nor were they exclusively responsible for the free trade reforms of the 1850s and 1860s. Equally important were the businessmen who stood to gain from the lowering of tariff barriers in France and abroad. In the 1840s these businessmen were mainly those engaged in international commerce: Lyons silk traders, Mulhouse cotton printers, and the merchants and merchant-bankers of Paris and the ports. The Bordelais, for example, hoped to open up new markets for their wine through the negotiation of trade treaties, especially with England, and in pursuit of this goal they joined the free trade movement. Indeed, it was at Bordeaux that Wolowski and other Parisian political

4. Information on the early corporate activities of the political economists as well as biographical data is found in Emile Levasseur, "La vie et travaux de M. Wolowski," *J des ec,* ser. 3, 44 (1876), 321–345; *Annales de la Société d'économie politique,* 16 (1880–1881), 90–94 and 304–314 (obituaries of Passy and Garnier, respectively); Arthur L. Dunham, *The Anglo-French Treaty of Commerce of 1860* (Ann Arbor, 1930), pp. 28–38 (on Chevalier). See also *DPF,* III, 113 (Garnier), IV, 1–2 (Léonce de Lavergne), and 556–557 (Passy).

5. On the free trade agitation of the 1840s, see André-Jean Tudesq, *Les grands notables en France, 1840–49,* 2 vols. (Paris, 1964), II, 607–620. The standard account of Chevalier's negotiations with Cobden remains Dunham, *The Anglo-French Treaty of Commerce,* pp. 38 ff.

economists—with the help of the zealous free trade advocate from the nearby Landes, Frédéric Bastiat—founded the Association du libre-échange in 1845. In the 1850s the enthusiasm for free trade of these business interests, in Bordeaux and elsewhere, continued to mount in response to the transport revolution—epitomized by the building of the railroads—that was breaking down age-old physical barriers to trade and, by integrating France into the international economy, was offering unprecedented opportunities for business expansion. Logically for those dedicated to linking the best source of goods with the most lucrative market for those goods, the fall of physical barriers to trade could only make artificial barriers to trade, such as tariffs, seem more intolerable. Consequently, the commercial interests continued to lobby for freer trade in the 1850s and ultimately played a crucial supportive role in the negotiation of the trade treaties, with the Bordelais again leading the way.[6]

The building of the rail networks not only strengthened the existing interests favoring free trade, but also created new interests, the most important of which were the railroad companies themselves. In the early 1850s, the railroads wanted to import iron rails and rolling stock in order to complete and open their lines as quickly and cheaply as possible and thus pressed Napoleon III to decree reductions in the tariffs on those items. He complied in 1853. At the same time, the companies were coming to realize that the institution of a broader, more inclusive free trade was the key to the future development of France's international commerce and that this was, in turn, the key to the long-term financial success of the railroads. As François Bartholony, director of the Paris-Orléans line, explained,

> The extension of commerce, the necessary consequence of greater freedom of exchange, will lead to a considerable increase in the traffic on the railroads, and to the most productive of increases, since it is foreign commerce which requires the longest—and hence

6. On the efforts of the Bordelais to mobilize public support for the Anglo-French commercial treaty, see Albert Charles, "Le rôle du grand commerce bordelais dans l'évolution du système douanier français de 1852 à 1860," *Revue historique de Bordeaux et du département de la Gironde*, n.s., 9 (1960), 65–88.

the most remunerative—traffic. In the matter of revenues, the railroads are far from having had their last word: the future holds for them all sorts of improvements if we continue along the path of prudently progressive free trade which we have entered.[7]

To maximize long-haul traffic and thereby maximize revenues, the railroads pushed for freer trade, not only in public, through pamphlets such as Bartholony's, but also in private, as in the decisive behind-the-scenes activities of Emile Pereire of the Midi railroad on behalf of the negotiation of the trade treaty with England in the fall of 1859.[8]

In the final analysis, then, it was in response to specific pressures from certain business interests—especially those rising with and presiding over the transport revolution and the resultant development of international trade—as well as in response to the ideological pressure of the political economists that Napoleon III used the extensive authority granted him under the Constitution of 1852 to enact the measures that ended high protection and pointed France toward free trade in the 1850s and 1860s. In the years following the enactment of these policies, the interests that had supported them initially continued to grow and prosper (to what extent they grew because of changes in tariff policy is impossible to calculate),[9] and consequently they became even more committed to the free trade system. Thus, from 1860 on, a

7. François Bartholony, *Simple exposé de quelques idées financières et industrielles,* 2d ed. (Paris, 1860), p. 15. The importance of foreign goods for the railroads is indicated in the structure of the traffic of the Chemin de fer du Nord. In the 1860s some 44 percent of the total freight shipped on the Nord consisted of coal. Of that, 60 percent originated in Belgium in 1861 and 39 percent in France (François Caron, *Histoire de l'exploitation d'un grand réseau: La Compagnie du chemin de fer du Nord, 1846-1937* [Paris, 1973], pp. 154, 159).

8. On Pereire's actions, see Barrie M. Ratcliffe, "Napoleon III and the Anglo-French Commercial Treaty of 1860: A Reconsideration," *Journal of European Economic History,* 2 (1973), 582-613.

9. While the economic development of France as a whole leveled off in the 1860s, according to estimates based on industrial production, French foreign trade burgeoned and, presumably, the free trade interests tied into that trade grew and prospered apace. Specifically, the total general commerce of France (imports and exports combined) averaged 5,313 million francs in 1856-1860; it averaged 7,937 million francs in 1865-1869, an increase of 50 percent (calculated from *Annuaire statistique de la France,* 13 [1890], 512-513).

permanent and growing nexus of interests supported the continuation of the commercial policies of the Second Empire. To be
sure, this nexus did not always take the form of an organized
lobby. In fact, once the reforms were completed, these interests
tended to recede into the background, leaving the day-to-day
defense of imperial policies to politicians and economists. Nevertheless, they remained on the scene, poised to respond to any
serious threat to the free trade system, and eventually, in 1878,
when tariff reform was again at issue and the commercial policies
of Napoleon III hung in the balance, they reemerged as part of a
visible free trade lobby. The character, aspirations, and conditions of those interests, as they stood at that time, will be
examined more thoroughly in Chapter 2. For now, it needs only
to be emphasized that the free trade revolution under the Second
Empire left a double legacy to the Third Republic: a commercial
policy and a party willing to defend that policy. In doing so, it
laid an important part of the groundwork for the later political
fight over tariffs.

The Protectionist Reaction

The ministers of Napoleon III were still putting the finishing
touches on the free trade system in 1867 when French protectionists launched a concerted attack on that system which dominated
economic politics in France for the next six years and, like the free
trade revolution before it, helped to set the stage for subsequent
tariff reform. This turn of events was hardly surprising, for
protectionists had constituted a coherent political force in France
for some time. To head off the negotiation of a trade treaty with
Belgium in the early 1840s, industrial protectionists had formed
three patronal organizations—representing, respectively, coal,
metallurgy, and textiles (or, more specifically, the flax and cotton
spinners of Normandy and the Nord). Later these came together
in the Association pour la défense du travail national to counter
the agitation of the free trade association in 1845–1848. In the
1850s the protectionists abandoned public campaigning, as was
de rigueur under the authoritarian Empire, but they remained
organized and politically powerful. Indeed, they blocked many of

Napoleon III's efforts to legislate tariff liberalization in the 1850s and even appeared to have reversed the trend toward freer trade by 1859, when the sliding scale duties were reapplied to grain imports. Ironically, however, these successes proved to be their undoing, for they prompted the government to take up extraparliamentary means to realize its plans (the negotiation of trade treaties) and thereby brought about a more thorough shift to free trade than might have occurred otherwise.[10]

The protectionists were taken by surprise by the "economic coup d'état" embodied in the Cobden-Chevalier treaty, and their response to it was ineffectual. To be sure, they organized a petition campaign against the signing of the treaty in January 1860 and protested further the following summer at the hearing to determine the exact level of import duties to be applied within the framework of the treaty. But, because the trade treaty did not require legislative approval and because the emperor skillfully diffused opposition by simultaneously putting forth an ambitious public works program—the so-called "Programme de la Paix"—the protectionists had neither the political means nor the popular support to undo it or the other free trade reforms in the early 1860s. All this changed after 1867, however. The progressive liberalization of the political system, including the granting to deputies of the right to question (interpellate)—and thus to challenge—ministers on policy matters, gave the protectionists a forum in which to reopen the tariff question. In addition, the industrial depression that began in 1867 and continued to the end of the decade, although stemming from causes other than tariff policy,[11] served to mobilize new opposition to liberal economic

10. On the protectionist party in the 1840s and 1850s, see Roger Priouret, *Origines du patronat français* (Paris, 1963), pp. 57–90, and Bertrand Gille, "Esquisse d'une histoire du syndicalisme patronal dans l'industrie sidérurgique française," *Revue d'histoire de la sidérurgie*, 5 (1964), 209–250.

11. A glut of raw cotton on the European market in 1866–1867, after four years of dearth during the American Civil War, rapidly depressed prices in all sectors of the textile industry and led to a series of bankruptcies, production cutbacks, and worker protests (Claude Fohlen, *L'industrie textile au temps du Second Empire* [Paris, 1956], pp. 373–397). At the same time, the slowdown in railroad building caused a general slump in the metals market and increased domestic competition which especially worked against technically backward producers (Bertrand Gille, *La sidérurgie française au XIXe siècle* [Geneva, 1968], pp. 216–279). Industrialists,

policies among industrialists and their workers in textiles and metallurgy.

This climate enabled protectionists politicians to launch a systematic campaign to destroy the free trade system. It began in the spring of 1868 with a parliamentary interpellation in which Augustin Pouyer-Quertier, the wealthy Rouen cotton spinner who had led the resistance to the Anglo-French trade treaty in 1860, along with Adolphe Thiers, Jules Brame, and Charles Kolb-Bernard of Lille, attempted to discredit the trade treaties by blaming them for the ongoing industrial depression.[12] It continued the following year, first with protectionist agitation in the parliamentary elections and then with a drive to pressure the government into renouncing the trade treaty with England that was to become eligible for renunciation in 1870. Throughout the fall of 1869, Pouyer-Quertier crisscrossed France mobilizing antitreaty sentiment and, in his wake, workers joined with patrons in numerous industrial cities to protest government tariff policy.[13] By January 1870, when the simultaneous but separate drive to liberalize the Empire culminated in the appointment of a responsible ministry under Emile Ollivier, the protectionists had wrung from the emperor an agreement to place all matters of economic policy in parliamentary hands. Yet the anticipated scuttling of the Anglo-French trade treaty did not follow. Ollivier refused to back renunciation and, in perhaps the key test of the protectionist offensive, an interpellation sponsored by Jules Brame to force the government to renounce the treaty was voted down in February.[14] A subsequent parliamentary inquiry into the crisis in industry proved to be anticlimactic. Although it provided a forum for further attacks on the trade treaties, the inquiry had

---

however, tended to blame the trade treaties, not these market conditions (Gustave de Molinari, "La réaction protectionniste," *J des ec*, 3d ser., 9 [1868], 177–198).

12. Augustin Pouyer-Quertier et al., *La vérité sur le régime économique de la France* (Paris, 1868); Gustave de Molinari, "Les interpellations sur la nouvelle politique commerciale: Appréciation générale de la discussion," *J des ec*, 3d ser., 10 (1868), 321–347.

13. Fohlen, *L'industrie textile*, pp. 418–437.

14. Gustave de Molinari, "Les interpellations économiques au Sénat et au Corps législatif," *J des ec*, 3d ser., 18 (1870), 295–305.

resulted in no changes of policy by July, when the outbreak of war with Prussia brought it to an abrupt end.

The political events of 1870–1871 in France caused only a temporary interruption in the protectionist campaign. Indeed, they actually promoted its resumption and intensification, not only by resulting in the overthrow of Napoleon III, but also by bringing to power his strongest protectionist opponents. Specifically, in February 1871, Adolphe Thiers became "Chief of the Executive" of the French government and promptly appointed Pouyer-Quertier minister of finance and another protectionist, Félix Lambrecht, minister of commerce. The protectionists had suddenly become insiders and could conduct their assault on the trade treaties with official sanction. Yet, as things happened, this advantage meant little. Thiers subordinated renunciation of the trade treaties and upward revision of tariffs to implementation of a raw materials tax that, he hoped, would solve the fiscal problems arising from the war with Prussia. Such a tax, however, was anathema to most industrialists, including the textile manufacturers who were the mainstays of the protectionist party. In a bitter confrontation with Thiers, representatives of these textilists in the National Assembly, led by Ernest Feray of Essonne (Seine-et-Oise), helped to defeat the tax when it first came up for consideration in January 1872 and only reluctantly approved a watered-down version the following July. In the process, the parliamentary protectionists became alienated from their leaders in the government and also began to fight among themselves, as legislative delegations such as those of the Seine-Inférieure and the Nord, which normally were united on matters of tariff policy, divided between "thieristes" and "antithieristes."

The drive to reinstate high protection thus never gained momentum. To be sure, the assembly approved the reestablishment of the *surtaxe de pavillon* (a tax on goods imported in non-French ships) to give French shipowners an advantage in their competition with foreigners. More important, the assembly authorized the renunciation of the trade treaties, and the government duly renounced the treaties with England and Belgium in March 1872. Thiers, however, was forced to negotiate new treaties in the fall because, in approving the raw materials tax in July, the assembly attached a rider forbidding its collection until compensatory duties were established on the manufactures whose raw materials were to be taxed. (This, in turn, could be done only through new treaties because the authorization to renounce the old treaties stipulated that the old conventional tariff would continue in effect until a new one was voted.) The protectionists, of course, expected more than mere compensation from the duties to be set in new treaties, but Thiers, anxious to meet the legal requirements to collect the raw materials tax and thereby solve his fiscal problems, did not drive a hard bargain with the British or the Belgians. Consequently, when the terms of the new treaties were announced, the protectionists were outraged. The cotton spinners of Rouen, for example, immediately protested the "obvious errors" and "practical impossibilities" in the new conventions and especially "the regrettable incompetence of the French commissioners who prepared them."[15] In March 1873, the protectionists in the assembly joined in rejecting the new treaties. Moreover, following Thiers's resignation in May, they joined in repealing the raw materials tax and the *surtaxe de pavillon* and in voting to extend the old conventional duties four more years, all of which effectively preserved the free trade system at least until 1877.

The ultimate result of this complex string of events was to deprive the six-year campaign for a return to protection of any immediate effect. French tariff policy remained in 1873 what it had been in 1867. Yet the "protectionist reaction" was not without influence on the subsequent course of tariff politics. First, it clearly demonstrated the permanence and perseverance of protectionists on the French political scene. More specifically, it demonstrated the continuing ability of the textile interests of Normandy, the Nord, and the East and the mining and metallurgical interests of the North, East, and Center to mobilize their political representatives in their behalf. The message was simple: the Third Republic could avoid accommodating these interests only at its own risk. Second, the events of 1867–1873 helped to

15. Quoted by (His) de Butenval, "Les nouveaux traités de commerce avec l'Angleterre et la Belgique," *J des ec*, 3d ser., 30 (1873), 34.

clarify what protectionists wanted in future tariff reform. Thiers's demand for renunciation of the trade treaties with England and Belgium raised the specter of a complete return to the pre-1860 tariff system that made protectionists, as well as free traders, recoil. Industrialists, in particular, realized that they had bene- fited from the removal of import duties on foodstuffs and raw materials and did not want them reimposed. Consequently, in January 1872, their representatives in the assembly joined in authorizing treaty renunciation only with the understanding that it would not lead to a return to the pre-1860 economic regime. Henceforth, to be a protectionist was to seek adjustments in the tariff system of the Second Empire (mainly the raising of duties on imported manufactures), not its wholesale destruction.

Beyond its effects on the protectionists themselves, the protec- tionist campaign—or rather the specific legislation in which it resulted in 1873—had additional consequences. By synchronizing the expiration dates of the trade treaties—all would become eligible for renunciation on the tenth anniversary of the last one negotiated (with Portugal, 1867)—this legislation established a pretext for tariff reform. From 1873 on, it was generally accepted that the French government would launch a systematic review of the tariff system no later than 1877—a review that would entail the reconsideration and consolidation of the hodgepodge of legislation, some dating back to 1815, that constituted the general tariff, as well as a decision on whether to abandon or renegotiate all the trade treaties simultaneously. Consequently, although the protectionist reaction did not determine the nature of future French tariff policy, it did determine that tariff reform would become a major item on the agenda of the emerging Third Republic.

Free Traders and the Launching of Tariff Reform

The extension of existing trade treaties in 1873 meant that no definitive reform of the French tariff system could begin before 1877. For this reason, the years 1873–1877 were quiet compared to the years of controversy immediately preceding and following.

Nevertheless, developments of great significance for the future course of tariff politics in France occurred during these years. The free traders, who had been on the outside politically and on the defensive ideologically during Thiers's presidency, returned to positions of power and began to redefine in liberal terms the concept of tariff reform that had been previously shaped in the protectionist mold. Reflecting this, in 1875 the government began to prepare specific plans for tariff reform that emphasized, not a return to protection, but the liberalization of the general tariff and the renewal of the trade treaties. Thus, because of the return and resurgence of the free traders between 1873 and 1877, tariff reform, as it reemerged on the political stage in 1877, was oriented toward preserving, instead of destroying, the policies of the Second Empire.

To say that the free traders "returned" with the fall of Thiers is perhaps misleading. Strictly speaking, they had never been away. Liberal economists and publicists had organized a vigorous propaganda campaign to counter that of the protectionists in the late 1860s and early 1870s and, in the National Assembly in 1871, free trade deputies formed a caucus that played an important role in frustrating Thiers's efforts to effect a return to protection.[16] Yet, despite this apparent continuity in the free trade presence, something did change in 1873. Amid an economic boom that restored prosperity after years of depression and thus restored a measure of confidence in the economic policies of the Second Empire, free traders, who had lost power and prestige under Thiers, became more active and more visible and entrenched themselves once again in policy-making positions within the government. At the same time, new figures emerged who would lead the drive to maintain and extend free trade policies in the years ahead.

One manifestation of this free trade revival was the redoubling of efforts by the political economists to spread the free trade ideology. Already, since the 1840s, they had been reaching the literate and affluent through the *Journal des débats* and the learned through the *Journal des économistes*. Beginning in the

16. On the founding and work of the free trade caucus, see *Annales de la Société d'économie politique*, 9 (1871–1872), passim.

1860s, they addressed the working classes through lecture series organized by the Société d'économie politique in various cities in cooperation with local learned societies. Then, in April 1873, they added an important new weapon to their public relations arsenal with the founding of a weekly, *L'économiste français*. Modeled on the British *Economist* and edited by the rising young liberal journalist Paul Leroy-Beaulieu,[17] *L'économiste français* was designed to capture a broad audience among French businessmen by providing accurate, up-to-date economic news and then to guide this captive audience, through its editorials, toward liberal views on economic policy. In other words, by serving as a "center of information and action"—its stated goal[18]—it ultimately sought to "defend the treaties of commerce against the attacks of protectionism," as one of its founders later admitted.[19] It succeeded admirably on both counts. Despite its relatively modest circulation,[20] *L'économiste français* came to exert unequaled influence on public opinion in France on economic issues, especially among professionals and businessmen. It thereby gave the free traders an important advantage over the protectionists, who lacked a comparable organ, in the ensuing battle over tariff reform.

In addition to again becoming aggressive in the realm of public information after 1873, the free traders increasingly reestablished themselves in position of power, first within the government of

17. Son of a Lisieux notable, Leroy-Beaulieu studied at the lycée Bonaparte in Paris and won an unprecedented string of prizes from the Académie des sciences morales et politiques in the late 1860s. He then joined the staff of the *Revue des deux mondes*, where he fell under the influence of Michel Chevalier (he married Chevalier's daughter in 1870). In 1871 he began what became a lifelong collaboration on the *Journal des débats*, and the next year he assumed a professorship at the newly opened Ecole libre des sciences politiques. Selection as editor of *L'économiste français* thus crowned a meteoric rise to prominence in the world of liberal academics and journalism (Réné Stourm, "Paul Leroy-Beaulieu," *Revue des deux mondes*, April 1, 1917, pp. 532–553).

18. "Programme," *L'économiste français*, April 19, 1873, pp. 1–3.

19. Gustave Roy, *Souvenirs, 1823–1906* (Nancy, 1906), p. 288.

20. In 1880, the circulation of *L'économiste français* was 2,600 copies per week, versus 99,500 for the *Moniteur financier* (France's largest business weekly) and 23,400 for *La réforme économique* (another free trade weekly). See Claude Bellanger et al., *Histoire générale de la presse française*, 3 vols. (Paris, 1972), III, 172.

duc Albert de Broglie and subsequently in the cabinets of Louis Buffet, Jules Dufaure, and Jules Simon. Indeed, free traders held at least one of the three cabinet posts most influential in the making of commercial policy—finance, commerce and agriculture, and foreign affairs—in every government between 1873 and 1877, while in the same period none of these posts was held by an active protectionist. Moreover, just as the renewal of free trade propaganda was led by a new group of political economists, the free traders' return to political power was led by new statesmen coming to office for the first time after 1870. The most important of these were duc Elie Decazes, who served as foreign minister continuously from November 1873 to November 1877, and Léon Say, who served as finance minister in five cabinets between March 1875 and December 1879.[21]

This return of free traders to power was, in part, the by-product of unrelated political developments: the fall of Thiers in May 1873 (for reasons other than his advocacy of protection) and the subsequent advent to power (again, for reasons unconnected to economic philosophy) of men who happened to be sympathetic to free trade, such as the duc de Broglie and Jules Simon.[22] At the

21. Son of Louis XVIII's favorite minister and the founder of the Decazeville industrial complex, Decazes entered politics as deputy for the Gironde, where the family estate was located. Reflecting the views of his constituents, he soon became a free trade spokesman in the National Assembly, for which he was feted by the Bordeaux Chamber of Commerce in October 1874 (L'économiste français, October 31, 1874, pp. 545–546). Léon Say was, by birth and by training, France's "compleat" free trader. Like his grandfather, Jean-Baptiste Say, he was a political economist and free trade publicist. Since the 1860s he had been an active member of the Société d'économie politique and had promoted liberal economic policies through the Journal des débats, which he directed on behalf of his wife's family, the Bertins. He and his family also had typical free trade business interests. His father, Horace, had been a wealthy Paris négociant. Léon, himself, received early training in finance in the Eichthal bank and then through the influence of a classmate, Alphonse de Rothschild, acquired a seat on the board of the Nord railway, which he retained the rest of his life (Georges Michel, Léon Say, sa vie, ses oeuvres [Paris, 1899], pp. 1–50; A. Delavenne, Recueil généalogique de la bourgeoisie ancienne [Paris, 1954], pp. 390–391; Joseph Valynseele, Les Say et leurs alliances [Paris, 1971], pp. 61–66).

22. As a great-grandson of the Geneva banker Jacques Necker, Broglie had family connections with the financial-commercial community and was sympathetic to liberal economics. He showed his free trade colors most conspicuously in May 1872, when he resigned as ambassador to England ostensibly to protest Thiers's trade policy, which he denounced in his memoirs as an attempt "to

same time, there was an element of inevitability in this return to power. France faced a severe fiscal crisis following the war with Prussia—brought on by war expenditures and payment of the indemnity to Prussia in combination with the interruption of tax collections—and Thiers and the Third Republic, from the outset, needed the assistance of the Parisian commercial-financial elite to float the loans that kept the government solvent. It was only a matter of time until members of this elite, as possessors of expertise in fiscal and financial matters, took over the economic ministries and, in so doing, reoriented them toward free trade (the exact linkage between Paris financiers and merchants and the free trade movement is given greater attention in Chapter 2). In fact, this process began even before the fall of Thiers, when Léon Say, despite his sharp differences with Thiers on economic philosophy, acceded to the Finance Ministry for the first time in December 1872.

Although the active reimplantation of free traders in key ministries undoubtedly contributed greatly to the shift in the government's outlook from protectionist to *libre-échangiste* after 1873, this shift also derived from the presence in the various bureaus of the government of a host of civil servants who were products of, and holdovers from, the Second Empire and who were thus sympathetic to its policies. The presence of such men made for a residual, built-in free trade orientation in certain ministries that surfaced not only when a free trader served as minister but also in the many instances when the ministries were headed by men without strong economic views. This was the case, for example, in the Ministry of Commerce and Agriculture under vicomte Camille de Meaux, an old friend of Broglie who held the post in the Buffet, Dufaure, and Seize Mai cabinets for strictly

---

rehabilitate protection and monopoly" (Duc Albert de Broglie, "Mémoires, IV: Difficultés avec M. Thiers," *Revue des deux mondes*, March 15, 1929, pp. 391–397).

The first truly outspoken free trader to hold the premiership under the Third Republic, however, was Jules Simon. Simon emerged as a free trade spokesman while serving as a deputy for Bordeaux in 1869–1870—his speeches of that period having been published in Jules Simon, *Le libre-échange* (Paris, 1870)—and he reaffirmed this commitment during the debate over the general tariff ten years later in *La question des traités de commerce* (Paris, 1879).

political reasons. At the outset of his tenure in 1875, Meaux confessed to his constituents in Saint-Etienne that he was ignorant of commerce and industry, and he later indicated in his memoirs that he found commerce "the least interesting ministry."[23] Therefore, he relied heavily in policy matters on his senior officials, chief of whom was Jules Ozenne, secretary of the ministry and director of foreign trade, whom Broglie described as "very devoted to commercial liberty."[24] It is likely that he also relied on Léon Amé, the general director of customs and the government's top tariff expert, who insisted, as did Ozenne, that though tariffs could still be used as sources of revenue, the day of protective tariffs was over and the reforms of 1860 were irreversible.[25] In this manner, the Ministry of Commerce continued to favor the policies of the Second Empire in the 1870s in spite of—or perhaps because of—the occasional lack of strong direction from above.

Having strengthened, in these various ways, their control over the formation of public opinion and the making of official policy in economic matters, the free traders soon turned to the task of preparing the tariff reform that, by the spoken and unspoken agreements of 1873, would become mandatory by 1877. Naturally they wanted to direct that reform toward continuation and even intensification of the free trade policies of the Second Empire. Therefore, they set out, first, to replace the excessively protective, even prohibitive, duties that still comprised France's general tariff with a new, comprehensive, and moderate general tariff based on the conventional tariff in the trade treaties; and, second, to use this new general tariff as the starting point for the negotiation of trade treaties establishing a new conventional tariff that presumably would be as low as, or lower than, the existing conventional tariff. In executing this two-stage plan, they proceeded deliberately and circumspectly, lest by acting too precipitously they would revive memories of the economic coup d'état of 1860 and thus stimulate excessive opposition. Therefore, in the first step toward tariff reform, the vicomte de Meaux, in a circular of April

23. Camille de Meaux, *Souvenirs politiques, 1871–77* (Paris, 1905), p. 258.
24. Broglie, "Mémoires, iv," p. 392.
25. Léon Amé, *Etude sur les tarifs de douane et sur les traités de commerce*, 2 vols. (Paris, 1876), i, 531–534.

7, 1875, committed the government to scrapping the old general tariff and to creating a new one, but at the same time he solicited the advice of France's chambers of commerce on the form and content of the new tariff. Specifically, he asked if the *ad valorem* duties remaining in effect—duties computed as a set percentage of value—should be replaced by specific duties, which were defined as a set tax on each unit of weight of a commodity (he carefully avoided asking for recommendations on the future level of duties on particular commodities, however). He also asked if France should rely exclusively on a legislative tariff in the future or if it should renegotiate the trade treaties.[26]

Some fifty-four chambers responded. Although a majority favored replacing all remaining *ad valorem* duties with specific duties—a protectionist move of sorts, since in an age of falling prices fixed duties would represent a larger and larger percentage of the values of imported items as time passed—the chambers nonetheless unanimously supported making the existing conventional tariff, with adjustments, the new general tariff. Moreover, the chambers showed surprising goodwill toward the trade treaties. Only fourteen—the diehard protectionist chambers, including those of Lille, Rouen, and Saint-Dizier—opposed negotiation of new treaties.[27] The responses clearly indicated that most of France's business community, if not ardently *libre-échangiste*, at least accepted the existing tariff system. Thus in February 1876, Meaux could confidently report to Marshal Mac-Mahon that "the government's line of conduct is determined. We must prepare new treaties and new tariffs, basing them on present treaties and present conventional duties."[28] With this decided and with the Conseil consultatif des arts et manufactures having worked out the desired conversion of *ad valorem* to specific duties, Meaux delegated the task of drawing up the government's tariff bill and fixing the exact level of duties to the Conseil supérieur du commerce in March 1876.

The Conseil supérieur du commerce, de l'agriculture, et de

26. "Lettre du Ministre de l'agriculture et du commerce relative à la revision des traités de commerce," AN, F^{12} 2488A.

27. "Analyse des réponses au circulaire du 7 avril 1875," AN F^{12} 2488A.

28. "Rapport du Ministre de l'agriculture et du commerce au Président de la République," *J des ec*, 3d ser., 41 (1876), 306.

l'industrie was an official consultative body, made up of business notables appointed by the head of government, which had played a role in economic policy making from time to time throughout the nineteenth century. At the outset of the Second Empire, Napoleon III used it to formulate the decrees that first lowered tariff rates. In 1869, he tried without success to quell the ongoing protectionist agitation by asking the council to organize an inquiry into the causes of the industrial depression. In the early 1870s, Thiers sought to use the council in developing his fiscal progam and, toward that end, expanded its membership (purging free traders and adding protectionists in the process). When MacMahon and Broglie succeeded Thiers in May 1873, however, they immediately restored the ousted free traders and commissioned the council to draw up plans to liquidate Thiers's fiscal and tariff policies.[29]

In 1876 the structure and composition of the council still reflected the contradictory manipulations of the membership by Thiers and Broglie. Free traders clearly controlled the section of commerce and, to a lesser degree, the section of agriculture. Protectionists, however, remained strong in the industrial section, and their leader, Pouyer-Quertier, served as presiding officer of the council in the absence of the minister of commerce and agriculture. Given this cleavage, the council's deliberations on the general tariff bill in the spring of 1876 proved to be highly contentious and did not always go the free traders' way. For example, an attempt to lower duties on coal and iron in the new general tariff below the level in the current conventional tariff failed, while Pouyer-Quertier succeeded in getting the conventional duty on cotton thread raised 10 percent before it was included in the general tariff.[30] On the whole, however, the free traders won more than they lost. The general tariff bill hammered out by the council and submitted to the Chamber of Deputies in

29. For the early history of the council, see (His) de Butenval, "Les conseils supérieurs de l'agriculture, de l'industrie, et du commerce," *J des ec*, 3d ser., 31 (1873), 60–85. On its actions in 1873, see Conseil supérieur du commerce, *Examen de la question des matières premières, des traités de commerce, etc.* (Paris, 1873), and Paul Leroy-Beaulieu, "Le conseil supérieur du commerce," *L'économiste français*, June 14, 1873, pp. 225–227.

30. Conseil supérieur du commerce, *Examen des tarifs de douane* (Paris, 1876).

February 1877 erased all prohibitive duties and, in most cases, established the old conventional duties, which were previously the minimum, as the new maximum. In the case of some items— steel rails, for example—the new general tariff was to be lower than the old conventional tariff.[31] Thus the threat of a sudden return to high protection seemed to have been averted once and for all, and the real possibility existed that, in the forthcoming trade negotiations, the tariff system could be even further liberalized by substituting new conventional tariffs for the revised general tariff. Indeed, it was with that goal in mind that the Simon government opened talks with the British and Italians in March 1877.

In the spring of 1877, it thus appeared that the free traders were about to achieve their version of tariff reform quickly and with a minimum of political conflict. This appearance soon proved illusory. Distracted by the issue of railroad repurchase and nationalization, the Chamber of Deputies failed to elect a committee to report on the tariff bill before its April recess. Rescheduled for May 19, the election was again postponed by the Seize Mai crisis and the ensuing prorogation of the Chamber. As a result, the bill was withdrawn and was not resubmitted until the following February, by which time the political and economic climate had changed considerably. Likewise, the trade negotiations that began in the spring of 1877 also became embroiled in the Seize Mai Affair and ultimately fell victim to it. But the free traders' efforts in 1873–1877 did not go unrewarded. In those four years, they had succeeded in reestablishing themselves in positions of power and in controlling the initial preparation of tariff reform, both achievements that served them well in the subsequent confrontation with the protectionists. Indeed, it is to these early successes that the free traders' later triumphs in 1881 and 1882 must ultimately be traced.

31. Ibid. In the cases where duties were converted from *ad valorem* to specific valuations—as with chemicals, dyes, pottery, glass and crystal, fine cotton, linen and woolen cloth, and various highly specialized manufactures—the level of the tariffs was thought to be 10 percent above the level in the conventional tariff (Paul Leroy-Beaulieu, "Le conseil supérieur du commerce et le renouvellement des traités," *L'économiste français*, April 8, 1876, pp. 449–452).

Depression, the Seize Mai, and the
Protectionist Resurgence

After four years of relative inactivity, protectionists returned to the French political arena in the summer and fall of 1877. Led by a combination of seasoned political veterans and eager young novices, the protectionists in parliament formed coherent, if informal, blocs in the Senate and the Chamber of Deputies. Outside parliament, industrialists favoring a return to protection experimented with various forms of lobbying and then founded a permanent pressure group, the Association de l'industrie française (AIF), in the spring of 1878. With the emergence of both leaders and organization, the protectionists came to represent a political force capable of countervailing the power of the free traders, and they began to challenge the free traders' control of economic policy making and to call into question the free traders' plans for tariff reform. By June 1878, they succeeded in forcing the French government to abandon its drive for rapid endorsement of the free traders' version of the general tariff and to postpone the negotiation of new trade treaties. Thereafter, tariff reform, which seemed to have been moving toward a quick resolution in early 1877, became a slow, painstaking process, the initial phase of which dragged on for four more years. Consequently, while the protectionist resurgence of 1877–1878 did not determine the ultimate content of tariff reform, it did affect the timing and pace of reform. Moreover, it brought to the fore the men and interests on the protectionist side who played key roles in the ensuing struggle, and it drew the lines between them and the free traders more clearly than ever before. As such, it represents the last in the long chain of developments, stretching back to the Second Empire, that made the tariff a major issue in the 1870s and defined the setting for tariff politics under the Third Republic.

The protectionist resurgence was, in part, the inevitable result of the submission of the general tariff bill in the spring of 1877. The importance of that bill to the protectionists alone would have ensured their increased activity in 1877, just as their apparent quiescence over the previous four years can be traced to the decision in 1873 to maintain the status quo in tariff policy until all trade treaties were eligible for renunciation in 1877. However, two unexpected developments outside the realm of tariff policy also stimulated and shaped the protectionist resurgence in 1877. One of these was the advent of economic depression; the other was the eruption of political crisis in the so-called Seize Mai Affair.

"The "Great Depression" that engulfed most of the industrialized world in the wake of the stock crashes of 1873—unlike the more severe Great Depression of the next century—did not result in cessation of production or massive layoffs of workers. Actually production continued at a steady or even accelerating pace and unemployment rates remained low in most industries. What was depressed, then, was not production or employment but prices—and ultimately profits and wages. The Great Depression was, in essence, the Great Deflation. The causes of this deflation remain obscure. A shortage of bullion in relation to total demand, the expansion of production worldwide, and the cost-cutting effects of technological advance all certainly played a part.[32] But what is important in this context is that, for continental Europe, the onset of depression was accompanied by—and perceived to be caused by—a rise in British imports. Indeed, in response to contracting demand for its products outside Europe and perhaps in response to the increased accessibility of European markets after two decades of railroad building and tariff reduction, the British exported some commodities (especially textiles) to Europe on a larger scale in 1871–1876 than in any other five-year period during the nineteenth century. In doing so, they undoubtedly helped to force down prices in European markets and added to the competitive pressures on European manufacturers. Not surprisingly, those manufacturers, in turn, soon began pressing their governments to raise tariffs.[33] As a result, by the late seventies, the

32. David Landes mentions several possible explanations for the depression in *The Unbound Prometheus: Technological Change and Industrial Development in Europe from 1750 to the Present* (Cambridge, 1969), pp. 232–234. In the end, however, he sees it as part of a secular trend of falling prices, brought on by the fall in real costs that accompanied rising productivity during industrialization.

33. An empirical description of British trade is found in S. B. Saul, *Studies in British Overseas Trade, 1870–1914* (Liverpool, 1960). The depression and protec-

return to protection was gathering momentum throughout the Continent, France included.

The depression did not hit France as quickly or as hard as other countries, perhaps because its economy was buoyed by the lingering needs of postwar recovery. Nevertheless, by 1876—1877 at the latest—most French industries were experiencing falling prices and contracting profits.[34] Many pointed to rising imports as the source of these ills and soon began seeking a cure in higher tariffs.[35] This is not to say, however, that the depression—more specifically the phenomenon of falling prices in conjunction with rising imports—was the sole cause of the protectionist resurgence in France. As we have noted, that was in the offing in 1877 regardless of economic conditions because of the timetable for tariff reform. The precise contribution of the depression, then, lay in providing added justification for higher tariffs to those who would have been demanding them anyway. Also, as it deepened and affected more and more businesses, the depression enabled committed protectionists to enlist a larger number of new recruits in their movement than would have been possible in good times. In short, the depression of the 1870s did not create the protection-

tionist resurgence on the Continent has been best studied for Germany. See Ivo N. Lambi, *Free Trade and Protection in Germany, 1868–1879* (Wiesbaden, 1963).

34. At Lille, number 40 cotton yarn which had sold for 5F10 per 100 kg in 1874 was bringing only 3F80 in September 1877, a decline of 25 percent ("La crise industrielle du Nord," *L'industrie française*, October 10, 1878). Similarly, forges that had sold steel rails to the Eastern railway at 414F per ton in 1874 were getting only half that price three years later (Jean Fourastié, *Documents pour l'histoire et la théorie des prix* [Paris, 1958], I, 118). The fall in iron and steel prices was, in turn, reflected in the balance sheets of the major metallurgical firms. Châtillon-Commentry, for example, yielded a return on invested capital of only 6.2 percent in 1877, versus a 50 percent return in 1873 (Jean Bouvier, François Furet, and Marcel Gillet, *Le mouvement du profit en France au XIXe siècle: Matériaux et études* [Paris, 1965], p. 421).

35. The value of cotton cloth imported annually into France, for example, rose from 19 million francs in 1868 to 47.7 million in 1873 and to 77.2 million in 1877. Although the major portion of the increase in the early 1870s resulted from the transfer of Alsace from France to Germany (which made what had previously been domestic production into a foreign import), the largest part of the increase between 1873 and 1877 came from a jump in British imports from 14.1 million francs (29 percent of the total) in 1873 to 38.3 million (50 percent of the total) in 1877 (figures from *Annales du commerce extérieur*, no. 102, 1867–1881).

ist groundswell, but it did sustain it and make it more pronounced.

Although the depression rendered the economic climate in France conducive to a resurgence of protectionism, the immediate cause of renewed protectionist agitation and organization was provided by the political crisis known as the Seize Mai Affair—or, more specifically, by actions on tariff policy taken by Broglie's Seize Mai government during the crisis. The affair began when the Republican prime minister, Jules Simon, resigned under pressure from the monarchist president of the Republic, Marshal MacMahon, on May 16, 1877 (hence its name). During the summer, it escalated with the prorogation and dissolution of the Chamber of Deputies and came to a climax in the fall with the election of a new Chamber. This turned out to be a virtual national referendum on whether the Third Republic was to be run by Republicans operating through parliament (and especially through the Chamber of Deputies) or by conservative monarchists operating through a strong executive. Thus the Seize Mai Affair was primarily a constitutional and political dispute; tariff policy was not directly at issue, and the cleavage between Republicans and *MacMahonistes* did not coincide with the cleavage between free traders and protectionists.[36] Nor did the replacement of Simon's government by a *MacMahoniste* government under the duc de Broglie signal a transfer of power from one to the other. Broglie may have been a less vocal free trader than Jules Simon, but he was a free trader, nonetheless, and like Simon he put free traders in key ministries.[37] As a result, during the Seize

36. The famous 363 Republicans who protested Simon's dismissal and Broglie's appointment in June and who thereafter formed the core of the anti-MacMahon party contained both free traders and protectionists. Likewise, there were both free traders and protectionists among the *MacMahonistes*. The MacMahonist slate in the fall election in the Loire, for example, included both the ribbon exporter Tezenas du Montcel, a free trader, and the ironmaster Alexandre Jullien, a protectionist. Thus there was no correlation between political philosophy—Republican or "monarchist"—and economic philosophy—free trade or protectionist—in 1877.

37. Broglie retained Decazes in Foreign Affairs. His finance minister, Eugène Caillaux, was a railroad administrator and economic liberal, as was the man he replaced (Léon Say).

Mai crisis, efforts to preserve free trade policies proceeded much as before, with the Broglie government picking up and continuing the commercial negotiations launched by Simon earlier in the spring.

Yet, despite the continuity in tariff policy during the Seize Mai crisis, the fall of the Simon government and the advent of Broglie proved to be a watershed in tariff politics. The reason lay in the fact that, although Simon and Broglie pursued the same ends, they used radically different tactics to achieve those ends, reflecting perhaps the difference between Simon's "parliamentary mentality" and Broglie's "executive mentality." Specifically, during the spring, Simon had negotiated with the British and Italians more or less openly and had skillfully disarmed protectionist opposition by setting up a council of industrialists, headed by Pouyer-Quertier and Ernest Feray, to "advise" the French negotiators (without, however, allowing it to participate directly in the negotiations). By contrast, Broglie affronted the protectionists, first by eliminating the advisory council, then by pursuing negotiations in secret during June, when the Chamber was prorogued (thus eliminating even nominal parliamentary oversight), and finally by demonstrating his willingness to conclude treaties at the industrialists' expense. On July 6, France signed a new trade treaty with Italy that, it was soon learned, allowed the Italians to raise their duties on French textiles, a chief item of export to Italy. More ominously, word was spreading at the same time that Broglie's government was about to conclude a new treaty with England that would concede a 50 percent reduction in French duties on imported iron and a 20 percent reduction in duties on cotton goods. Obviously this would have constituted a coup on the scale of the original Anglo-French treaty.[38]

These maneuvers by the Broglie government, within the tense political atmosphere of Seize Mai, shocked the industrial protectionists out of their four-year lethargy and set them to organizing their forces and to attacking the policy initiatives of the free traders. At first, this renewed activism took the form of a campaign against Broglie's trade negotiations, reminiscent of the

38. The various rumors and the protectionist response to them are described in *L'industrie française* in this period, especially in the issue of July 12, 1877.

campaigns of 1860 and 1869. Starting in late June, industrialists from all over Normandy and the Nord deluged MacMahon with petitions protesting the trade talks. On July 1, a congress of chambers of commerce of the Nord convened at Lille and dispatched a delegation to Paris for a similar purpose. Like-minded delegations followed from Epinal, Condé-sur-Noireau, Nancy, and other industrial towns. There was talk of a national assembly of chambers of commerce, and the chambers of Normandy met at Rouen the end of August to lay the ground for it.[39] This incessant pressure ultimately took its toll; in mid-September, Broglie suspended the talks with England (which, in any case, had been stalled for months). Heartened by this first victory, however small, the protectionists looked forward to building on it and taking control of tariff policy in the months to come.

When the Senate and Chamber of Deputies reconvened in November, following the decisive defeat of Broglie and the *MacMahonistes* in the October elections, the rising protectionist campaign shifted from the public to the parliamentary arena. It was first manifested in the Senate, which in December launched an inquiry into the ongoing economic crisis. The initial purpose of the inquiry was to discredit the Seize Mai regime by demonstrating its bad effect on business, but protectionists won control of the committee of inquiry and quickly turned the proceedings into what one liberal journalist later called "a striking manifestation of the doctrine, aspirations, and power of the protectionist party."[40] From December to March, the committee heard a veritable "collection of lamentations" as a carefully selected group of industrialists paraded to the witness stand to tell of their economic troubles and to blame them on increased importation of foreign manufactures.[41] Drawing the predictable conclusion from this testimony, the committee recommended that existing trade treaties be prorogued (and thus no new treaties negotiated) until after the passage of a new general tariff law. More important, it recommended that, in any future general or conventional

39. *L'industrie française*, July 5, July 12, and September 6, 1877.
40. E. Fournier de Flaix, "L'enquête industrielle," *J des ec*, 4th ser., 3 (1878), 306.
41. Sénat, *Enquête*.

tariff, duties on a long list of manufactures be pegged substantially above current levels.[42] These recommendations had no immediate effect because the Chamber, not the Senate, had authority to initiate legislation in fiscal matters, including tariffs. Nonetheless, they did serve to restate and publicize the protectionist concept of tariff reform that had lain dormant since 1873 and to give it the imprimatur of an official parliamentary commission. Thus the inquiry and the resulting report added to the momentum of the protectionist resurgence.

While the protectionists in the Senate were calling into question the existing plans for tariff reform and were setting forth their own alternative plans for reform, the protectionists in the Chamber took practical steps to put those alternatives into operation and thereby greatly influenced the future course of tariff reform. First, on March 21, 1878, in the election of the committee of thirty-three to report on the general tariff bill (which had been resubmitted to the Chamber in February after the hiatus of Seize Mai), the protectionists won a clear majority of the seats and installed as chairman Jules Ferry of the Vosges, "whose protectionist tendencies [were] well known."[43] With control of this committee, they then set out to modify the general tariff bill to their specifications. To this end, they immediately organized another parliamentary inquiry to obtain advice from interested parties on what constituted a "fair" level of protection for various commodities. (Their chief grievance against the government's tariff bill was that its schedule of duties was set by the Conseil supérieur du commerce without benefit of such an inquiry and was thus by definition arbitrary, even though, in resubmitting it, the government had raised many duties 24 percent over the original level, in accordance with the demands of Pouyer-Quertier.) Going along with and complementing this effort to take control of the general tariff bill were efforts to undercut the trade treaties. On this front the protectionists won a signal victory on June 6, when in a close vote the Chamber rejected the Franco-Italian trade treaty signed the previous summer. This vote hardly struck a fatal blow to the system of

42. "Rapport de la commission du Sénat," *L'industrie française*, May 30, 1878.
43. *L'industrie française*, March 28, 1878.

trade treaties—*Le Temps* cautioned that "one [should] not interpret this as the abandonment of the commercial policy inaugurated in 1860"[44]—but it did put the government on notice that no commercial negotiations would be tolerated until the legislation of the general tariff was completed.

None of the protectionists' actions in the Senate and Chamber during the spring of 1878 was of great importance in itself. Cumulatively, however, they had enormous import. They effectively stymied the government's drive to accomplish tariff reform quickly, along the lines laid down in 1875 and 1876, and they guaranteed that henceforth tariff reform would follow the protectionists' timetable, with consideration of the general tariff coming first and negotiation of the new trade treaties coming later (if at all). Of course, this did not mean that reform would necessarily bring a return to protection, but it did mean that the continuation of free trade policies was no longer a foregone conclusion. In sum, tariff reform was again up for grabs in France in the summer of 1878 and the protectionists as well as the free traders were in a position to influence the outcome.

The protectionists' success in revising the agenda of tariff reform and in regaining a measure of control over the process of reform resulted in large part from the emergence of effective leaders and cohesive organization in their ranks, both inside and outside parliament, in the fall of 1877 and the spring of 1878. Within parliament, the success of resurgent protectionism—as manifested in the Senate inquiry, the election of the Chamber Tariff Commission, and the defeat of the Franco-Italian trade treaty—was the work of many men but was directed by five in particular: Ernest Feray, Nicolas Claude, and Augustin Pouyer-Quertier in the Senate; Richard Waddington and Jules Méline in the Chamber. Of these, the eldest and most distinguished was Ernest Feray. Grandson of the celebrated Oberkampf of Jouy, who had supplied printed cloth to the court of Louis XVI, Feray had presided over extensive textile, paper, and machine works at Essonne since the 1830s and since the 1840s had been a leading

44. *Le Temps*, June 9, 1878.

national spokesman for French industry.[45] In the early 1870s, as a member of the National Assembly, he led the opposition to Thiers's raw materials tax while continuing to support protectionism generally. As senator for the Seine-et-Oise after 1876, Feray took the lead in mobilizing opposition to the trade talks in early 1877 and in December sponsored the Senate inquiry into the economic crisis. His most important backer in launching the inquiry was Nicolas Claude, senator for the Vosges. Scion of an Epinal Protestant family involved in the Alsatian cotton prints industry since the eighteenth century, Claude had made his fortune first as an employee, then as proprietor, of the Géhin cotton mills at Saulxures-sur-Moselotte. In the 1860s, he played a prominent role in the eastern cotton syndicate and helped finance the Parisian daily, Le Temps. In the 1870s he continued to devote most of his time to local industrial interests in the Vosges—completely renovating his plant at Saulxures and supervising the transfer of the Alsatian finishing industry to Thaon-les-Vosges—but he also entered national politics, first as a member of the National Assembly and, after 1876, as a senator. By 1877, he had emerged as a major spokesman for the textile industry in hearings such as those of the Conseil supérieur du commerce and helped to organize and orchestrate the protectionist testimony before the Senate commission.[46]

Clearly the most important leader of the protectionist bloc in the Senate—indeed, the most famous and most energetic protectionist spokesman in France—was Augustin Pouyer-Quertier, who chaired the inquiry into the economic crisis. Pouyer-Quertier was a millionaire cotton spinner who had started with small, water-driven mills in the Andelle valley in the 1840s, but in 1859 in Rouen opened La Foudre, at the time the largest cotton mill in Normandy and probably in France.[47] Struck personally by

45. DPF, ii, 627; Feray, letter to Jules Simon, in L'industrie française, March 6, 1879. On the eighteenth-century origins of the Feray industrial dynasty, see Guy Richard, Noblesse d'affaires au XVIIIe siècle (Paris, 1974), pp. 104–106, 210–214.

46. DPF, ii, 120–121. On the Claude family, see Philippe Mieg, "Les réfugiés protestants lorrains et de Sainte-Marie à Mulhouse et en Suisse au XVIIe siècle," Trois provinces de l'Est (Paris, 1957), pp. 13–36. Claude described his industrial activities in the 1870s in Sénat, Enquête, pp. 149–151.

47. Augustin Pouyer was something of a self-made man, but he was helped

the Anglo-French trade treaty the following year, he had taken command of the protectionist forces in the Corps législatif in the 1860s and had organized the public campaign against imperial tariff policy in 1868–1870. As Thiers's finance minister in the early 1870s, he had been forced to support the raw materials tax and had lost credibility as an industrial spokesman as a result. After 1873, however, he rapidly restored his reputation through vigorous advocacy of high tariffs in the hearings of the Conseil supérieur du commerce. And in skillfully turning the Senate hearings of December 1877–March 1878 into a vehicle for protectionist propaganda, he again established himself at the head of parliamentary protectionists on the eve of the battle over tariff reform.

Whereas the leading protectionists in the Senate were veterans of many previous battles over tariffs, most of the protectionists in the Chamber of Deputies had entered politics since 1870 and were becoming involved in the tariff issue for the first time in 1877 and 1878. Of these, two in particular—Richard Waddington and Jules Méline—quickly came to dominate the others through their work as members of the Chamber Tariff Commission and, especially, as floor managers in the successful opposition to the Franco-Italian trade treaty. Waddington headed one of the foremost industrial families of Normandy. His great-grandfather, an English immigrant, had founded cotton mills in association with Henry Sykes at Saint-Rémy-sur-Avre (Eure-et-Loir) in 1792. His father, Frédéric, the first naturalized Frenchman in the family, had brought the plant to its maximum size—some thirty-three thousand spindles and three hundred mechanized looms—in the 1840s and 1850s.[48] Born in 1838, Richard took over management of the firm in the 1860s. While his older brother, William, was

---

along (as are so many "self-made" men) by marriage into a well-established business family. The Quertiers were already prominent in Norman business—specifically, shipping and insurance at Le Havre—in the late eighteenth century (Pierre Dardel, *Commerce, industrie, et navigation à Rouen et au Havre au XVIIIᵉ siècle* [Rouen, 1966], pp. 168, 173). In the 1840s they owned a dyeworks in Rouen and a cloth printing works at Fleury-sur-Andelle, which nicely complemented Pouyer's spinning mill at Fleury and his weaving plant in Rouen (*Statistique de la France*, 1st ser., 12 [1850], 32–35, 208).

48. Waddington dossier, AN F¹² 5298.

pursuing the literary and diplomatic careers in Paris and London that would bring him to the Foreign Ministry in December 1877 and to the premiership in December 1879, Richard settled in Rouen, seat of the family's business connections, where he was elected a member of the chamber of commerce, a judge on the tribunal of commerce, and in 1876 a member of parliament.[49] Reelected in 1877 as one of the 363 anti-*MacMahoniste* Republicans, Waddington subsequently devoted his political life to economic issues—railroads and, above all, tariffs—in a continuing effort to defend and promote the Norman cotton industry.

Defense of the French cotton industry also brought Jules Méline to the protectionist party. Also born in 1838, Méline was the son of a clerk in the justice of the peace court of Remiremont. Despite his humble origins, he managed to study law in Paris, where, during the siege of 1870, he procured a minor position in the Government of National Defense, probably with the aid of Jules Ferry, who was then mayor of Paris. At the same time he began building his political base back home by founding the *Memorial des Vosges*. After failing in his initial bid for the National Assembly in February 1871, he won a by-election in Remiremont the following year. From then until 1877, Méline concentrated on purely political issues like the Communard amnesty.[50] He remained close to Ferry, his first political mentor, and eventually served as minister of agriculture in his second cabinet. At the same time, however, he was working more and more closely with Nicholas Claude. It was probably Claude who taught him the economics of the cotton industry, of which Méline had no firsthand knowledge. As one journal later commented, Méline entered the tariff commission "as the representative of the old *filature* of the Vosges which spins only yarn of common gauge using obsolete machinery purchased from the Alsatians,"[51] an accurate description of Claude's operation. Although other men would serve as chairman—first Jules Ferry, then François

---

49. *DPF*, v, 553.
50. Jean-Paul Gérard, "Jules Méline, député des Vosges à l'Assemblée nationale et à la Chambre des députés, 1872–1877," *Annales de l'Est*, 5th ser., 16 (1964), 329–349.
51. *La Liberté*, May 21, 1880.

Malézieux of Saint-Quentin—Méline would dominate the deliberations of the tariff commission, write its crucial report on textiles, and thereby establish himself as the foremost spokesman of the protectionists in the Chamber, a position he held throughout the ensuing struggle over tariff reform.

By the summer of 1878, Feray, Claude, Pouyer-Quertier, Waddington, and Méline had emerged (or reemerged) as the unofficial directors of the protectionist "party" in parliament through their actions in undermining the free traders' tariff program. In the months and years ahead, dozens of other politicians grouped around them to fight for legislation of high protective tariffs and against the negotiation of new trade treaties. In this effort, they received vital support from an extraparliamentary lobby, the Association de l'industrie française, which, like the protectionist blocs in the Chamber and Senate, came into being in response to the political and economic circumstances of 1877 and 1878.

At the beginning of 1878, industrial protectionists had been without any form of national organization for three decades, ever since the demise of the Association pour la défense du travail national. However, the resubmission of the general tariff bill to the Chamber in February prompted them to fill this lacuna. The founding of the Association de l'industrie française was the result. By March 18, when its first plenary session convened in Paris, the AIF had attracted some 128 members from mining, metallurgy, textiles, and shipbuilding. The various specific grievances and demands of these members will be examined in succeeding chapters. Suffice it here to say that all found the schedule of duties in the government's tariff bill "insufficient and illusory," despite the government's raising of many duties 24 percent above the level proposed in 1877. All hoped, moreover, to use the AIF to mobilize public opposition to the bill and to convince the government of the danger of "persevering in these errors . . . so disastrous and prejudicial to [French] industry."[52] To this end, the AIF prepared a resolution demanding the maintenance or raising of all duties on industrial products; this was presented to the Chamber Tariff Commission in June, amid a wave of pro-

52. Deposition of J.-B. Martelet, Chambre des députés, Commission du tarif général des douanes, *Procès-verbaux des séances* (Paris, 1878–1879), p. 387.

protection testimony by various members of the association. Simultaneously, the AIF took its case for increased protection to the public through the weekly newspaper, *L'industrie française*, which had been its official organ from the outset, and through a campaign, financed by members' dues, aimed at discrediting free trade and the free traders. Henceforth, throughout the battle over tariff reform in the next fifteen years and well into the twentieth century, the AIF was to be an indispensable part of the protectionist movement in France.[53]

The rise of protectionist blocs in the Senate and Chamber and, even more, the founding and early activities of the AIF forced the free traders to define and tighten their organization. Of course, free traders remained government insiders after the Seize Mai Affair as they had been since 1873. They continued to control the making of government economic policy through Léon Say, who returned to the Ministry of Finance in the Dufaure and Waddington cabinets (December 1877–December 1879), and through Pierre Teisserenc de Bort, Pierre Tirard, and Maurice Rouvier who, among them, controlled the Ministry of Commerce from December 1877 to August 1882.[54] Consequently, the free traders did

53. In 1892 the AIF became the AIAF—Association de l'industrie et de l'agriculture française—but continued to attract mostly industrialists (see *fichier* of members in AN 27 AS 11). It was active in French economic politics until 1919. After that, until its dissolution in January 1961, it continued to serve as an information agency for other lobbies, notably the CGPF (Confédération générale de la production française). A sketch of the AIF's overall history is found in the introduction to the catalog of holdings, AN 27 AS. On its beginnings, see the weekly issues of *L'industrie française* in early 1878, especially that of March 28, 1878.

L'industrie française was first published on May 21, 1877, at the height of the trade negotiations with England and, coincidentally, at the outset of the Seize Mai crisis. Billed as the "organe de la défense du travail national," it sought to combat the "pro-English" trade theory it thought had dominated France since 1860. Its backing and management were obscure. It was published by the publishers of several trade journals, including *Le moniteur des fils et tissus* and *La métallurgie*. The editor was one Edmond Rousset (*L'industrie française*, May 21, 1877). The journal's exact connection to the industrialists who founded the AIF remains undetermined.

54. Teisserenc de Bort was not an outspoken free trader, but as a former director of the P-L-M railroad he seemed to share the liberal viewpoint of the railroad fraternity. In any case, as minister of agriculture and commerce, he deferred on tariff policy to the finance minister, Léon Say. Pierre Tirard was a Parisian politician whose free trade views dated from his early involvement in the gold and jewelry export business in the 1860s. Maurice Rouvier got his start in commercial

not need parliament and parliamentary committees as forums
and power bases as much as the protectionists did. Nonetheless,
the Senate inquiry and the formation of the Chamber Tariff
Commission brought parliamentary spokesmen for free trade to
the fore, just as they brought protectionists to the fore. In the
Senate these included Stanislaus Dupuy de Lôme, Louis Hubert-
Delisle, Emile Fourcand (all of the Gironde), Jean-Simon Dauphinot of Reims, and Louis Léonce de Lavergne—who together
formed a vocal minority on the Senate inquiry commission,
gamely resisting Pouyer-Quertier's efforts to turn the hearings
into a protectionist demonstration.[55] They also included the
deputies who formed an equally vocal and politically more
important minority on the Chamber Tariff Commission: Tirard,
Rouvier, Napoleon III's former minister Eugène Rouher, the
sugar magnate Gustave Lebaudy, the *chocolatier* Emile Menier,
Pierre Brélay of Paris, and Edouard Millaud of Lyons. More
important than the emergence of free trade blocs in parliament,
however, was the formation outside of parliament of a free trade
lobby, the Association pour la défense de la liberté commerciale
(Free Trade Association), in response to the founding of the AIF.
Organized in mid-June at the offices of Fould Frères, Paris export
merchants, the association brought publicists and politicians,
such as Leroy-Beaulieu, Tirard, and Rouvier, together with
representatives of free trade business interests, under the presidency of Adolphe d'Eichthal, a leading Paris banker and railroad
administrator.[56] Just as the AIF sought to raise tariffs and
discourage trade treaties, the Free Trade Association set out to

---

banking in Marseilles and continued to represent a Marseillais constituency, and
his commitment to commercial liberty reflected this.

55. Sénat, *Enquête*, pp. 41, 55.

56. On the founding of the Free Trade Association, see Arthur Mangin,
"L'Association pour la défense de la liberté commerciale," *L'économiste français*,
June 22, 1878, pp. 789–790.

Two of the most important members of the association were Edgar and Fernand
Raoul-Duval who, like Léon Say, were grandsons of J.-B. Say (their mother was
Octavie Say). A lawyer and former deputy of the Seine-Inférieure, Edgar Raoul-
Duval was tied to Le Havre shipping interests through his marriage into the
Foerster family and to Bordeaux wine interests through his son's marriage into the
Johnston family. Fernand Raoul-Duval was president of the Compagnie pari-
sienne du gaz, vice-president of the board of Decazeville, regent of the Banque de
France, and a member of the Conseil supérieur du commerce (Valynseele, *Les Say*,
pp. 77, 91, 99–104, 112–113, 121, 133).

block efforts to raise the duties in the government's tariff bill and, more important, to bring about the renewal of the trade treaties. In pursuing these goals, they quickly emulated the AIF by organizing testimony before the Chamber Tariff Commission and by launching a publicity campaign in the summer and fall of 1878.[57] Thus, because of the protectionist resurgence of 1877–1878, free traders, as well as protectionists, were better organized than ever before by mid-1878.

In the summer of 1878, the French were at last beginning the first comprehensive review of their tarif system since the Revolution. Moreover, eighteen years after the signing of the Cobden-Chevalier treaty, they were about to examine, and decide the fate of, the network of trade treaties that constituted the Second Empire's free trade legacy to the Third Republic. As we have seen, they came to these tasks in response not merely to short-term economic fluctuations (the depression), but to a wide range of economic and political developments unfolding over a period of years. By 1878, the interplay of these developments had defined an agenda of reform and determined possible alternatives for future tariff policy; it had created the machinery by which reform would be worked out and had mobilized the human agents of reform. For the next fifteen years, the process of tariff reform and the struggle between free traders and protectionists associated with it would be key elements in the politics of the Third Republic and prime factors in the larger process of creating a stable economic and political order in France.

57. The association's manifesto was published in *Journal des débats*, June 21, 1878; *L'économiste français*, June 29, 1878; and *J des ec*, 4th ser., 3 (1878), 121–123. The testimony of its leaders before the Chamber Tariff Commission appeared in *Journal officiel*, November 28, 1878, pp. 11110–11114.

2

The Interests and the Tariff (I)

From a survey of French tariff politics in the 1860s and 1870s, one might conclude that institutionalizing economic principles through the enactment of tariff laws and through the negotiation of trade treaties had become an end in itself for both free traders and protectionists by 1878. But this was not the case. Almost everyone involved in tariff reform continued to view the establishment of his preferred policy—whether free trade or protection—as a means to higher ends. For some these ends were political: they saw tariff reform as a part of the ongoing struggle between Left and Right, for and against the Republic.[1] For the great majority of French politicians, however, the higher ends of tariff reform were clearly economic. They believed that tariff policy played a crucial role in the economic development of the nation, and, more important, a crucial role in the economic life of their own town or region. Indeed, most politicians involved in tariff politics were either businessmen protecting their own interests or spokes-

---

1. For example, Eugène Rouher, Napoleon III's former "vice-emperor" and leader of the Bonapartist party in parliament, steadfastly defended the policies of the Second Empire and urged their extension to preserve the good memory of the emperor and to sustain the dwindling hopes for a Bonapartist restoration. See his speech on the general tariff bill in *Journal officiel,* February 21–23, 1880. On his wider political activities, see John Rothney, *Bonapartism after Sedan* (Ithaca, N.Y., 1969), passim.

men for the dominant interest of their district. This meant that, for all its ideological overtones, the struggle between free traders and protectionists was at root a struggle among rival interests to decide which would be favored of disfavored by government policy and even to decide which would survive and which would perish. To comprehend this political process, it is necessary to identify the intersts most concerned with tariff reform, describe their economic circumstances, and determine how their demands on the tariff fit in with their long-term business strategies.

The identity of the interests involved in tariff reform is best ascertained by examining the background, constituencies, and connections of the members of the free trade and protectionist blocs in parliament and, more directly, the memberships of the AIF and the Free Trade Association. Such a survey reveals, first, the relative uninvolvement of agricultural interests in tariff politics. The great mass of small farmers in central and southern France remained indifferent to national economic policy in the 1870s because they produced for local markets (or only for themselves), not for national or international markets, and because the incomplete status of the railroad system protected those markets from outside competition. By contrast, the big commercial farmers of the West and North, who did produce for the national and international market, were interested in national economic policy and in 1868 formed the Société des agriculteurs to influence its formulation. Amid the prosperity of the late 1860s and early 1870s, the society had supported the tariff policy of the Second Empire. By the mid-seventies, however, the first signs of impending agricultural depression sufficiently undercut their faith in free trade so that, of the leaders of the society, only Edouard Lecouteux, the general secretary, joined the Free Trade Association in 1878. The others, however, were not necessarily ready to join the industrialists of the AIF in the protectionist movement. Rather, most members of the society, along with the representatives of agriculture in parliament, stood apart from both the free traders and the protectionists in the late 1870s. Although both free traders and protectionists wooed the Société des agriculteurs and the agricultural bloc in parliament between 1878 and 1882, agriculture became a decisive force in tariff politics only in the mid-eighties, when the increased importation of foodstuffs in conjunction with the building of the third railroad network made the mass of French farmers aware of national economic policies for the first time.

Meanwhile, in 1878, the commercial and industrial interests dominated tariff politics. These interests formed three distinct clusters. One cluster consisted of the commercial, financial, and transport interests that consituted the core of the free trade party. Another consisted of the heavy industrial interests—mining, metallurgy, and construction—that formed an important segment of the protectionist party. The third cluster consisted of textile industries that divided sharply on the tariff issue and provided an important element of both parties. The analysis of these clusters—as well as the analysis of the "fiscal interest" embodied in the French state—is the subject of this chapter and the next. Each cluster will be broken down into its component parts because only by looking at the various industrial and commercial specialties, and even at individual capitalists and enterprises, can one fully appreciate what was at stake economically in tariff reform. Such a disaggregation of interests will allow us to comprehend not only the basis of cleavage between free traders and protectionists but also the basis for cooperation among the disparate interests that gravitated to each side of the tariff question. The latter is especially important because it was in the formation of alliances among interests—particularly in the AIF, which managed to unite natural economic adversaries such as coal and metallurgy, linen and cotton, on the tariff issue—that we find the beginnings of the accommodation of interests which, in time, not only led to the resolution of the tariff controversy but also contributed to the larger process of economic and political stabilization in France at the end of the nineteenth century.

The Free Trade Nexus: Commerce, Finance, and Transport

As we saw in Chapter 1, the initial establishment of a free trade policy by Napoleon III was supported by the leaders of international commerce and transport. Not surprisingly, it was representatives of these interests, along with representatives of banking and finance, who set out to preserve and extend that policy through the Free Trade Association in 1878 and thereby formed the core of the free trade nexus in France. Why the *grands négociants*—the wholesale dealers in diverse commodities on the international market—would support free trade should be obvious. High tariffs would be anathema to anyone in the import business. Likewise, for exporters, the reduction of domestic import duties could be (and had been) useful in gaining similar concessions abroad and, in any case, removed the cause of tariff retaliation by foreign countries. That the *négociants* would draw certain bankers into the free trade camp along with them is perhaps less obvious. The nature of international trade had long required that the commercial houses of Europe discount paper, advance credit, and, in short, do all the work normally associated with banks. The expansion of world commerce in the eighteenth and nineteenth centuries brought some specialization, with merchant banks assuming a distinct identity, but even then it was difficult to distinguish between merchants and bankers. They usually belonged to the same family, and indeed many pursued both professions at once. François Arlès-Dufour of Lyons, for example, got his start by marrying the daughter of a Leipzig merchant who set him up in the silk trade. Business was good, and Arlès soon added banking to the functions of his trading house. In 1863 he participated in the founding of the Crédit Lyonnais through which he eventually invested in a wide range of commercial and industrial ventures in France and elsewhere in Europe. Despite diversification, he continued in business as a silk merchant. It probably never occurred to him to make too great a distinction among his diverse interests. The interests of merchant banking were inseparable from those of international commerce. The merchant bankers were free traders to the same extent that their clients, or cousins, in commerce were free traders.[2]

2. An excellent discussion of the relationship between the commercial and banking communities of France is found in David S. Landes, *Bankers and Pashas* (Cambridge, Mass., 1958), pp. 1–52. See also Bertrand Gille, *La banque et le crédit en France de 1815 à 1848* (Paris, 1959), and Maurice Lévy-Leboyer, *Les banques européenes et l'industrialisation internationale dans la première moitié du XIXᵉ siècle* (Paris, 1964). On Arlès-Dufour: Jean Bouvier, *Le Crédit Lyonnais de 1863 à 1882*, 2 vols. (Paris, 1961), I, 130–131.

The rise of a modern transport industry through the construction of the railroads added another element to the free trade nexus. The railroads were financed and controlled by merchants, who needed them to move merchandise in bulk over long distances, and by merchant bankers, who needed them as a place to invest their accumulated capital. This connection to commerce and finance in itself oriented the transport industry toward free trade, but the railroad companies would have favored low customs duties in the 1860s and 1870s in any case. As François Bartholony pointed out in a previously quoted passage, railroads needed a consistently high volume of traffic in order to turn a profit. Only the import and transit trade in coal and manufactures from England and Belgium and in raw materials from overseas offered such volume. Therefore, in the 1860s, all French trunk lines devised special rates for long-haul traffic to capture a share of this trade. Because they were competing with Belgian and German lines to supply eastern France and central Europe with cotton and British goods, the Western and Eastern Railways combined to set low rates on traffic between Le Havre and Strasbourg. Likewise, the Northern and Paris-Lyons-Mediterranean (P-L-M) lines adjusted their freight rates to attract the trade of England and Belgium with southern France, Italy, and the Levant.[3] Obviously, to be effective, such tactics required a simultaneous reduction of customs duties. For this reason, those railroad owners and managers not already in the free trade movement as merchants or bankers were inevitably drawn to it.

A similar pattern obtained in steam navigation. Steamship lines were really only extensions of railroad companies; the same group of financiers controlled both. Both depended on international commerce, and the steamship companies often made freight rate agreements with French railroads to improve their position in the competition for trade between the interior of Europe and overseas areas.[4] Likewise, anyone involved in steam navigation would sooner or later become involved in the free

---

3. André Lefevre, *Sous le Second Empire: Chemins de fer et politique* (Paris, 1951), pp. 119–168.

4. The Compagnie générale transatlantique, for example, sought preferential freight rates in order to funnel Swiss and German exports bound for America to Le Havre and onto its vessels (Marthe Barbance, *Histoire de la Compagnie générale transatlantique* [Paris, 1955], p. 87).

trade movement. Thus, just as banking, commerce, and transport interests were bound together by financial and familial ties, they also were bound together by a common desire to liberalize French trade policy. The diversity and interconnectedness of these interests and their importance for the free trade movement can be further demonstrated by determining who represented these interests within the Free Trade Association. As one would expect, most came from France's centers of trade, finance, and transport—Paris, Lyons, and the seaports (particularly Marseilles and Bordeaux)—and these figures can best be examined within the context of those cities' economic activities.

Paris was France's largest city and its most lucrative marketplace. As such, it naturally attracted diverse industries, some of which produced exclusively for the home market and sought protection from foreign competition there.[5] Most industries of Paris, however, were somehow tied to international commerce and favored free trade. More important, the Parisian economy was dominated less by industry in the 1870s than by commerce, banking, and transport. On one hand, Paris was a center for the importation of foreign commodities, some of which were consumed in Paris, some of which were transshipped to other parts of France and Europe. On the other hand, Paris was a center for the export of French goods, both those produced in Paris and elsewhere.[6] Paris was also the financial nerve center of France and the hub of its transportation system. In line with all these functions, Paris naturally attracted a large community of merchants, bankers, shipping specialists, and manufacturers for

5. Parisian industrial firms in the protectionist pressure group (the AIF) included Oeschger et Cie (zinc, copper, and lead); Cail, Farcot, Laveissière, and Mignon-Rouart-Delinières (metallurgical manufacturing); and Bolay-Morot and Cartier-Bresson, both manufacturers of cotton sewing thread. See the AIF membership list in *L'industrie française*, March 21, 1878, pp. 89–90, reproduced in Appendix 1.

6. Of France's top twenty imports in 1876, as ranked by value in the *Annuaire statistique de la France*, 1 (1878), 451–452, the trade in at least seven (coal, skins and leather, woolens, cottons, silk cloth, and sugar) was run from Paris. Of France's twenty leading exports, the trade in at least six (including *articles de Paris*, silverware and jewelry, dressed and worked leather, lingerie, and pottery, glass and crystal) centered on Paris. Paris was also involved in three other major exports: woolen cloth, silk cloth, and metalwork.

export who came to dominate both the economic and political life of the city and the free trade movement nationally. As noted earlier, free trade's leading parliamentary spokesmen, Léon Say and Pierre Tirard, rose from the milieu of Parisian big business. So, too, did two senior members of the free trade party in France, the bank and railroad administrators Adolphe d'Eichthal and Isaac Pereire.

Both Eichthal and Pereire came to free trade through Saint-Simonism, although only the latter had a disciple of Saint-Simon. As the serious young director of his family's bank, Eichthal had violently rejected the philosophical and religious tenets that had drawn his brother Gustave to the Saint-Simonian cult in the late 1820s.[7] Nevertheless, he was obviously sympathetic to the Saint-Simonian dream of securing economic progress through investment banking and expansion of transport facilities. In the 1830s he financed the first railroad-building schemes of the Pereires, whom he had met through his brother, and subsequently backed their Chemin de fer du Midi and the Crédit Mobilier. Although he broke with the Pereires in 1863 over their attack on the Banque de France (Eichthal had been the first Jewish regent of the bank), he kept his seat on the board of the Midi railroad until his death in 1895 at the age of ninety.[8] Throughout this long career, Eichthal exhibited the support for free trade characteristic of railroaders. As a member of the Conseil supérieur du commerce in the 1870s, he consistently voted with the free traders on the tariff question. More important, in 1878 he took the lead in organizing the Free Trade Association and served as its first president. Meanwhile, his old associate, Isaac Pereire, was emerging as an even more vocal advocate of free trade.

The Pereire brothers, Emile and Isaac, had been leaders in baking and railroad building in France and throughout Europe during the early Second Empire. As noted earlier, they also had been involved in the formulation of Napoleon III's liberal

7. Barrie M. Ratcliffe, "Saint-Simonism and Messianism: The Case of Gustave d'Eichthal," *French Historical Studies,* 9 (1976), 484–502.

8. Rondo E. Cameron, *France and the Economic Development of Europe, 1800–1914* (Princeton, 1961), p. 192 and passim; Jacques Boudet, ed., *Le monde des affaires en France de 1830 à nos jours* (Paris, 1952), p. 680.

economic policies in 1859–1860. In 1867, however, their public careers and private fortunes suffered severe reversals. Amid a public clamor stirred up by their numerous enemies, led in parliament by Pouyer-Quertier, the Pereires lost control of the Crédit Mobilier and the Compagnie générale transatlantique and only barely managed to retain control of the Chemin de fer du Midi. For the next eight years they lived in obscurity. But then in 1875—a few months after Emile's death—Isaac staged a remarkable comeback. Cornering two-thirds of the shares of the faltering Transatlantique, he installed his son, Eugène, as president. He then overhauled the administration and poured 25 million francs into modernization and expansion of the fleet. The volume of passengers doubled by 1880, and the CGT again took its place among the foremost Atlantic carriers.[9]

While regaining his position in big business, Pereire also launched a new career in journalism by taking charge of the Paris daily, *La Liberté*, early in 1876.[10] His editorial line was pure Saint-Simonian: the evils of revolution and social turmoil were the products of poverty, said Pereire, and poverty could be eliminated by proper social organization and by economic progress encouraged by enlightened government policy.[11] To help define that policy, Pereire turned out a steady stream of editorials and pamphlets on the railroad question, fiscal reform, and the tariff between 1876 and his death in 1880. His program for tariff reform was straight free trade and included a demand for the elimination of all import duties on coal, iron, textiles, and sugar.[12] In stating these views, Pereire emerged as a free trade publicist second only to Leroy-Beaulieu. And, although never a member of Eichthal's

9. Barbance, *Histoire de la Compagnie générale transatlantique,* pp. 92–100. The rise and fall of the Pereires is also chronicled in Cameron, *France and the Economic Development of Europe,* pp. 134–195, and Louis Girard, *La politique des travaux publics sous le Second Empire* (Paris, 1952).

10. In 1871, *La Liberté* was purchased by a stock company headed by Pereire. Management of the paper remained in the hands of Léonce Detroyat, nephew of the original owner, Emile de Girardin, until May 1876, when Detroyat was removed and Pereire became editor (Claude Bellanger et al., *Histoire générale de la presse française,* 3 vols. [Paris, 1972], III, 202–203).

11. "Notre programme—II," *La Liberté,* June 20, 1876.

12. Isaac Pereire, *Politique industrielle et commerciale: Budget des reformes* (Paris, 1877), pp. 6–14.

Free Trade Association, he must be considered a leader of the free trade party in the late 1870s.

Ranked close behind Eichthal and Pereire among Parisian free traders and dominating the Paris contingent in the Free Trade Association was an eclectic group of import-export merchants and manufacturers for export who controlled the Paris Chamber of Commerce and the Chambre syndicale du commerce d'exportation. This group included such men of moderate wealth and purely local influence as Louis-Adolphe Houette, a leather merchant and president of the Chamber of Commerce in 1878; Pierre-Eugène Brélay, a cloth merchant and deputy for the Seine; Camille Marcilhacy, a dealer in silks; J. Levois, an exporter of *articles de Paris*; the jeweler Léon Hiélard; and a necktie manufacturer, Jules Hayem.[13] The contingent was led by five men of great wealth and national—even international—influence: the manufacturers Ernest Gouin, Gustave Lebaudy, and Emile Menier, and the *négociants* Henri Fould and Gustave Roy.

Ernest Gouin came from an important banking family of Tours which produced two other major figures in the nineteenth century: Alexandre-Henri Gouin, deputy and senator for the Indre-et-Loire, a director of the Paris-Lyons railroad, and commerce minister in 1840; and Alexandre's son and Ernest's cousin, Eugène, who founded the Banque de Paris et des Pays-Bas.[14] Ernest sprang from the Paris branch of the family and, although a regent of the Banque de France late in his career, he was not directly involved in the family bank, but made his way as an engineer. Graduating from the Ecole polytechnique in 1836, he was first employed by the Pereires in building the Paris-Saint Germain railroad, 1839–1845. In 1846, he set up a firm to manufacture railroad equipment with the backing of the Rothschilds, Hottinguers, and Eichthals. This company, which be-

13. These and subsequent names are taken from the membership list of the Free Trade Association found in a memorandum to the minister of commerce, December 30, 1878, in AN F^{12} 6385, and reproduced in Appendix 1. On this group little biographical data is available. On Brélay, see *DPF*, I, 477; for Houette, Marcilhacy, J. Levois, Hiélard, and Hayem, see their dossiers in AN F^{12} 5169, 5201, 5194, 5168, and 5166, respectively.

14. André Delavenne, *Recueil généalogique de la bourgeoisie ancienne* (Paris, n.d.), pp. 212–215; *DPF*, III, 213–215.

came the Société des constructions des Batignolles in 1871, built locomotives, bridges, tunnels, and earth-moving equipment not only for French railroads, but also for railroads in eastern Europe, South America, and North Africa.[15] This wide-ranging business brought Gouin into the free trade camp in two ways: because the trade treaties of the 1860s opened markets for him in Italy, Switzerland, and Austria-Hungary, he naturally favored their renewal, and he needed to import cheap iron and steel from England in order to compete for foreign contracts. Indeed, in the early 1870s, Gouin had imported virtually all iron and steel used in constructing locomotives for Brazil, Portugal, and Austria under the temporary admissions system, whereby certain semifinished goods could be imported duty-free if used in finished goods to be exported.[16] Ideally, Gouin wanted permanent reductions in duties on iron, and in 1877, when he served as president of the Paris Chamber of Commerce, he pushed for such a reduction. Realistically, he was willing to settle for a more liberal policy on temporary admission of iron and argued for such a liberalization before the Conseil supérieur du commerce in January 1877.[17]

The importation of foreign raw materials and the exportation of finished products brought other Parisian capitalists to the free trade party. One of these was the sugar refiner Gustave Lebaudy; another was the *chocolatier* Emile Menier. Lebaudy was the son of Guillaume Lebaudy, who, in association with his brothers, made a fortune importing and refining cane sugar in the early nineteenth century. The Lebaudys began with trading houses in Le Havre and Paris and a refinery at La Villette; through marriage alliances with the Derosne and Cail families, they added the manufacture of refining equipment to their purview; in 1844, with the banker, Jacques Laffitte, they created the Société des Antilles—a veritable colonial sugar trust—to assure supplies.[18]

15. Cameron, *France and the Economic Development of Europe*, pp. 99–100; François Caron, "Les commandes des compagnies des chemins de fer en France, 1850–1914," *Revue d'histoire de la sidérurgie*, 3 (1965), 170–171.

16. Gouin et Cie dossier, AN F¹² 2582.

17. Conseil supérieur du commerce, *Admissions temporaires* (Paris, 1877), pp. 8–11.

18. Bertrand Gille, *Recherches sur la formation de la grande entreprise capitaliste* (Paris, 1959), p. 123.

Gustave Lebaudy inherited the refining end of this business, centered in the 1870s at Mantes (Seine-et-Oise). Throughout the seventies, as a member of the Paris Chamber of Commerce, as a deputy, and as a member of the Chamber Tariff Commission, Lebaudy pressed for maintenance of the liberal tariff system. In doing so, he reflected the viewpoint of the cane sugar importer at odds with the protectionist beet sugar interests of the métropole. Menier's free trade convictions had similar origins. In 1853, Menier had inherited a prosperous chocolate factory at Noisiel. Subsequently he added factories in the Somme and participated in the construction of a huge sugar refinery at Villenoy-les-Meaux. In the 1870s, he was the biggest chocolate and candy producer in Europe. In contrast to Lebaudy, he used domestic sugar (Villenoy processed sugar beets), but he imported cacao from plantations in Nicaragua and marketed his products world-wide.[19] Consequently, as deputy for the Seine-et-Marne and as a member of the Chamber Tariff Commission, he, too, supported continued free trade.

Gouin, Lebaudy, and Menier were manufacturers led to support a free trade policy by the needs of their industries; Henri Fould and Gustave Roy are classic examples of free traders drawn from international commerce. Henri Fould came from the cadet branch of a renowned family of Alsatian Jews. The elder line of Foulds—Beer-Léon and his sons—had founded the Fould-Oppenheim bank in the capital and had soon risen to the top of the Parisian banking community, with Achille Fould serving as Napoleon III's finance minister in the 1850s. Henri's grandfather (Beer-Léon's brother) had remained in the cloth trade in eastern France, and Henri's father had contented himself with a relatively modest career as a grain dealer in the Paris market. Thus, although Henri and his younger brother Léon did not inherit great wealth, they were able to utilize extensive family connections in trade and finance in setting up a business in Paris specializing in the export of *articles de Paris* (luxuries and novelties, such as chess sets and umbrellas). Founded in 1858, their firm prospered in the next two decades. By the 1870s, Fould

19. *DPF,* iv, 337–338; Philippe Bernard, *Economie et sociologie de la Seine-et-Marne, 1850–1950* (Paris, 1953), pp. 105, 110–111.

Frères annually exported 15 million francs worth of *articles de Paris* (one-tenth of the total) and had branches in the United States, South America, and the Orient. As an adjunct to this commerce, Henri Fould joined in 1872 with Jean Vignal of Le Havre to form the Chargeurs réunis, a steamship company operating between Le Havre and the ports of Brazil and La Plata. By 1880, Fould Frères could be described as "the most important firm in France from the standpoint of exports."[20] In defense of the export business and his own firm, Henri Fould vigorously pushed for tariff liberalization as a member of the Paris Chamber of Commerce and as vice-president of the Chambre syndicale d'exportation.[21]

While Fould was rising through the export of Parisian luxuries, Gustave Roy had already made his fortune in the international trade in cloth and yarn. Roy descended from a long line of Huguenot cloth merchants. In the early 1800s, his maternal grandfather, Charles Carcenac, had founded in Paris a firm for the manufacture and sale of cotton cloth which his father, Auguste-Emmanuel Roy, and his uncle, Henry Carcenac, continued to run into the 1840s. At first, Roy and Carcenac had put out cotton to be spun at Chantilly, woven in Picardy, and bleached by Davillier et Cie at Gisors, and had then marketed the finished product in Paris. With the rise of the Alsatian cotton industry, however, they abandoned manufacture to become middlemen between Alsace and the Paris market. It was as contact man with Alsatian cotton manufacturers—especially Boigeol-Japy of Giromagny—that Gustave Roy entered the firm in 1845. In 1847, he became Carcenac's partner and, after suffering through hard times in 1848–1850, he struck it rich in 1851 when he bought up thirty thousand pieces of cotton cloth at Mulhouse—virtually cornering the market immediately prior to the coup d'état in December (of which he apparently had advance notice)—and then

20. Letter of Charles Lecomte, June 30, 1880, in Henri Fould dossier, AN F[12] 5148. On the Fould family, see Delavenne, *Recueil généalogique*, pp. 181–182, and Boudet, ed., *Le monde des affaires*, pp. 316, 656. On the Chargeurs réunis, see Alphonse Courtois, *Manuel des fonds publics et des sociétés par actions*, 7th ed. (Paris, 1878), p. 653.

21. See his testimony before the Chamber Tariff Commission on November 6, 1878, in *Journal officiel*, November 28, 1878, pp. 11110–11118.

sold at a hugh profit during the business upswing of 1852. By 1858, Roy was a millionaire. Subsequently, he diversified into insurance and winegrowing and also turned to "public service," as a member of the Conseil consultatif des arts et manufactures and the Commission des valeurs de douane. However, his basic interest—and the generator of his free trade views—remained the cloth and yarn trade headquartered in Paris with branches in Rouen, Manchester, and, until 1871 Mulhouse.[22] Roy did not describe the exact structure of this trade in his memoirs, but from his testimony before the Chamber Tariff Commission in 1878, one can infer that the chief business of G. Roy et Cie in the 1870s was the importation of cotton yarns from England and Alsace for use by the weaving industries of Saint-Pierre-lès-Calais and Tarare and perhaps the marketing of the finished cloth in France and abroad. Certainly his demand for reduction of tariffs on yarn but maintenance of tariffs on cloth was consistent with such a business orientation.[23]

Despite the diversity of their enterprises, Gouin, Lebaudy, Menier, Fould, and Roy all prospered under the tariff policy of Napoleon III, and it is thus not surprising that they worked together to preserve and extend that policy. In 1873, Fould and Roy joined with merchants of Bordeaux, Lyons, Marseilles, and Le Havre to finance *L'économiste français,* and they subsequently served on its board of directors. At the time, Lebaudy, Gouin, and Roy entered the Paris Chamber of Commerce and, with Fould and Louis-Adolphe Houette, formed a free trade bloc that controlled the Chamber for the next ten years (Gouin, Houette, and Roy each served as president between 1877 and 1883). During this time, the Chamber aggressively defended the liberal trade policy.[24] Outside the Chamber these men pursued similar goals through such organs as the Chambre syndicale d'exportation and, of course, the Free Trade Association, which

22. For full biographical details, see Roy's remarkably frank memoirs: Gustave Roy, *Souvenirs, 1823–1906* (Nancy, 1906).
23. Roy deposition, Chamber Tariff Commission, *Journal officiel,* July 18, 1878, pp. 7971–7976.
24. The position of the Paris Chamber of Commerce on the tariff is best seen in "Revision du tarif général," Chambre de commerce de Paris, *Avis: 1877* (Paris, 1878), pp. 149–225.

first met at Fould Frères in June 1878. In this manner, the economic power of the industrial, financial, commercial, and transport interests of Paris and the commitment of those interests to free trade were translated into effective political support for a moderate general tariff and for renewal of the trade treaties.

Although Paris furnished most of the founders of the Free Trade Association and the largest single contingent of its members, Lyons and its environs provided the second largest contingent. Like Paris, Lyons was not only a center of commerce and finance, but also the hub of a regional industrial complex encompassing the Rhône and its neighboring departments, especially the Loire and the Isère. This complex included mining and metallurgy (especially in the Loire), chemicals, and textile manufacture (silks and blends in Lyons and its suburbs, ribbon in the Loire, cotton goods in Roanne and Tarare). Indeed, in the 1860s and 1870s the Lyonnais was France's most important industrial region in terms of total product and total work force. Because of their economic circumstances, most of the industries of the region—all textiles and, for a while, even metallurgy—were sympathetic to free trade, and many Lyonnais industrialists joined in the Free Trade Association in 1878. Yet, because the focus of this analysis is on interests, not on locales or communities per se, discussion of these industries and their leaders' position on tariff policy will be reserved for the sections on metallurgy and textiles. Here we will focus on the capitalist elite—the merchants and merchant-bankers—who headed the free trade forces in Lyons. Many of these were investors in the industry of their area, but their essential interests lay in international commerce, banking, and transport, and, like the Paris free traders, they derived their free trade convictions from those interests.

From the beginning, the economy of Lyons rested on international (that is, trans-European) trade. Located at the confluence of the Rhône and Saône rivers, Lyons was ideally situated to organize and exploit the trade in Italian and Levantine goods coming over the Alps and down the Rhône Valley en route to markets in France, the Netherlands, and England. The establishment of four annual fairs to handle this commerce in the Middle Ages led, in turn, to the rise of a cosmopolitan community of merchants in Lyons. As the Levant trade shifted from inland trade routes to the Atlantic in the sixteenth and seventeenth centuries, these merchants increasingly specialized in the importation and reexport of Italian silks. Eventually they organized the manufacture of silk in Lyons itself, first using imported raw silk and later silk grown in the Rhône Valley. Since the market for these silks was largely foriegn, the Lyonnais's new interest in manufacturing reinforced their involvement in international trade. Continued involvement in international trade, in turn, made Lyons a center of merchant banking, equal in stature to Paris, Geneva, and Basel in the eighteenth century. Although Paris somewhat eclipsed Lyons in banking and finance in the early nineteenth century, the founding in 1863 of the Crédit Lyonnais, France's first modern deposit bank, reestablished the city's financial importance in the 1860s. At the same time Lyons remained an important transport center. In the 1840s and 1850s it was headquartered for the steamboat traffic on the Rhône and Saône and the entrepôt for goods moving from one river to the other. Although the completion of the P-L-M and Geneva-Lyons-Paris railroads by 1859 killed the steamboat business and undercut Lyons's status as a national entrepôt, the Lyonnais compensated in the 1860s through the building of a regional railroad network that enhanced their city's position as a regional transport and trade center.[25]

As in Paris, the commerce, finance, and transport interests of Lyons were interrelated; anyone involved in one was usually involved in the others as well. Also as in Paris, involvement in this nexus of interests in Lyons invariably fostered free trade sentiments, as is well illustrated in the life and interests of Oscar Galline, the leader of the Lyonnais free traders in the late 1870s. The firm of Galline et Cie was founded in 1821, with the backing of Geneva bankers, to exploit the discount and haulage business in Lyons. By the 1850s, Oscar Galline, heir and head of this firm, had developed a wide range of interests of international

25. Pierre Léon, "La région lyonnaise dans l'histoire économique et sociale de la France: Une esquisse," *Revue historique*, 237 (1967), 31–62; Jean Bouvier, "Aux origines du Crédit Lyonnais: Le milieu économique et financier lyonnais au début des années 1860," *Histoire des entreprises*, 6 (1960), 41–64.

scope in transport and banking. He ran an important inland navigation company and was a director of the Lyons-Geneva railroad, the Messageries Imperiales, and the Compagnie des docks de Marseille; he was also a regent of the Lyons branch of the Bank of France. In 1859 he joined with Arlès-Dufour in the founding of the Magasin général des soies, a precursor of the Crédit Lyonnais, and later he took a place on the board of the Crédit Lyonnais itself.[26] Involvement in international transport and finance naturally molded his views on tariff policy. Following the lead of other Lyons bankers who were defending the trade treaties as members of parliament in the 1870s—including Henri Germain, Eugène Flottard, and Edouard Millaud—Galline, as president of the Lyons Chamber of Commerce, led a Lyonnais contingent into the Free Trade Association and defended the free trade system before the Chamber Tariff Commission in 1878.[27]

In this endeavor, Galline was strongly supported by various *marchands de soie,* representatives of that characteristically Lyonnais subspecies of merchant banker which had produced so many prominent financiers (including Henri Germain) and had long controlled the commercial organs of the city. In the 1870s there were some eighty *marchands de soie* operating in Lyons. Then as previously, they provided the capital and contacts to move raw silk into Lyons for spinning and weaving and to move finished silk goods from Lyons to markets throughout France, Europe, and the world. Of course, in doing so, they became closely bound up with the manufacture of silk, although they rarely owned spindles and looms themselves or directly employed weavers (this was the function of the master weavers).[28] Thus they had a clear

26. Gailline dossier, AN F¹² 5150; Gille, *La banque et le crédit,* p. 58; Bouvier, "Aux origines du Crédit Lyonnais," p. 57.

27. Eugène Flottard was an administrator of the Lyons branch of the Banque de France and a co-founder of *L'économiste français.* As deputy for the Rhône, he helped to organize the free trade caucus in the National Assembly in 1871. Henri Germain, president of the Crédit Lyonnais and deputy for the Ain, joined that caucus and participated in the resistance to the raw materials tax in 1872–1873. Edouard Millaud, of a prominent Jewish banking family, was deputy for the Rhône after 1876 and a member of the Chamber Tariff Commission. For Galline's deposition to the Chamber Tariff Commission, see *Journal officiel,* June 22, 1878, pp. 6931–6932.

28. Invariably the president of the Association de la fabrique lyonnaise was a *marchand de soie* (Auguste Sévène in 1878) and not a master weaver.

interest in maintaining the health of the silk industry in general and the export trade in silk cloth in particular. This interest provided sufficient rationale for supporting free trade. It was not their only interest, however, nor their only rationale for supporting free trade. The value of silk cloth exported from France was declining rapidly in the late 1870s, from a peak of 478 million francs in 1873 to 293 million francs in 1877, a result not of a decline in production—the quantity of silk production continued to rise—but rather of a decline in the unit price of silk goods caused by growing competition in the world market. In any case, for most *marchands de soie*, the export of silk cloth, which had been the single most lucrative element of their business as late as 1873, had taken a back seat to the import and export of raw silk by 1876.[29]

The raw silk trade had risen because of the pebrine blight of the 1850s which had devastated the silkworms of the Rhône, thereby ruining many landed proprietors of the region and causing no small inconvenience for the silk industry of Lyons. For the *marchands de soie*, however, it provided new business opportunities. One of them, Francisque David—who, atypically, also ran a textile mill in the Loire—took advantage of the crisis and the recent opening of trade with Japan to initiate the importation of silkworm eggs from Oshio and Yanagawa in partnership with the Dutch trader who had a monopoly in all Japanese-European transactions.[30] More important, as the blight continued (despite the infusion of Japanese stock) and as raw silk prices rose, David joined other *marchands de soie* in organizing and financing the importation of Oriental cocoons—and operation made possible by the completion of the Suez Canal. As a result, French silk imports jumped dramatically—from 4.7 million kilograms in 1867 to 9 million kilograms in 1876—and the Oriental share in French silk imports doubled from 15 to 30 percent.[31] Soon the *marchands de soie* were able not simply to replace the domestic

29. Between 1873 and 1876, the value of all silk imports (mostly raw silk) rose from 445 million francs to 664 million francs. In the same period, the value of exported raw silk rose from 193 million to 295 million francs, but the value of exported silk cloth fell from 478 million francs to 295 million (*Tableau décennal*, I xciv ff.).

30. Francisque David dossier, AN F¹² 5120.

31. *Annales du commerce extérieur*, no. 102, p. 170; John Laffey, "Les racines de

supplies lost to pebrine but also to supply raw silk to manufacturers throughout Europe. Between 1867 and 1876, French exports and reexports of raw silk rose in value from 190 million to 293 million francs and Lyons regained from London control of the world silk trade. It was to keep channels open for all of this trade, not just to encourage the export of Lyons silk cloth, that the *marchands se soie* favored free trade. In the 1870s they joined with Galline to mobilize the chamber of commerce against any "revolution anti-économique et retrograde," that is, any return to protection, and under the leadership of Lilienthal, president of the Union des marchands de soie, they formed a subcommittee withing the Free Trade Association to lobby continuously in favor of a mild general tariff and renewal of the trade treaties.[32]

Beyond Paris and Lyons, the chief centers for international commerce, finance, and transport were the seaports. In Bordeaux, Marseilles, Le Havre, and Nantes—the major ports for transoceanic commerce—as well as in smaller ports like Dunkirk and Boulogne, there were communities of traders, commission agents, and merchant bankers, who were often linked to the merchant families of Paris and Lyons. Because these communities lived off the movement of goods across national boundaries, they naturally abhorred high tariffs and instinctively favored free trade. But their presence in a port city did not always assure that the official organs of that city, such as the chamber of commerce, would support the cause of free trade. Other interests sometimes swung the chamber of commerce the other way. Shipbuilders and shipowners constituted such an interest in the 1870s. In particular, the builders and operators of sailcraft were becoming aggressively protectionist as their economic position declined in the 1870s. At first, they hoped to maintain their viability in the face of foreign (British) competition and technical obsolescence through the imposition of taxes on foreign shipping. Led in the National Assembly by Daniel Ancel of Le Havre and Louis Babin-Chevaye of Nantes, they had won a brief victory in January 1872, when the

l'imperialisme français en extrême-orient. A propos des thèses de J-F Cady," *Revue d'histoire moderne et contemporaine*, 16 (1969), 287–288.

32. *L'économiste français*, April 8, 1876, pp. 463–464; "Déclaration du comité lyonnais, Association pour la défense de la liberté commerciale," AN F[12] 2488A.

surtaxe de pavillon—a tax on goods imported in foreign holds—
was reestablished. However, the surtax was scrapped in 1873, and
thereafter shipbuilders and shipowners put their hopes in winning outright government subsidies. In April 1876, they captured
national attention by staging a maritime congress in Paris to put
forth their demands. Two years later, they returned under the
leadership of Arthur Petitdidier of Honfleur and Emile Bossière
of Le Havre to plead their cases in the Senate inquiry on the
economic crisis. In 1878 they flocked to the AIF and eventually,
with the support of the industrial protectionists, they won
subventions for both construction and navigation.[33] Meanwhile,
back home, they vied with the local merchants to decide their
ports' stand on tariff policy. In Nantes and Le Havre, they, along
with other protectionist interests, succeeded in blocking any
official participation in the free trade party.

In the eighteenth century, Nantes had been France's most
prosperous port, the center of trade with the Antilles in slaves and
sugar. But the Revolution and the blockade, not to mention the
abolition of the slave trade, had ruined this commerce. Although
in the nineteenth century Nantes continued to import and refine
as much cane sugar as Marseilles, it no longer exported anything.
Coupled with its inaccessibility to ships over three hundred tons,
this meant that the new Atlantic steamers passed it by. The great
merchants soon departed, leaving local shipbuilders, who were
preoccupied with the search for subsidies, in control of the port
almost by default. Thus, though Lechat, the mayor of Nantes,
joined the Free Trade Association in 1878, the chamber of commerce did not participate. On the contrary, when it spoke on
commercial policy, it tended to favor protection.[34]

In Le Havre the situation was less clear-cut. Unlike Nantes, Le
Havre possessed the largest, most modern port facilities in France

33. On the plight of sail navigation, see the testimony of Arthur Petitdidier,
Sénat, *Enquête*, pp. 453–473. On the *congrès maritime: La Liberté,* April 27, 1876.
For a brief introduction to French shipping subsidies, consult Royal Meeker, *The
History of Shipping Subsidies* (New York, 1905), pp. 43 ff.
34. Deposition of Babin-Chevaye, president of the Nantes Chamber of Commerce, Sénat, *Enquête*, pp. 441–447. On the economic situation of Nantes in the
1870s, see Louis Simonin, "Les grands ports de commerce de la France: Nantes et
le bassin de la Loire," *Revue des deux mondes,* November 15, 1877, pp. 409–436.

and was a center of transatlantic steam navigation. It was from Le Havre that Pereire's Compagnie generale transatlantique sent packet boats to New York biweekly and that Fould's Chargeurs réunis dispatched steamers to the Caribbean and South America. The maintenance and repair of steamships supported two major shipyards in Le Havre: the Chantiers Normand and a branch of the Forges et chantiers de la Méditerranée. Moreover, it was to Le Havre that foreign steamers delivered much of the overseas products imported into France, first and foremost raw cotton, but also English coal and manufactures, Norwegian timber, Brazilian coffee, and American grain and meat (the importation of Argentine beef in refrigerated ships began at Le Havre in 1876). To protect this trade—especially the transit trade in English and American goods bound for Paris, eastern France, and central Europe—the merchants of Le Havre naturally favored free trade policies in France and elsewhere. During the protectionist reaction of 1869, they had persuaded the chamber of commerce to go on record for the trade treaties.[35] Presumably they continued to favor free trade after 1870 and yet, curiously, they ceased to speak in its defense and turned instead to other aspects of economic policy. For example, Jules Siegfried, a onetime cotton importer and a rising leader of the commercial community of Le Havre, who helped prepare the 1869 endorsement of the trade treaties, spoke and wrote almost exclusively on the railroads in the seventies.[36] There were two reasons for this, however. First, Siegfried and others were increasingly concerned that Le Havre was losing its battle with Antwerp for dominance of the transit trade with central Europe, and they increasingly sought the solution in the reform of railroad rates, not in tariff reform. Second, their soft-pedaling of free trade rhetoric reflected Le Havre's growing involvement in the protectionist cotton industry of Normandy. Le Havre had always depended on Normandy as a market for the raw cotton it imported, but that dependence was increasing in the

35. The chamber of commerce's position was indicated in Robert Quesnel, *Protection et libre-échange* (Le Havre, 1870).

36. Jules Siegfried, *Rapport sur la question des tarifs des chemins de fer français* (Le Havre, 1869); idem, *Quelques mots sur la question des chemins de fer* (Le Havre, 1875); idem, *Tarifs des chemins de fer* (Le Havre, 1877).

1870s as other cotton centers (such as the Vosges) were turning to other sources of supply (such as Antwerp). Moreover, Le Havre itself was becoming a center for cotton manufacture (the Siegfried family ran a spinning mill there). For these reasons, plus the influence of protectionist shipbuilders and shipowners, Le Havre remained outside the free trade camp in the 1870s. Indeed, no Le Havre businessman joined the Free Trade Association, although several—including Henri Fould's partner in Chargeurs réunis, Jean Vignal, and Jules Siegfried's brother, Ernest—joined the AIF. And when voices emanated from Le Havre on the tariff question in the late 1870s, they were voices of protection, such as Amédée Marteau's in the *Journal du Havre*. Consequently, although commercial, financial, and transport interests existed in all of France's major ports, only in Marseilles and Bordeaux were they sufficiently strong and committed to mobilize their city's official organs on behalf of free trade. Therefore, among the seaports, only those two played a role in the free trade movement comparable to that of Paris and Lyons.

In the 1870s, Marseilles was France's busiest port. Its harbor facilities had been enlarged and modernized in the 1860s so that, in contrast to its reputation as France's most backward port as late as 1857, it had become its most modern by 1870. At the same time, it had become France's center for the importation and transshipment of a variety of foreign goods thanks to a series of fortuitous changes in tariff policy, national production, and international trade. First, the destruction of Rhône silkworms made Marseilles the port of entry for Oriental cocoons bound for Lyons. Then the abolition of the sliding scale duties on wheat in 1861 opened Marseilles to east European grain for the first time. Simultaneously, the "cotton famine" on the Continent led to increased importation of Egyptian jumel. And after 1865, Marseilles served as entrepôt for Algerian ore on its way to the smelters of central France.[37]

37. Marseilles experienced a sixfold increase in the importation of raw silk and cocoons between 1855 and 1874 (from 9,319 to 58,036 bales). Its annual average of cotton imports rose from 60,000 bales in 1855–1859 to 156,210 bales in 1865–1869. Iron imports, nonexistent in 1860, amounted to some 4 million quintals a year in the early 1870s (Octave Teissier, *Histoire du commerce de Marseille pendant vingt ans, 1855–1877* [Paris, 1878], pp. 119–123, 240, 297).

The opening of the Suez Canal in 1869 offered Marseilles the promise of limitless growth, especially in the transit trade, although it was apparent as early as 1871 that Marseilles would profit less from the canal than Genoa would, because its rail facilities remained underdeveloped whereas Genoa possessed excellent connections, via the Saint Gothard Pass, with all of central and northern Europe. Nonetheless, Marseilles had all the business it could handle. Its merchants did not worry as much about Genoese competition as about the problem of providing outbound steamers with a cargo to replace the grain, ore, cotton, and silk that they had delivered. No one profited from empty holds, and merchantmen forced to leave a port carrying only ballast would not call again there soon. To attract the steamers, Marseilles had to export something. Lyons silks had been shipped out through Marseilles for years, but they did not furnish the bulk required to sustain maritime trade in the steam age. The wines of the Midi were exported from Marseilles until 1876, when phylloxera started taking its toll; thereafter Marseilles was an importer of Spanish, Italian, and Algerian wines.[38] To this critical situation the Marseillais responded imaginatively: they started producing their own exports from the raw materials that they imported. The decade of the seventies witnessed the birth of myriad construction and manufacturing industries around Marseilles: chemical plants, sugar refineries, flour mills, tanneries, seed oil distilleries, iron smelters, and shipyards, all constituting an industrial revolution unique among French port cities. To an observer writing in 1877, Marseilles had the unmistakable appearance of a boom town:

> In a hundred places, even within the city itself, which dares not complain, clusters of smokestacks higher than obelisks belch forth smoke which blackens the sky and fouls the air. All-conquering industry spreads everywhere and has overrun the entire coastline. The saltworks of Bouc and the Berre pool work for Marseilles; it is because of Marseilles that there are workshops at La Ciotat constructing and repairing the ships of the mighty Messageries

38. Report of the Marseilles Chamber of Commerce to the Conseil supérieur du commerce, 1890, AN F^{12} 6916.

maritimes. The élan has even gripped the neighboring department of the Var. At the port of La Seyne, near Toulon, stand the shipyards of the Société des forges et chantiers de la Méditerranée which maintains its headquarters and principal workshops at Marseilles.[39]

Because the source of raw materials and most of the markets of these new industries lay overseas, their continued prosperity depended on good commercial relations and on the minimization of restrictions on maritime traffic. Consequently most industrialists of Marseilles joined with the local mercantile community in defending the tariff policy of the Second Empire. In 1869, a local board of trade was formed to support the embattled trade treaties. In 1875 the Marseilles Chamber of Commerce came out for renewal of the treaties. And three years later Alphonse Grandval, president of the chamber of commerce, led a contingent from Marseilles, including Alexandre Clapier and Maurice Rouvier, into the Free Trade Association.[40]

In the realm of commercial policy, the chief concern of the Marseilles Chamber of Commerce in the 1870s was the future of the temporary admissions system, which directly affected Marseilles's grain trade and its milling industry. Between 1864 and 1873, Marseilles imported an average of 6.4 million hectoliters of grain yearly, constituting as much as 86 percent of France's total annual grain imports. Approximately one-tenth of this was processed and reexported; the rest was consumed domestically. The whole of this enterprise owed its existence to the commercial legislation of the Second Empire, and its continued success depended on the mechanics of temporary admissions which exempted grain to be milled and reexported from the 60 centime duty, provided it was accompanied by a custom permit. Marseilles was able to bring in grain for domestic consumption, as well as grain for reexport, under this system because it could discount the cost of permits by selling them at a reduced price to Dunkirk millers, who redeemed them for full value when they exported

39. Louis Simonin, "Les grands ports de commerce de la France: Marseille et le golfe de Lyon," *Revue des deux mondes,* July 15, 1877, p. 394.
40. Ibid., p. 404; *L'économiste français,* May 8, 1875, pp. 592–593.

flour milled from French wheat. The Marseilles importers profited because the net cost of the permits was less than would have
been paid in tariffs. Because this traffic produced a quasi-export
subsidy on French flour going to England, Belgian millers
considered it unfair competition. When the Franco-Belgian trade
treaty was renewed in 1873, they managed to have inserted in it an
intricate system of zones whereby permits purchased for the
importation of grain at a port in one zone could not be redeemed
on flour exported from a port in another. Obviously directed at
the lucrative partnership of Marseilles and Dunkirk, this system
threatened to undermine the Marseilles grain trade. Consequently, when the Conseil supérieur opened hearings on temporary admissions in December 1876, the president of the Marseilles
Chamber of Commerce, Grandval, and a contingent of grain
merchants were on hand to denounce the zone system and to
demand restoration of the traffic in permits. Grandval argued that
temporary admissions, as they existed from 1861 to 1873, were
mandatory for the well-being of French agriculture and for the
survival of the grain import business, and he easily rallied the free
traders on the council to his side. The council voted, seventeen to
fourteen, to restore the trafficking in permits after the expiration
of the treaty with Belgium in June 1877—at best a moral victory
for Marseilles, however, since the subsequent controversy on the
general tariff and trade treaties indefinitely postponed the implementation of this decision.[41]

Marseilles backed free trade because of the needs of its import,
milling, and manufacturing businesses. Bordeaux came to free
trade for other reasons. Like Nantes, Bordeaux had risen on the
Antilles trade in the eighteenth century and had seen that trade
destroyed between 1789 and 1815. In the nineteenth century,
Bordeaux shipowners met with some success in their efforts to
open new markets in Africa, South America, and the Orient. In
the 1860s and 1870s, Le Quellec and Bordes sent three-masted
schooners to the Plate River for wool and to Valparaiso for
copper, guano, and nitrates while Maurel and Prom traded flour

41. Alexandre Clapier, "Des admissions temporaires: La question des blés,"
L'économiste français, June 30, 1877, pp. 803–805; Conseil supérieur du commerce, *Admissions temporaires*, pp. 94–109.

and cloth for gum and peanuts in Senegal. Yet such trade was at best marginal in the age of steam, and in the realm of steam navigation Bordeaux remained backward. To be sure, the steamers of the Messageries maritimes and the Transatlantique called at Bordeaux en route to South America, but Bordeaux for a long time lacked the port facilities to properly accommodate the new scale of oceanic transport. Construction of vertical quays and docks began only in 1867, well after the initial modernization of Marseilles and Le Havre was completed. As a result, the main currents of transatlantic commerce continued to bypass Bordeaux for some time.[42] Despite these drawbacks—and in contrast to what happened in Nantes—a dynamic community of international merchants, descendants of the Spanish Jews and German and English Protestants who ran the colonial trade in the eighteenth century, remained in Bordeaux and, by overcoming the protectionist influence of local shipbuilders, succeeded in orienting the city toward free trade. The reason for their presence and their free trade sentiments was simple: the Gironde produced some of the most coveted wines in the world, and Bordeaux was the center for their export.

Bordeaux had sent its wines abroad for centuries, but the wine trade there took on new dimensions in the late 1850s. The oidium blight of 1850 had done no permanent damage to the vines, but by wiping out several harvests it raised the price of Bordeaux vintages. This, in turn, attracted heavy investment in Bordeaux wineries (it was in this period that Achille Fould, Michel-Frédéric Pillet-Will, and Alphonse de Rothschild bought châteaux in the Médoc). The upshot was that wine production in the Gironde almost doubled, rising from 1,263,000 hectoliters in 1852 to 2,350,000 in 1869.[43] The growth of wine exports was equally dramatic—rising from 700,000 hectoliters in 1859 to 1,261,000 in 1876—despite a decline in exports to the United States. This overall increase derived from substantial increases in exports to

42. Louis Desgraves and Georges Dupeux, *Bordeaux au XIXe siècle* (Bordeaux, 1969), pp. 35–83; Marthe Barbance, *Vie commerciale de la route du Cap Horn au XIXe siècle: L'armement A-D Bordes et fils* (Paris, 1969); Albert Charles, "La modernisation du port de Bordeaux sous le Second Empire," *Revue historique de Bordeaux*, n.s., 11 (1962), 25–49.
43. Desgraves and Dupeux, *Bordeaux au XIXe siècle*, pp. 179–186.

continental Europe and South America, but most of all from a tenfold increase in exports to England. Indeed, by 1876, England stood second only to Germany as a foreign market for Bordeaux wine.[44]

In the eyes of the Bordelais, the growth of their wine exports clearly sprang from the trade treaties negotiated in the 1860s, particularly the Anglo-French treaty, and renewal of those treaties preoccupied the Bordeaux Chamber of Commerce in the 1870s. By then it had been agitating for free trade for decades. As seen earlier, it had helped organize the first national free trade association in 1845. Throughout the 1850s the chamber supported a paid lobbyist in Paris to pressure the government to liberalize trade policy. In 1860, Chevalier relied heavily on the enthusiasm of the Bordelais to counteract the opposition to the treaty with England, and in 1868–1870 Bordeaux led the defense of the treaties against the protectionist assault.[45] After 1870 this defense continued in the National Assembly under the leadership of Nathaniel Johnston, a descendant of English traders, who was reputedly the wealthiest wine exporter in France. When Johnston retired from parliament and from public life in 1876, leadership passed to Armand Lalande, another major wine merchant and the owner of several "grand cru" vineyards, who also had extensive interests in transport (the Bordeaux–New York Steamship Company, the Orleans railway).[46] During Lalande's presidency, the Bordeaux

44. Lalande deposition, *Journal officiel*, December 5, 1878, pp. 11458–11461. Breaking down the export of Gironde wines by destination, Lalande gave the following figures (in hectoliters):

	1859	1876
England	28,500	248,000
Germany	164,700	252,700
Belgium	70,250	95,200
United States	149,000	60,500
Plate River	35,200	154,700
The Netherlands	59,800	109,000

45. Albert Charles, "Le rôle du grand commerce bordelais dans l'évolution du système douanier français de 1852 à 1860," *Revue historique de Bordeaux*, n.s., 9 (1960), 65-88.

46. *DPF*, iii, 546–547.

Chamber of Commerce emitted a steady stream of free trade propaganda as well as a twelve-point program for tariff reform which not only called for renewal of the trade treaties but also demanded the elimination of all protective duties, thereby reaffirming the Bordelais's traditional position as the most extreme of French free traders.[47]

These, then, were the commercial, financial, and transport interests that stood at the heart of the free trade party. Together they formed a coherent nexus—centered in Paris and Lyons with major branches in Marseilles and Bordeaux—which possessed economic and political influence far out of proportion to the number of its members and far in excess of its weight in the economic life of the country. This influence was in part a matter of position: bankers and merchants naturally held a position of command within the economic system and, through their presence and connections in the capital, they wielded great influence in politics as well. Influence also stemmed from the cohesiveness of the free trade interests, which, in turn, derived partially from the personal interconnections (business and family ties) that united bankers, merchants, and transport magnates and partially from the nature of the free trade doctrine itself. Unlike protectionist systems where preferential treatment of one product often prejudiced the production of another and made it difficult to find common ground among interests on the basis of tariff policy, free trade by definition meant the absence of special treatment and could easily unite all interests with the strength to survive and prosper in an open system (thus it was often easier for the strong and expansive to unite behind a specific set of free trade policies than for the weak and threatened to unite behind a specific set of protectionist policies). In any case, it was clear in 1878 that the free trade nexus—whatever the source of its strength—was already well entrenched in the political and economic landscape of France and would subsequently play a crucial role in the making of tariff policy under the Third Republic.

47. Chambre de commerce de Bordeaux, *Voeux exprimés de 1872 à 1879 au sujet des tarifs douaniers, des traités de commerce, du commerce extérieur, et de la marine marchande* (Bordeaux, 1880).

The Protectionist Consensus in Heavy Industry: Mining, Metallurgy, and Construction

Turning from free trade interests to protectionist interests, we leave the large, cosmopolitan centers of trade and finance and enter France's provincial cities and mill towns. We also shift our focus from merchants and merchant bankers involved in world trade to manufacturers producing for the domestic market (local, regional, or national). Just as the free traders mobilized within a national association in 1878, the protectionist industrialists entered the political arena through a new pressure group of national scope, the Association de l'industrie française, formed in the spring of 1878. The largest contingent within the AIF—accounting for half of the total membership—was the textile manufacturers: cotton and flax spinners and the makers of carded woolens, jute, and burlap. These will be examined along with the entire French textile industry in Chapter 3. Meriting initial consideration, however, is the second most numerous contingent, formed by representatives of mining, metallurgy, and construction. This group provided many of the founders and officers of the AIF, including the president, six of the eight vice-presidents, two of the three secretaries, and thirteen of the twenty-four members of the action committee. As such, it furnished much of the leadership of, and had the greatest leverage within, the protectionist bloc. Indeed, heavy industry held a position within the protectionist movement comparable to that of commerce, finance, and transport interests within the free trade movement, and an analysis of it provides the proper accompaniment to the foregoing discussion of the free trade nexus. This analysis will follow the sequence of manufacture beginning with the most basic, mining, and proceeding to metallurgy (smelting and refining), metallurgical manufacturing, and construction. As in the previous section, the goal here will be to identify the interests involved, describe their circumstances, pinpoint their demands for tariff policy, and explain how those demands fitted into their broader business strategies. In addition, we will explore the cooperation among these interests on economic policy in the late 1870s—an important development because it foreshadowed the larger accommodation of interests in France in the 1890s.

The mining interest in the AIF included producers of metallic ores, such as Parron of the Mokta-el-Hadid iron mine and Bourlon de Sarty of the Compagnie des mines de fer de Camerata, but it centered mostly on coal. Directors of the fifteen coal companies joined the AIF, including directors of five of the six largest (Anzin, Grand'combe, Blanzy, Firminy-Roche-La Molière, and Aniche) as well as directors of another five in the top twenty (Lens, Courrières, Le Creusot, Béthune, and Decazeville).[48] Colliers also played an active role in the leadership of the organization. Arthur Joly de Bammeville of the Houillères de l'Aveyron (Decazeville) and Emile Vuillemin, administrator of Aniche and president of the Comité des houillères du Nord et du Pas-de-Calais, were vice-presidents of the AIF; Paul Schneider of Decazeville was a secretary. On the action committee sat Alfred Dupont of Courrières, vice-president of the Nord–Pas-de-Calais coal syndicate, Paul-Ferdinand Delaville le Roulx of Grand' combe, Henri Schneider of Le Creusot (which included an important coal mine, as well as a metallurgical and manufacturing complex), and Amédée Burat, chief engineer of the Blanzy mines and spokesman for the Comité des houillères françaises.

The presence of France's foremost colliers in the protectionist party was, of course, not surprising. The French coal industry had grown continuously through the nineteenth century, yet in the 1870s it was no larger than Belgium's and considerably smaller than England's and Germany's.[49] It included various minor fields scattered through France, but production centered on two major beds—that of the Massif Central (Allier, Saône-et-

48. This ranking derives from figures in Jean Bouvier et al., *Le mouvement du profit en France au XIXe siècle: Matériaux et études* (Paris, 1965), pp. 316 ff., and Marcel Gillet, *Les charbonnages du nord de la France au XIXe siècle* (Paris, 1973), p. 118.

49. French coal production advanced from 881,587 tons in 1815 to 17.1 million tons in 1876 (*Annuaire statistique*, 13 [1890], 506–507). According to Alfred Dupont's testimony before the Chamber Tariff Commission (*Journal officiel*, July 23, 1878, p. 8083), both Belgium and France produced 17 million tons in 1878, whereas Germany produced 40 million and England 140 million.

Loire, Loire, and Gard) and the "Australasian" field in the North (Nord and Pas-de-Calais)—where all the largest mines were located. These mines not only served local markets but also aspired to serve the national market—Paris especially. To do so, however, they had to compete continuously with foreign colliers, which created and sustained a protectionist mentality in the industry throughout the century. In the 1840s and 1850s colliers organized in a Union des houillères to fight tariff liberalization, and in the 1860s politicians linked to coal (especially Adolphe Thiers, longtime spokesman for Anzin) led the attack on the trade treaties.

If it is thus not surprising that the colliers favored protection in the 1870s, the relative moderation of their protectionism *is* surprising. The Second Empire had aimed at reducing the colliers' control of the domestic market. In 1854, the government broke up the monopolistic coal combine in the Loire, the Compagnie de la Loire, and further discouraged concentration by keeping existing companies from picking up additional conces-sions, which led to the fragmentation of the newly opened Pas-de-Calais field among a number of competing firms. At the same time it opened the way for increased foreign competition in the home market by reducing the coal duty from 5.5 francs per ton in the early 1850s to 1.2 francs per ton in 1863. Yet the colliers had no intention of reversing these policies in the 1870s. Rather than demanding a return to previous levels of protection, spokesmen for the industry, appearing before the Chamber Tariff Commis-sion in 1878, sought only to maintain the existing nominal duty.[50] The colliers had not converted to free trade, but they apparently accepted the mildly protective system set up by Napoleon III. Why this was so can be discovered by looking at the development of the industry in the 1860s and early 1870s and by considering the economic and political realities of the industry in 1878.

Despite the reduction of the tariff, the French coal industry had in no way been undercut by foreign competition after 1860. Quite the contrary. Although importation of English, Belgian, and

50. Testimony of Paul Schneider et al., Chamber Tariff Commission, *Procès-verbaux*, pp. 416–445.

German coal rose 50 percent between 1859 and 1873, so great was the growth of domestic demand, undoubtedly due to the building and operation of the railroads, that domestic production had risen 100 percent in the same period.[51] Prices remained steady in the 1860s and shot up dramatically in the early 1870s. This combination of rising demand and rising prices produced unprecedented growth of revenues and profits among the major companies in the period 1860–1873. Even in the mid-seventies, when production was leveling off and prices declined from their 1873 peak, revenues and profits remained well above the level of the previous decade.[52]

The lesson of these years was that French coal did not need protective tariffs to keep prices and production high enough to assure the industry's survival and prosperity. This was particularly true in the south and southwest. The building of the P-L-M and Midi rail systems, the rapid industrial development of the Lyons region (especially in metallurgy), and the equally rapid development of Marseilles together produced an enormous rise in the demand for coal. With foreign producers unable to supply this demand economically because of the distance factor, the local mines—Blanzy, Firminy, Grand'combe, and Decazeville (reopened in 1867 to produce coal rather than metals)—were able to exploit and, indeed, to control this demand. Dividing up the market and fixing prices by agreement,[53] all proceeded to enjoy the expanding production and rising profits. Demand slackened in the seventies as metallurgical production slackened, but with

51. *Annuaire statistique*, 1 (1878), 362; Gillet, *Les charbonnages du nord*, p. 425.

52. Grand'combe's production, for example, rose from 397,752 tons in 1859 to 588,000 tons in 1873 and 709,634 tons in 1878; its declared profits rose from 1.8 million francs in 1859 to 3.48 million in 1878, with the rate of return advancing from 31 percent to 54.6 percent. Firminy-Roche-La Molière did even better: production rose from 174,828 tons (1859) to 638,616 (1878); revenues increased 500 percent, 1859–1873, and, although they slumped thereafter, they were still in 1878 three and a half times what they had been in 1859 (Bouvier, *Le mouvement du profit*, pp. 348, 407). In the fast-growing Pas-de-Calais field, the largest company, Lens, saw production rise from 159,000 tons (1859) to 654,000 tons (1878) with dividends rising from 450,000 francs in 1859 to 3 million in 1873 before leveling off at 1.5 million in 1878 (Gillet, *Les charbonnages du nord*, pp. 499–500).

53. Pierre Guillaume, "Aux origines du Comité centrale des houillères de France: La Comité des houillères françaises de 1851," *Actes. Congrès des sociétés savantes, 1962* (Paris, 1963), p. 599.

no foreign competition to complicate the situation tariff protection remained irrelevant. The only problem was internal competition to serve the contracting domestic market, but this was solved, again, by overt collusion. by 1878, Blanzy, Bessèges, and other major mining companies had formed a cooperative to market "excess" coal abroad, thereby keeping domestic competition down and domestic prices up.[54] As a result, production and profits remained high.[55]

To the north, in the Nord and the Pas-de-Calais, the situation was somewhat less favorable in the 1870s. Importation of British and Belgian coal had always focused on the Nord colliers' markets in northern France and Paris. The high coal duties of the early nineteenth century were expressly designed to give Anzin some respite from this competition and increased control over its market. The reduction of the coal duties unquestionably reduced this market control in the 1860s and 1870s. Indeed, as Alfred Dupont pointed out in the Chamber of Deputies' tariff hearings, prices in the Nord were largely dictated by prices in Belgium and in England.[56] Still, despite this competition, the Nord–Pas-de-Calais field was the fastest growing in France in the 1860s, and the companies of the region experienced no less growth in production, revenues, and profits than the companies of the South which were insulated from foreign competition. To be sure, the vulnerability of the Nord was revealed in the 1870s, when prices there declined much more sharply than in the rest of France and when companies of the region—especially the new ones of the Pas-de-Calais—suffered a decrease in revenues and profits despite rising production.[57] Yet there remained little doubt that coal mining

54. Testimony of F. Chalmeton, *Journal officiel*, July 23, 1878, p. 8090. The effect of the southern colliers' entente was clearly felt at Marseilles. According to Teissier (*Histoire du commerce de Marseille*, p. 333), France's overseas neighbors were receiving coal from southern France, shipped from Marseilles, at prices below those charged to Marseilles factories.

55. Grand'combe's performance was noted above. Blanzy's production rose from 580,531 tons to 618,305 tons between 1873 and 1877, with revenues rising from at least 628,727 francs to at least 813,608 francs (Bouvier, *Le mouvement du profit*, pp. 338–339).

56. Alfred Dupont, *Journal officiel*, July 23, 1878, p. 8083.

57. Prices declined for France as a whole from 16.16 francs a ton to 14.06 francs a ton, 1873–1877, but they declined even faster in the North. In the department of the Nord, the decline was from 16.99 francs to 12.51; in the Pas-de-Calais, from

was a profitable business and a good investment in the North. Although the rate of return would have been higher if tariffs had been higher, an increase in tariff protection was not necessary to maintain production and profitability—even in the late 1870s.

The clear lack of necessity for protection did not, in itself, keep colliers form seeking higher tariffs, but it did make it politically inexpedient to do so. In light of the industry's strong performance—seen most clearly in the continuing rise of domestic output as imports remained steady—the colliers realized that the public would not tolerate an increase in protection. More important, they realized that metallurgists would not tolerate such an increase and that to insist on it might jeopardize the metallurgists' support for the existing coal tariff. In any case, those colliers seeking to maintain their share of the domestic market and to keep profits up (such as Commines de Marsilly of Anzin), as well as those seeking to win a greater share of the domestic market at the expense of foreign competitors (such as Paul Schneider of Decazeville, who aspired to market coal in the Bordeaux-Toulouse corridor then controlled by the British), emphasized reduction of taxes and improvement of the transport system, especially canals. The Pas-de-Calais colliers, for example, sought construction of the long-delayed Canal du Nord to link them to the Paris market and simultaneously sought to block deepening of the lower Seine, which would have given English coal better access to Paris.[58] All colliers sought, in addition, the reform of railroad freight rate schedules that forced them to pay relatively high charges on short hauls from the pithead to the trunk lines while importers of foreign coal benefited from proportionately lower long-haul rates.[59] At the same time, they also insisted on the maintenance of the 1F20 duty, which Schneider conceded would be "sufficient" provided the proper reforms in the transport

19.13 francs to 13.98 (Gillet, *Les charbonnages du nord*, pp. 478–581). The impact is seen in the balance sheet of Béthune: its production rose from 236,000 tons to 424,000 tons, 1873–1877, but the value of its production rose only from 4.5 million francs in 1873 to 5.9 million in 1877, and its yearly profits dropped from 1,275,000 francs (1873) to 765,000 (1877) (ibid., p. 492).

58. Marcel Gillet, "The Coal Age and the Rise of the Coalfields in the North and the Pas-de-Calais," in François Crouzet et al., eds., *Essays in European Economic History, 1789–1914* (London, 1969), p. 196.

59. Testimony of Paul Schneider, Chamber Tariff Commission, *Procès-verbaux*, p. 418.

system were realized. For the southern colliers, this duty had no immediate value, but it did offer insurance against any future changes in the market. For the northern colliers, the duty did not offer protection, in the sense of keeping foreign coal out of France, but it did provide compensation for the various "surcharges" on domestic production (the higher cost of mining convoluted beds, the additional expense of maintaining relief funds for workers, the higher cost of transport), all of which their competitors did not have to pay. Thus it allowed them to meet foreign competition without cutting too far into their generous profit margins. In reality, the 1F20 duty was in the seventies what it had always been for the colliers of the North: a roundabout subsidy, a government-sponsored device enabling them to peg their prices about 10 percent above the international price for coal, whatever it might be. In 1878, French colliers joined the AIF to protect this combination buffer and subsidy against its possible abolition by the free traders (already, in the Conseil supérieur du commerce deliberations on the general tariff in 1876, the free trader Fernand Raoul-Duval—a cousin of Léon Say—had tried unsuccessfully to have the coal tariff deleted from the new schedule of duties). Just as important, the colliers also joined the AIF to support the protection of other French industries. For, in 1878, they realized that their prosperity depended in the long run on their customers' prosperity. They also realized that the foremost of those customers—French metallurgy—faced a genuine crisis in the late seventies and that, for some sectors of that industry, tariff protection seemed to be the best remedy.

The crisis in French metallurgy (particularly ferrous metallurgy) was in part the result of long-developing technological changes and in part the result of short-term changes in world supply and demand. Certainly for the less advanced forms of metallurgy the root of the problem was technological change. As early as the 1840s, the increasing use of coke to smelt pig iron (*fonte*) from iron ore—a process introduced into France at Le Creusot in the late eighteenth century and reestablished there in 1818—and the use of coal to refine wrought iron from pig— introduced by Georges Dufaud around 1820—placed in jeopardy those who used the traditional but more expensive fuel, charcoal, to smelt and refine iron. Moreover, the appearance of the Bessemer and Siemens-Martin processes for the mass production of steel in the 1860s threatened to undercut all iron production, whether based on coal and coke or charcoal. Yet through the 1850s and early 1860s the rising demand for all forms of iron and steel muted and even suspended the process of economic natural selection by which producers of low-cost iron and steel would kill off producers of high-cost iron and steel through price competition. It was only with the downturn of the market in the 1870s that the less advanced producers faced the full consequences of their obsolescence. And this downturn was so severe that even the technologically advanced metallurgists also faced hard times by 1878.

The origins of the market crisis in metallurgy lay in the curtailment of railroad building in America and Europe. The resulting decline in demand forced French iron and steel exports, which had burgeoned between 1872 and 1874, to contract rapidly, falling to one-sixth of their 1873 value by 1876. At the same time, an oversupply of iron and steel was created worldwide which soon produced a rise of imports into France, especially from England.[60] Surprisingly, France was able to absorb both the rising foreign imports and the redirection of its own exports back to the home market and still maintain or increase its level of production.[61] But the resultant increase of competition in the domestic market had a devastating effect on prices. Indeed, in the mid-seventies French metallurgists witnessed a dramatic, even precipitous, decline in domestic prices on virtually every form of iron and steel. For example, a ton of pig iron that brought 110 francs in 1875 brought only 90 francs a year later (and would bring only 70 francs by 1880). Steel rails priced at 349 francs a ton in 1868 cost only 217 francs ten years later. The price of tinplate fell from 720 francs to 650 francs in 1875–1876; the price of bar

60. France exported 36.3 million francs worth of pig iron, iron, and steel in 1872 but only 6.1 million francs worth in 1876. Meanwhile, imports of iron and steel which amounted to 7.4 million francs in 1869 rose to 15.5, 14.0, and 13.8 million francs per annum in 1874, 1875, and 1876 (*Tableau décennal*, i, xciv–v, xcix).

61. French pig iron production increased from 1.2 million tons in 1872 to 1.52 million tons in 1878; iron and steel production rose from 1.02 million tons to 1.156 million, 1872–1878 (*Annuaire statistique*, 13 [1890], 506–507).

steel fell from 700 to 600 francs in the same period.[62] As a result, the total value of production of the various kinds of iron and steel either declined absolutely or rose at a slower rate than did the quantity of production.[63] With production costs holding steady or declining gradually, this meant either declining profits or actual deficits for individual firms.[64]

How could metallurgists combat this depression? One obvious way was to demand the continuation or increase of duties on imported iron and steel, and in 1878 no one was eschewing this course of action. As we will see, all sectors of metallurgy favored tariff protection in 1878 and sent representatives to the AIF in rough proportion to their relative size and importance within the industry as a whole. Yet, in the end, tariffs could be of real importance only for those who operated primarily in the domestic market and who were threatened in that market primarily by foreign competitors. For those whose problem was internal competition or a loss of foreign markets, tariffs were of limited value. Instead, their best response lay in technical adjustment or innovation. That is, they could either switch to new products less vulnerable to price competition or they could take steps to reduce production and marketing costs on existing products to allow their continued production and profitability in the face of falling prices.[65] In general, technical solutions had greatest appeal to those firms and sectors that were already technically advanced. Tariff protection was more important to the less technically

62. For steel rail prices, see Jean Fourastié, ed., *Documents pour l'histoire et la théorie des prix* (Paris, 1958), I, 122–123; other prices are from *Annales du commerce extérieur, Valeurs arbitrées*, no. 89 (1875–1876), pp. 500–501.

63. From 1877 to 1878, steel production rose 16 percent but the value of that production rose only 4 percent; pig iron production rose from 1,506 million tons to 1,521 million, but its value declined, 142.6 million francs to 133.7 million (*Annuaire statistique*, 1 [1878], 362–363; 6 [1883], 316–317).

64. Fourchambault's balance sheet went from 661,000 francs in the black in 1873 to 488,000 francs in the red in 1877 (Guy Thuillier, *Georges Dufaud et les débuts du grand capitalisme dans la métallurgie en Nivernais au XIXe siècle* [Paris, 1959], p. 108). Similar stories are told by the balance sheets reconstituted in Bouvier, *Le mouvement du profit*, pp. 411–430.

65. Because the cost of fuel and raw materials comprised the bulk of production costs at all levels of metallurgy, steps to reduce those costs, such as increasing fuel efficiency and reducing transport costs, were of greatest value. See the breakdown of production costs for iron in Statistique de la France, Industrie, *Resultats généraux de l'enquête, 1861–1865* (Nancy, 1873), p. xxxv.

advanced firms and sectors, which could not or would not modernize, and to those close to the borders of France and thus most vulnerable to foreign competition. However, the exact mix of technical improvement and tariff protection in the metallurgists' strategies for survival, and thus the precise meaning of their participation in the protectionist movement, can only be understood and appreciated by breaking down metallurgy into its various specialties and examining each in turn.[66]

The hardest pressed metallurgists in France, those most dependent on tariff protection for their survival and most strident in demanding higher import duties in 1878, were the producers of charcoal iron and pig iron located in the East and in the Pyrenees. The production of charcoal iron and pig iron had reached its highest level in France during the boom of the 1850s. After 1860, when the boom ebbed and tariff barriers fell, increased competition from coke pig iron, iron, and steel, both domestic and foreign, initiated the industry's rapid and irreversible decline. Of the some 100 Catalan forges operating in the Pyrenees in 1853, only 12 remained in 1878. Likewise, only 214 refining furnaces using charcoal—less than half the number in 1864, less than one-third the number of the 1840s—still operated in 1878.[67] The blast furnaces using charcoal held out a bit longer because of the Loire steel industry's demand for high-quality pig iron. But as competitors such as the Société des hauts-fourneaux de Marseille perfected the production of high-grade pig iron with coke and as Loire steelmakers began to set up their own pig iron production (as did the Marine steelworks at Givors after 1870), this sector also declined. Where there had been 142 charcoal-fired furnaces in 1867 (one-half of the total blast furnaces in France), only 64 (one-third of the total) were left in 1878.[68]

By 1878, only the strongest, most efficient, and best adminis-

66. Nonferrous metallurgy—zinc, copper, lead—experienced hard times in the 1870s along with ferrous metallurgy. Its representatives also joined the AIF and lobbied before the Chamber Tariff Commission. Iron and steel, however, constituted by far the largest segment of French metallurgy, and iron and steelmakers dominated the metallurgical section of the AIF; therefore this analysis focuses on them alone.

67. Jean Vial, *L'industrialisation de la sidérurgie française, 1814–1864*, 2 vols. (Paris, 1967), I, 214–221; Comité des forges de France, *La sidérurgie française, 1864–1914* (Paris, n.d.), p. 130.

68. Comité des forges, *La sidérurgie française*, pp. 115–130.

tered charcoal iron producers survived—in most cases those who combined smelting and refining and used a combination of charcoal and coal to produce fine iron. Producers of *fer fin* included various *maîtres de forges* of the Meuse and Haute-Marne. They also included the Société de l'Ariège, founded and administered by Paul Aclocque; the Morvillars-Grandvillars complex of François Viellard-Migeon; and Audincourt, directed by Honoré Reverchon. The largest of these firms—Ariège and Audincourt—had resisted the competition of coke iron and steel in the 1860s by specializing in high-quality iron for naval and land artillery. However, the War Ministry's decision in 1876 to switch to steel for the casting of cannon signaled the end of this market.[69] Henceforth Ariège and Audincourt sought to turn to the production of fine iron wire used in the manufacture of telegraph cables, nails, and needles (Morvillars and the Champenois had already specialized in this production). This strategy—and indeed the survival of the entire French fine iron industry—was threatened by the growing importation of charcoal iron from Sweden. In 1878 these imports amounted to 15 million kilograms, as compared to the total French production of 21 million kilograms, and the Swedish cut of the market promised to increase. The Swedes consistently priced their iron below French iron because the availability of cheap charcoal rendered their production costs lower and because the cost of transporting iron by steamer and rail from Stockholm to French markets was usually less than the freight charges on iron sent to the same markets from the rather inaccessible French forges.[70] Thus the French charcoal iron producers, who were no strangers to protectionism (baron Lespérut of Saint-Dizier was a leader in the attack on the trade treaties in the 1860s), looked to a steep increase in import duties as their last refuge against this competition. Specifically, they sought a doubling of the duty on fine iron (from 60 francs per ton to 120 francs) and a tripling of duties on drawn iron (from 60 francs to 180 francs). In search of this increase in protection, Aclocque,

69. Saglio deposition, Sénat, *Enquête*, p. 312.
70. For example, it cost the Swedes 10 francs to send a ton of iron from Stockholm to Bordeaux, whereas it cost Aclocque 18 francs by rail from Pamiers (Aclocque deposition, Sénat, *Enquête*, pp. 326–328).

Reverchon, Viellard-Migeon, and various Champagne iron masters, including Paul Jamin, heir of Lespérut's forge at Eurville, joined the AIF and testified before the Chamber Tariff Commission. Meanwhile, J.-B. Danelle-Bernardin, *maître de forges* at Buisson and successor to Lespérut as deputy for the Haute-Marne, pushed for higher tariffs from within the Chamber Tariff Commission. Yet, because their production was becoming a smaller and smaller part of France's total metallurgical production (charcoal iron constituting only 7 percent of the total in 1878) and because their numbers were declining as more and more forges closed down, the charcoal iron producers, however vocal and well organized, ultimately took a back seat in the protectionist party to the producers of coke iron and steel.

In the 1870s the smelting of pig iron with coke and the refining of iron with coal constituted the principal branches of French metallurgy in terms of the quantity and value of their output.[71] Like the producers of charcoal iron and pig iron, the producers of coke iron and pig iron faced falling prices in the domestic market in the 1870s. However, most were in a stronger position to deal with this problem than were the charcoal ironmakers because their fuel costs were lower, their plants newer and more efficient, and their financial resources broader. The smelting of pig iron and refining of iron with coal were dominated by certain big joint stock companies founded earlier in the century, which had the ability to respond technologically to changing market conditions. Most of these, including Le Creusot, Denain-Anzin, and Commentry-Fourchambault, were shifting to steel production by the 1870s, and, even though they continued to produce iron as well as steel, it will be best to consider them below along with firms exclusively in steelmaking. Among the firms that continued to produce only iron or pig iron, those of the Center and Massif Central were bothered mostly by internal competition; importation did not affect them directly. Although some iron producers

71. In 1878 the total value of pig iron production (96 percent of which was coke pig) amounted to 134 million francs; the value of iron production (93 percent of which was coke iron) amounted to 182 million francs. Steel production amounted to only 84 million francs (*Annuaire statistique*, 1 [1878], 362–363; 6 [1883], 316–317; 13 [1890], 507).

of the Loire (La Rochette of Givors, Lescure of the Horme foundry and forges) joined the AIF, they did not campaign actively for increased tariff protection. Consequently, among the producers of coke iron and pig iron, only the tinplate producers of northern France and the *fonte* producers of the periphery—especially in the Meurthe-et-Moselle—played a major role in the protectionist movement.

In the 1860s and 1870s, the manufacture of tinplate (*fer blanc*) was a growth industry whose rise paralleled that of the canning industry. By 1878 eleven firms in France produced tinplate, including Audincourt and Châtillon-Commentry. The most important of these, however, was the Société des forges de Montataire (Oise). Founded in 1812 to produce pig iron and sheet iron with coal, Montataire experienced its real takeoff only in 1864 when the Strasbourg financier, Renouard de Buissière, became chairman of the board and installed an engineer, Alfred-Camille Martellière, as managing director. Martellière proceeded to refurbish Montataire's blast furnaces and to relocate them at Frouard (near Nancy) and at Boulogne-sur-Mer, closer to cheap sources of iron and coal, thereby significantly reducing the production cost of refining pig (*fonte d'affinage*), the raw material for the tinplate and other forms of iron manufactured at Montataire.[72] But the anticipated rise in profits did not follow this reduction of costs because in the 1870s domestic prices fell as the importation of cheap British tinplate increased.[73] To meet this challenge and to shore up profit margins, Martellière sought changes in the tariff. In the spring of 1878 he joined the AIF and formulated a three-point program calling for curtailment of the temporary admission of tinplate for the Breton canning industry, an end to the fraudulent import of *fer noir* (untinned *fer blanc*) at sheet iron duties, and, most important, an increase in the import duty on *fer blanc* from 130 francs a ton to 150. With the unanimous support of the other tinplate producers, he submitted this program to the Chamber Tariff Commission in June 1878.[74]

72. Martellière dossier, AN F¹² 5203.
73. Imports of British plated iron, which included tinplate, rose from 1,332 tons in 1873 to 4,366 tons in 1876 (*Tableau décennal*, I, 119); domestic prices of tinplate fell from 720 francs a ton to 650 francs a ton in 1875–1876 alone (*Annales du commerce extérieur, Valeurs arbitrées*, no. 89 [1875–1876], pp. 500–501).
74. Martellière deposition, *Journal officiel*, July 31, 1878, p. 8342.

Also interested in raising tariffs, or at least in applying existing tariffs more effectively, were the operators of independent pig iron plants recently installed on the periphery of France, who found domestic prices falling and foreign imports rising.[75] These included Sampson Jordan, administrator of the Compagnie des hauts-fourneaux de Marseille, which had set up the first blast furnaces in France using Mediterranean haemitite (mainly from Algeria) to produce high-quality coke pig iron. In the 1860s Jordan's firm had supplanted the charcoal blast furnaces of the Pyrenees in supplying high-quality pig iron to the steelmakers of the Loire and likewise had "rescued [French] forgemasters"— notably Denain-Anzin in the Nord—"from the Prussian monopoly."[76] By the 1870s, however, Jordan was feeling renewed pressure from both the Germans and the English, who by then were also smelting high-grade pig from Algerian and Spanish ores and who could often market this pig in France more cheaply than Marseille could, apparently because of high transport costs and high taxes in France. To gain compensation for these disadvantages, Jordan sought continuation of the 20 francs per ton duty on *fontes*. Just as important, he supported continued protection of the iron and steel refined by his customers, on whose orders his prosperity depended.[77]

Even more active in the protectionist cause than Jordan were the pig iron producers of Nancy and Longwy. Founded after 1860, the pig iron industry of the Meurthe-et-Moselle produced 226,000 tons of pig iron, one-sixth of the French output (1,416,000 tons), in 1874. It would, of course, achieve its true takeoff with the introduction of the Thomas Gilchrist basic steel process in 1880 (which created an enormous market for its phosphoric *fontes*) and would account for 55 percent of French pig iron production (940,000 tons) by 1889.[78] But in 1878 the industry remained small. Plagued by technical problems and by a chronic shortage of coal

75. The domestic price of pig iron fell from 110 francs a ton to 70 francs a ton in 1880 (*Annales du commerce extérieur, Valeurs arbitrées*, no. 89, pp. 500–501; no. 101 [1880–1881], pp. 113–114). Pig iron imports fell as low as 6,871 tons in 1868 and were still only 32,000 tons in 1874, but they had risen to 101,401 tons by 1877 (*Tableau décennal*, i, 117; ii, 131).

76. Jordan dossier, AN F^{12} 5175.

77. Sénat, *Enquête*, pp. 321–325.

78. Report of Xavier Rogé, Nancy Chamber of Commerce, AN F^{12} 6916.

and coke, it struggled to capture a market for its pig iron against strong competition from nearby Luxembourg. Its only advantages in this struggle were aggressive leadership and strong organization. In 1876 the ironmasters of the region, led by Joseph Labbé of Gorcy and baron Oscar d'Adelsward of Hersange, formed the Comptoir de Longwy, a cooperative agency, to market their products. Simultaneously, Labbé and Adelsward, along with Alphonse Fould of the Pompey forges, and Martellière, representing Montataire's blast furnaces at Frouard, sought to defend their industry's interests within the AIF. Although they favored continuation of the existing duty on pig iron, their main preoccupation was to end the policy of temporary admissions which allowed pig from Belgium and Luxembourg to cross the border duty-free for use by the metal refiners of the Nord and Nancy who might otherwise have been their clients. From 1876 to 1878, in the hearings of the Conseil supérieur du commerce, the Senate, and the Chamber Tariff Commission, the Meurthe-et-Moselle *fonte* producers, led by the pugnacious Adelsward, repeatedly attacked the temporary admission system. In doing so, as will be seen below, they came into conflict not so much with free traders as with other metallurgists in the AIF.

After 1860, steel was the most technologically progressive and most rapidly expanding sector of French metallurgy, and all major metallurgical firms, including the ten largest, were involved in its production by the 1870s.[79] Although the steelmakers were by no means the most protectionist of metallurgists, their size and economic influence determined that they would dominate the AIF in 1878, as witnessed by the election of Alexandre Jullien of Terrenoire as its first president and Jean-Baptiste Martelet of Denain-Anzin as a vice-president and as spokesman for its metallurgical section.[80] The steel firms in the AIF repre-

79. The average annual production of iron rose only 2 percent from 1865–1869 to 1875–1879, but steel production quadrupled and steel's share of the total production of refined iron (pig iron excluded) rose from 7 to 25 percent (calculated from figures in the *Annuaire statistique*, 13 [1890], 507).

The ten largest metallurgical firms in the 1870s, according to Robert Pinot (Comité des forges, *La sidérurgie française*, p. 135), were, in order, Le Creusot, Terrenoire, Petin-Gaudet (Marine), Firminy, Holtzer, Marrel Frères, Châtillon-Commentry, Fourchambault, Wendel, and Denain-Anzin.

80. The metallurgical section of the AIF was largely a subsidiary of the Comité

sented two distinct specialties: high-quality steel, produced in small amounts by various processes (cementation, crucible, puddling), and lower quality cast steel, mass produced by the Bessemer and Siemens-Martin processes.

High-quality steel was first produced in quantity in France at Saint-Etienne and Rive-de-Gier (Loire) by the Jackson brothers of Sheffield, using the crucible method, in 1816. Thereafter this became a specialty of the department of the Loire. Expanding rapidly in the 1850s, as steel was increasingly used in naval guns, armor plate, and railroad equipment, the Loire crucible and puddled steel industry produced two-thirds of all French steel by 1860.[81] Many important Loire firms continued to specialize in crucible steel in the 1870s, including Marrel Frères, who produced armor plate for the navy, and J. Holtzer et Cie, France's largest producer of high-quality steel castings.[82] These firms were protectionist. Pierre Dorian, brother-in-law of Jacob Holtzer and co-director of Holtzer et Cie, had been active in the campaign against the trade treaties in the late sixties as a deputy for the Loire, and in 1878 Holtzer, Marrel Frères, and others joined the AIF. Yet none was highly visible in the ensuing campaign for tariff protection because imports posed little threat to them: only 3,493 tons of steel bars were imported into France in 1877, in contrast to 4,659 in 1873.[83] If prices were falling, it was because of internal competition which could best be countered by cost reduction and product differentiation. Thus Allevard of the Isère, unable to compete in steel rail production with companies equipped with Bessemer converters, turned to the production of magnets after 1865, while in the mid-1870s Marrel Frères turned to the production of cannon barrels with crucible steel at the expense of the charcoal iron producers.[84]

---

des forges. The recommendations on metals duties presented to the Chamber Tariff Commission by the AIF in June 1878 were originally drafted by the Comité des forges and had been incorporated into the AIF program without discussion at its April 15, 1878, meeting (Martellière deposition, Chamber Tariff Commission, *Procès-verbaux*, p. 447).

81. L. Babu, "L'industrie métallurgique dans la région de Saint-Etienne," *Annales des mines*, 9th ser., 15 (1899), 368–389.

82. Marrel dossier, AN F[12] 5203; Holtzer dossier, AN F[12] 5169.

83. *Tableau décennal*, I, 121; II, 135.

84. Marrel dossier, AN F[12] 5203; on Allevard: Pierre Léon, *La naissance de la grande industrie en Dauphiné*, 2 vols. (Paris, 1954), II, 824–825.

The steelmakers most active in the AIF were those who operated Bessemer converters and Siemens-Martin hearths and who, ironically, were recent converts of protectionism. These included the managers of older joint-stock firms that were shifting from iron to steel production (Le Creusot, Denain-Anzin, Commentry-Fourchambault) and also the directors of new joint-stock companies organized in the Loire in the 1850s. Of the latter, the most important were the Hauts-fourneaux, forges, et aciéries de la Marine et des chemins de fer, created in 1854 by the merger of Petin et Gaudet of Saint-Chamond and Jackson Frères of Rive-de-Gier, which set up France's first Bessemer converters in 1861, and the Compagnie des fonderies et forges de Terrenoire, la Voulte, et Bessèges, an amalgam of a formerly separate iron mill (Terrenoire), pig iron smelter (la Voulte), and coal mine (Bessèges), which set up Bessemer converters in 1860–1865 and by 1867 was France's largest producer of Bessemer steel.[85] Initially all these producers of Bessemer and Siemens-Martin steel specialized in rails and thus depended on railroad building. When domestic construction slowed in the late 1860s, they came to rely on foreign markets and therefore became advocates of free trade or, at least, defenders of the trade treaties. Indeed, Alexandre Jullien of Terrenoire and Adrien de Montgolfier, who became director of the Marine steelworks in 1874, both joined the free trade caucus in the National Assembly and fought Thiers's protectionist schemes as deputies for the Loire in 1871–1876. Both continued to support the existing tariff system as late as 1877.[86] Their free trade orientation, however, did not survive the depression of the late seventies.

In 1876–1877 the roof fell in on the big steel companies. First, the remaining domestic demand for rails disappeared with the collapse of local railroad companies. Then foreign demand for rails, after reaching a peak in 1873, severely contracted. As competition for the remaining contracts increased, French pro-

85. Babu, "L'industrie métallurgique," pp. 402–422.

86. Jullien deposition, Conseil supérieur du commerce, *Admissions temporaires*, pp. 48–49; Deposition of the Saint-Etienne Chamber of Commerce, Sénat, *Enquête*, pp. 589–590; L.-J. Gras, *Histoire économique de la métallurgie de la Loire* (Saint-Etienne, 1908), pp. 141–148.

ducers were pushed out of the international market. The value of Le Creusot's annual exports declined from 22 million francs to 7 million francs between 1874 and 1877, and whereas its exports accounted for 35 percent of its total sales in 1874–1875, they accounted for only 13.9 percent in 1876–1877.[87] Amid this debacle, profits fell precipitously for Le Creusot and the others. Marine, for example, paid no dividends to either its directors or its stockholders between 1873 and 1876; its rate of return on invested capital, which had been more than 20 percent in 1872–1873, declined to less than 7 percent in 1876–1877.[88]

The crisis in the steel industry was eventually remedied by the resumption of railroad building under the Freycinet plan and by the development of the steel armaments industry.[89] But before that, in 1878, steel companies faced the grim prospect of depending on the general domestic market for the first time, and, in the face of rising foreign competition plus the free traders' efforts to abolish existing duties on iron and steel, even that market was far from secure. To shore up their position at home, some firms turned to product improvement and diversification. Terrenoire, for example, was already producing sheet steel for marine boilers for the CGT in the late 1860s, and in the 1870s it pioneered the production of stainless steel and manganese steel using Siemens-Martin hearths.[90] Others sought to stay competitive in existing lines by cutting production costs. The outstanding example of this approach was provided by the Marine steelworks. In taking over as director in 1874, Adrien de Montgolfier brought in as head engineer Claudius Magnin, an expert on the Bessemer process previously associated with Terrenoire, who succeeded in lowering the cost of Marine's steel production at Givors and Assailly 30 percent. More important, Montgolfier launched the transfer of all of Marine's pig iron and Bessemer production to Boucau near

87. Henri Schneider, Sénat, *Enquête*, p. 401; Yasuo Gonjo, "Le 'plan Freycinet' 1878–1882: Un aspect de la 'grande dépression' économique en France," *Revue historique*, 248 (1972), 49–51.

88. Bouvier, *Le mouvement du profit*, p. 411.

89. Gonjo, "Le 'plan Freycinet'"; François Crouzet, "Remarques sur l'industrie des armements en France: Du milieu du XIXe siècle à 1914," *Revue historique*, 251 (1974), 409–422.

90. Babu, "L'industrie métallurgique," pp. 410–412.

Bayonne to take advantage of cheap Spanish ore and English coal. When this move was completed in 1881, Marine emerged as France's largest producer of Bessemer steel.[91]

Such massive changes in production required huge capital investments that not all firms were willing or able to make. Once radical reorganization or technological improvement was ruled out, there was only so much that steelmakers could do to reduce production and marketing costs. Indeed, in 1878, steelmakers insisted that, in competing with foreign producers in the French market, they faced four handicaps which they had little power to correct: higher labor costs, higher taxes, higher coal and coke prices,[92] and higher transport costs deriving from a discriminatory freight rate schedule and from the longer distances raw materials had to be shipped (unlike Germany and England, coal and iron were in close proximity nowhere in France except in the Northeast, but the pig iron produced there was still unsuitable for steelmaking in 1878; thus haemitite ore had to be shipped from Algeria or Sardinia, far inland to the blast furnaces of the Loire, Center, and Nord). The steelmakers believed, as Martelet expressed it to the Chamber Tariff Commission, that "it [was] only equitable that the authorities compensate [them] in just measure for these forced inequalities."[93] In their estimation, such compensation should involve eventually the reform of railroad freight rates. In the short run, however, it was a matter of sustaining a pro-steel tariff policy that would include maintenance of the temporary admission of pig iron by customs permits which allowed Denain-Anzin to use low-cost imported *fontes* and produced, through trafficking in permits, an export subsidy for the rail manufacturers of the Center and Loire. It would also include maintenance of the 60 franc per ton duty on imported iron and steel (versus the reduction discussed by the Conseil supérieur du commerce in 1876 and which, as late as 1877, Alexandre Jullien had indicated might be feasible). In 1878, steelmakers insisted that "the least lowering of the barriers which

91. Montgolfier dossier, AN F¹² 5198.
92. According to Jullien (Sénat, *Enquête*, p. 298), coke cost 15 francs per ton in the Loire versus 6 francs in Germany and 11–12 francs in England.
93. Martelet, Chamber Tariff Commission, *Procès-verbaux*, p. 460.

defend us will put the existence of our industry in peril."[94] To defend those barriers, representatives of most of the major steel companies—including Le Creusot, Terrenoire, Marine, Alais, Denain-Anzin, and Commentry-Fourchambault—joined the AIF and lobbied vigorously before the Chamber Tariff Commission in 1878.

The final segment of the metallurgical industry—and the most important in terms of the value of its production[95]—was metallurgical manufacturing and construction. This was a diverse industry that included the manufacture of various kinds of hardware and light machinery. More important, it included the big joint-stock companies—such as Société des Batignolles (Gouin et Cie) and Le Creusot—that manufactured heavy machinery and transport equipment (locomotives and steamships, bridges and tunnels). Traditionally these firms had been the least protectionist and the most favorable to trade treaties in metallurgy because, on the one hand, they consumed various kinds of imported metals,[96] and, on the other hand, they had become increasingly dependent on foreign markets. Thus, as seen earlier, one of the leaders of this industry, Ernest Gouin, had become a leader of the free trade party in the 1870s.

By the late seventies, however, the metallurgical manufacturers were experiencing the same contraction of foreign markets that other sectors of metallurgy were experiencing and, like the others, they fell back on the domestic market. To defend that market, many flocked to the AIF in 1878. These included two manufacturers of iron gas pipes and water mains—Mignon, Rouart, et Delinières of Montluçon, represented in the AIF by Alphonse Grimault, and the Usines de Pont-à-Mousson (Meurthe-et-Moselle), represented by Xavier Rogé—as well as hardware and

94. Ibid.

95. In terms of value added, iron production amounted to 126 million francs annually in the period 1865–1874, but metallurgical manufacturing amounted to 484 million francs annually (T. J. Markovitch, "L'industrié française de 1789 à 1964," in Jean Marczewski, "Histoire quantitative de l'économie française," *Cahiers de l'I.S.E.A.*, ser. AF, 6 [1966], table 3).

96. For example, in 1874 alone Cail et Cie imported—or requested to import under the temporary admissions system—7,667 tons of foreign metals, mostly pig iron for casting, bar and sheet iron, and rolled copper, which constituted the bulk of its raw materials (Cail et Cie dossier, AN F[12] 2577).

light machinery manufacturers, the most important of which was Japy Frères of Beaucourt, which produced household utensils and clock and watch movements. They also included the leaders of the French engineering industry: Henri Schneider of Le Creusot (locomotives and other railroad equipment), Augustin Farcot of Maison J. Farcot (naval artillery, giant pumps for municipal water systems, refitting equipment for ports), J. Mignon of Mignon, Rouart, et Delinières and the Société des constructions navales du Havre (refrigeration equipment, ships), Emile Cail of Cail et Cie (refining equipment), and Félix Moreaux of the Compagnie de Fives-Lille (heavy construction—including Paris bridges and the gare des Batignolles—plus locomotives and sugar refining equipment).

In petitions and testimony before the Chamber Tariff Commission, representatives of construction and engineering spelled out a two-part program to minimize costs and maximize the prices on their finished products. First they demanded maintenance of the temporary admissions system on pig iron (this was especially important to Xavier Rogé of Pont-à-Mousson, who imported Luxembourg and Scottish *fontes* for pipe casting).[97] Second, they demanded the maintenance or increase of import duties. Shipbuilders, like Mignon, sought a raise from 2 francs per ton to 8–12 francs; a doubling of proposed tariffs on their products was sought by the manufacturers of textile and sewing machinery and locomotives (including even Gouin et Cie which was represented in the petitioning by a certain Fauquet).[98] Thus did the metallurgical manufacturers join with all other sections of French mining and metallurgy in the protectionist movement in 1878.

For the various sectors of mining or metallurgy to gain a favorable tariff policy, it was not enough that each enumerate its demands before government inquiries and parliamentary hearings. They also had to work together and form a common front in which all would support, or at least tolerate, the others' demands for protection. On one level, of course, it was easy to form a common front: all could agree that the trade treaties should be

97. Xavier Rogé, *Journal officiel*, December 5, 1878, p. 11447.
98. Chamber Tariff Commission, *Procès-verbaux*, pp. 512–517.

eliminated and that France should henceforth rely exclusively on legislated tariffs. On the crucial point of the level of duties, however, agreement was harder to obtain. Indeed, it seemed to make little sense for those downstream in the sequence of production to support protection of those upstream. For pig iron smelters, protection of coal and coke served only to raise their production costs. Similarly, protection of pig iron, as well as protection of coal, raised costs for iron and steel refiners, and protection at any level of mining and metallurgy seemed detrimental to manufacturers and constructors. Consequently, many metallurgists were susceptible to the free trade argument that it was better to protect no level of industry than to prejudice the position of some (especially those high in the sequence of production) by protecting others (especially those low in the sequence). But in the view of Jullien, Martelet, and other leaders of the AIF, such reasoning, if embodied in public policy, would have spelled disaster. They argued instead for a program in which each would sacrifice its maximum demands in exchange for mutual support of minimum demands. A close examination of the demands of mining and metallurgy in the summer of 1878 reveals a conscious and highly successful effort to mold the demands of each sector to the situation of other sectors up and downstream from them and thereby to achieve solidarity on the basis of moderate protection.

The most fundamental and, ultimately, the most successful accommodation was between coal and metallurgy. For a time in the 1860s, colliers in the business of supplying coal to railroads were tempted to support free trade on the theory that it would foster expanded railroad traffic and thus increase the demand for (and price of) coal. Such reasoning especially appealed to Alfred Deseilligny, director of the Houillères de l'Aveyron (Decazeville), which supplied the Orleans railroad. In the late 1870s, however, most colliers—including Paul Schneider, Deseilligny's successor at Decazeville—saw their interests served best by the protection of national industry, especially metallurgy, and in joining the AIF they came out in favor of such protection. More important and more surprising, the Comité des forges voted to support the 1F20 duty on coal and coke—metallurgy's chief raw material—and the ironmasters in joining the AIF concurred.[99] According to Mar-telet, this was a sacrificial act in the name of industrial solidarity. But, in point of fact, the metallurgists had logical reasons for opposing the abolition of the coal duty. On the one hand, as has been shown, the coal duty was not really protective, so its abolition would not have substantially increased coal imports. Even if it had, only those firms located near foreign sources of supply, namely those in the Nord and the Meurthe-et-Moselle, would have benefited. For the Loire and the Center, transport costs made the use of imported coal uneconomical even in the absence of import duties. And since the Nord had its own coal supplies, only the Meurthe-et-Moselle actually imported its coal. For this reason, the Lorraine metallurgists did object to continua-tion of the coal duty. But the rest of French metallurgy, rather than pursue the minor lowering of coal prices that might accom-pany the elimination of the coal duty, chose to live with a mild subsidy to domestic coal in return for the considerable benefit of the coal producers' goodwill and their support for the protection of metallurgy.

A similar process of trade-offs allowed manufacturers and metallurgists to form a common front. Ostensibly, of course, the interests of these two groups diverged considerably. Iron and steel would benefit from high tariffs and abolition of all temporary admissions; manufacturers had already benefited from the lower-ing of iron and steel duties in the 1860s and the expansion of temporary admissions and would have benefited from further tariff reductions in 1878. Conciliation and solidarity were made possible by the moderation of the iron and steel producers. Rather than seeking an increase in duties, almost all simply demanded the maintenance of the status quo (that is, the 60 franc duty on iron and steel).[100] This moderate attitude, coupled with the *maître de forges'* acceptance of continued temporary admissions of iron, made it relatively easy for the manufacturers to support protec-tion for iron and steel. As in the case of the metallurgists'

99. Martellière, Chamber Tariff Commission, *Procès-verbaux*, p. 461.

100. Had the free traders not sought massive reductions in iron and steel duties in the trade negotiations of 1876–1877, steel producers may have ended up on the side of the government in 1878. In any case, it was the fear of losing the existing 60 franc duty—not the desire to gain a higher duty—that brought them into the protectionist camp.

acceptance of coal duties, they considered metallurgy's support for protection of their home market fair compensation for whatever elevation in their production costs resulted from continued protection of iron and steel. This, of course, presumed reliance on the home market. Those manufacturers still operating in foreign markets (such as the Société des Batignolles) would not benefit from this deal and, not surprisingly, Batignolles did not adhere to the AIF, although it was the only major metallurgical construction company not to do so.

In the final analysis, the most serious conflict on tariff policy among metallurgists—and the only one not substantially resolved in 1878—pitted the pig iron producers of the Meurthe-et-Moselle against a coalition of steel refiners, headed by Terrenoire, and metallurgical manufacturers, Pont-à-Mousson in particular. The issue was temporary admissions of pig iron. The *fonte* producers of the Meurthe-et-Moselle found that this system opened their markets to cheap pig iron from Luxembourg and, led by baron Oscar d'Adelsward, they repeatedly demanded its abolition, or at least its modification from *admissions temporaires à l'équivalent* to *admissions temporaires à l'identique*.[101] Iron manufacturers— such as Xavier Rogé of Pont-à-Mousson, who imported *fontes de moulage* for the casting of water conduits—just as vociferously defended the prevailing system. They, in turn, were supported by certain steel producers—especially Alexandre Jullien of Terrenoire, whose ability to export steel rails to Switzerland and Italy depended on the traffic in the customs permits associated with the temporary admission of *fontes* along the northern border.[102]

101. As seen in the case of the grain trade of Marseilles and Dunkirk, *admissions temporaires à l'équivalent* allowed the importation of a given commodity to be offset by the exportation of a similar commodity (not necessarily the imported commodity itself). This led to trafficking in customs permits. Importers purchased permits and used them to import the desired commodity "temporarily" without any intention of reexporting it. Then they discounted the cost of the permit by selling it to others who redeemed it on their domestically produced exports. *Admissions temporaires à l'identique* ended the trafficking in permits by allowing them to be redeemed only on the reexport of the exact item imported.

102. Jullien and other rail exporters would buy permits from Rogé, who had used them to import foreign pig iron for domestic use (not for reexport). They would then redeem them when they exported rails made with domestic pig iron, thereby obtaining a kind of export subsidy (equal to the difference between the face value of the permits and the price they paid to Rogé). Jullien insisted that this

Throughout the tariff hearings of 1877–1878, the various interested parties fought bitterly over this issue, but it was finally resolved only in the succeeding decade. In the meanwhile, the feud, although bitter, was of sufficiently limited scope that it did not undermine the solidarity of metallurgy. Indeed, even as they fought over temporary admissions, Adelsward, Rogé, and Jullien could agree on the larger issue of tariff protection for pig iron, which Jullien produced at Vienne and La Voulte and Rogé produced at Pont-à-Mousson, as well as protection of iron and steel. This, in turn, allowed them all to coexist and to work together within the AIF.

French mining and metallurgy thus had achieved a remarkable degree of solidarity on tariff policy by the summer of 1878. One could argue that such solidarity stemmed from the relatively minor role that tariffs played in the success or failure of metallurgical enterprise, compared to public works programs, railroad contracts, and railroad freight rates; that is, since tariffs were unimportant to metallurgists, they could afford to accommodate each other concerning tariffs. To some extent, this was true (certainly more in the case of metallurgy than textiles, considered below). Yet this should not negate the significance of the formation of the common front among mining and metallurgical interests. In the short run, their solidarity measurably strengthened the protectionist movement. Moreover, it drew a line between certain industrialists (rail and railroad equipment manufacturers) and certain commercial-financial capitalists (railroad owners), who were formerly linked, and thereby made the tariff controversy more of a conflict between industry and commerce than it had been previously. At the same time it showed the way for the eventual resolution of this conflict. For the process of accommodation among metallurgists foreshadowed the process by which the reconciliation of all major interests—free trade and protectionist—would be effected later on. It represented the first step away from laissez-faire individualism and toward the solidarity of interests which would come to be a hallmark of the political and economic system of the later Third Republic.

"subsidy" was crucial to his ability to export rails at all (Conseil supérieur du commerce, *Admissions temporaires*, pp. 48–49).

3

The Interests and the Tariff (II)

The tariff demands put forth by interests in the free trade and protectionist parties in the late 1870s often turned out to be surprisingly compatible. As we have seen, most mining and metallurgical interests were seeking little more than the preservation of existing import duties. They joined the protectionist party in 1878 and campaigned against the trade treaties mainly out of fear that free traders would obtain further reductions if the trade treaties were renewed. Yet, in defending the treaties, most free traders were also seeking to preserve the existing system—a hybrid of free trade and protection—and did not really aspire to absolute free trade. Thus in many cases the dispute hinged not on the level of import duties but only on the method of setting up those duties (through trade treaties or through legislated tariffs). However, the apparent compatibility in the policy position of some free traders and protectionists should not be overemphasized, even though that compatibility eventually provided the basis for an accommodation on tariffs. In the 1870s the incompatibility of the free traders' and protectionists' economic interests and outlook mattered most. Free traders were in the business of international commerce or were tied to foreign markets as buyers and sellers, and they wanted to continue France's integration with the world economy. Protectionists, by contrast, operated mainly in the domestic market, and they wanted to insulate that market from outside competition as much as possible. This conflict of interest was of fundamental importance. It precluded any quick settlement of the tariff question in the late 1870s and thus constituted a major hindrance to the achievement of solidarity within the capitalist bourgeoisie of France in the last quarter of the nineteenth century. The nature of this conflict has been partially revealed in the juxtaposed analyses of the commerce-finance-transport nexus and the heavy industry nexus in Chapter 2. It can be further elucidated by an examination of French textiles, which traditionally had the greatest stake in tariff policy of all French industries.

Free Trade and Protection in French Textiles

By the 1870s the textile industry was France's fourth largest in terms of the value of output, but in terms of influence in matters of economic policy it was surely France's most important industry.[1] Involving the manufacture of a wide variety of yarns and fabrics, the industry can be viewed most clearly if subdivided into five components, corresponding to the five basic fibers used in textile production: wool, cotton, flax (linen), silk, and jute.[2] The largest of these—in quantity and value of production—was the woolens industry, situated primarily at Reims, Sedan, Elbeuf, and Roubaix-Tourcoing in northern France and secondarily at Mazamet and Carcassonne in the South. Close behind woolens came

---

1. Building, garment making, and food processing were each larger than textiles in the "added value" of their output, but they were much less concentrated and less "capital intensive" than textiles, produced fewer powerful industrialists, and therefore were less influential in economic politics. Coal and metallurgy were just as concentrated as textiles and growing at a considerably higher rate but remained much smaller in the value of their output. For estimates of growth rates and average value of production for these industries, see tables 2 and 3 in T. J. Markovitch, "L'industrie française de 1789 à 1964," *Cahiers de l'I.S.E.A.*, ser. AF, 6 (1966).

2. The production of various blended yarns and fabrics was important in the 1870s, but this production was usually subsumed under that of the basic fibers. Thus production of silk-cotton blends was considered part of the silk industry; production of cotton-wool blends was part of the woolens and worsteds industry.

cotton and linen. In the 1870s they were of roughly comparable size because of the expansion of linen during the "cotton famine" of the early sixties and the loss of the Alsatian cotton industry—France's largest—in 1871. Linen, however, was declining and cotton was expanding. Indeed, by 1878 cotton possessed the largest physical plant (that is, the most spindles and looms) of any French textile industry. Most of that plant was located in northern France, especially in the departments of the Nord, Seine-Inférieure, and the Vosges, while linen was increasingly concentrated in and around Lille in the Nord. Fourth largest, but politically coequal with the others because of its important place in foreign commerce, was the silk industry, centered primarily in the Rhône and Loire. Finally, there was jute and burlap, a small but growing industry located mostly in the department of the Somme in northwest France.[3]

Like metallurgy, all these textile industries were feeling the effects of the Europe-wide depression by 1876 or 1877. Between 1867 and 1876 the volume of woolens, cottons, and silks imported into France rose markedly as England's exports were diverted from America to Europe and as modern mechanized textile industries capable of competing with the French appeared in Switzerland and Germany (the rise of the German textile industry resulted in large part from the annexation of Alsace). With

---

3. Total Textile Production (from Markovitch, "L'industrie française," table 16):

		Wool	Cotton	Linen	Jute	Silk
A.	Average annual					
	quantity of out-	1865–1874	163	152	174	36	6.9
	put (thousands	1875–1884	207	179	168	52	7.2
	of tons)						
B.	Average annual					
	value of output	1865–1874	1748	1101	902	51	682
	(millions of	1875–1884	1839	974	809	65	418
	francs)						

Size of Plant, 1875 (from *Annuaire statistique*, 1 [1878], 374–381):

	Wool	Cotton	Linen and Jute	Silk
spindles (in thousands):	2,969	4,922	730	1,059
power looms (in thousands):	30	56	24	43
hand looms (in thousands):	57	68	55	133

competition increasing in both foreign and domestic markets, prices began to fall for all French textiles and, in the case of cottons and silks, they fell precipitously. As a consequence, the value of French textile production and exports also fell, and profits contracted or, at least, ceased to rise. Of course, in such economic circumstances, all French textile manufacturers became increasingly concerned with government commercial policies. Yet, unlike the metallurgists, who responded to the business slump by joining together to seek protection of the home market, textilists did not form a common front on tariff policy. Instead, adversity simply hardened the long-standing division between those in textiles who favored free trade and those who favored protection. Thus the manufacturers of silk cloth and silk-based blends (*tissus mélangés*), plus worsteds and tulle, continued to support the trade treaties and joined the Free Trade Association in 1878. Cotton, linen, and jute spinners and producers of carded woolens, however, increased their demands for the high protective tariffs they had favored throughout the nineteenth century; their representatives rallied to the AIF and, indeed, formed the largest section of that organization. To illuminate the economic basis of this split within the French textile industry on tariff policy—and to demonstrate the significance of the tariff issue for the future development of French textiles—the remainder of this section will examine the conditions, goals, and strategies of the textile interests active in tariff politics in the late 1870s, starting with those on the free trade side.

The foremost textile industry in the free trade movement in the 1870s was the silk industry of the Rhône and Loire, which consisted of the manufacture of pure silk cloth in Lyons and its environs, the weaving of various silk-based blends in Lyons, Saint-Etienne, and Tarare, and the production of velvet and ribbons in and around Saint-Etienne. Its representatives in the Free Trade Association included several *marchands de soies* of Lyons, those international silk dealers who, as mentioned earlier, also controlled the manufacture of silk cloth. Foremost among these was Auguste Sévène, president of the Association de la fabrique lyonnaise. The industry was also represented by Thivel-

Duvillard, a manufacturer of muslins and president of the Tarare Chamber of Commerce; Claudius Gerontet and Auguste Tezenas du Montcel of the Saint-Etienne Chamber of Commerce; and Francisque David, a silk trader, inventor, and industrialist who operated modern mechanized plants for velvet and ribbon production at Saint-Etienne, Boën (Loire), and Pont-de-Chéruy (Isère).[4]

The third quarter of the nineteenth century was a period of growth and prosperity for the Lyons silk industry primarily because of the burgeoning demand for its products abroad (in any given year from the 1850s to the 1870s, three-fourths of the silk fabrics produced in the Rhône and Loire were exported, with most going to England and America). The silk manufacturers' reliance on foreign markets naturally spurred the Lyons Chamber of Commerce to promote trade liberalization and to support the trade treaties in the 1860s and 1870s. The chamber had an additional reason to support free trade after 1860: the silk industry's growing dependence on imported raw materials, including not only raw silk from the Orient but also cotton yarn imported from England for the manufacture of blends. English cotton yarn was also important for Saint-Etienne, where production shifted from pure silk ribbon to ribbon of cotton and silk after 1860, and where, to gain and maintain access to English cotton yarns, the traditionally protectionistic chamber of commerce converted to free trade and threw its support to the trade treaties in the 1860s.[5]

In contrast to the prosperity of the 1860s and early 1870s, the Lyons textile industry faced serious problems after 1873. For one thing, the rising importation of Swiss and German silks threatened its sales in the once secure home market. More important, competition abroad—again from the Swiss and Germans—undercut exports, especially exports of pure silk cloth (the value

<hr/>

4. David's Legion of Honor dossier (AN F^{12} 5120) contains extensive data on his enterprises.

5. Léon Permezel, "L'industrie lyonnaise de la soie, sa situation actuelle, son avenir," Société d'économie politique de Lyon, *Compte rendu analytique, 1882-83*, pp. 131–175; Ernest Pariset, "La Chambre de commerce de Lyon au XIXe siècle," *Mémoires de l'Académie de Lyon*, 27 (1890–1891), 1–254; Louis-Joseph Gras, *Histoire de la Chambre de commerce de Saint-Etienne* (Saint-Etienne, 1913), pp. 175–178.

of which fell from a peak of 357.2 million francs in 1873 to 154.8 million francs in 1877).[6] The decline in pure silks was offset somewhat by the overall rise in the production and exportation of blends.[7] Yet even within that category certain specialties were in trouble. Tarare, which normally exported half of its total production, witnessed a 50 percent decline in the export of its muslins, tarlatans, and embroideries between 1874 and 1878 when these products began to be manufactured outside of France for the first time.[8] The ribbon manufacturers of Saint-Etienne experienced an even more catastrophic drop in the value of their exports, from a high of 103.5 million francs in 1873 to less than 23 million francs per year in the late seventies. As a result, production was cut back and eight thousand of Saint-Etienne's seventeen thousand silk weavers were unemployed or were being forced to seek jobs in the coal mines and iron mills in 1877. The latter was a particularly ominous turn of events in the eyes of Tezenas du Montcel because "when they returned to the silk industry . . . these workers, having taken up the pickax or file to avoid beggary [would] have lost the delicacy of touch needed to handle silk."[9]

This business slump inevitably raised the issue of government commercial policy in the minds of the Rhône-Loire textile manufacturers, but it did not prompt them to join the movement for higher tariffs. Quite the opposite. In the late 1870s Lyons textilists were seeking to continue and extend free trade policies. Their reasoning was simple: the domestic market remained secondary for most branches of their industry, and in any case

6. *Annales du commerce extérieur*, no. 102 (1867–1881), p. 171. The falling value of exports reflected not a decline in the volume of exports (this remained constant) but a decline in the unit price of pure silk in the world market. The official price, as calculated by the Commission permanente des valeurs de douane, of a kilogram of pure silk cloth imported into France fell from 113 francs in 1875 to 77 francs in 1880 (*Annales du commerce extérieur, Valeurs arbitrées*, no. 89 [1875–1876], pp. 483–486; no. 101 [1880–1881], pp. 88–92).

7. The value of the average annual production of blends at Lyons rose from 39 million francs in 1873–1877 to 151 million francs in 1878–1882 ("Fabrique lyonnaise de soieries mélangés," AN F^{12} 6879A).

8. Deposition of the Tarare Chamber of Commerce, Sénat, *Enquête*, pp. 683–687; testimony of Thivel-Duvillard and Victor Godde, *Journal officiel*, May 23, 1878, pp. 5611–5615.

9. Conseil supérieur du commerce, *Admissions temporaires* (Paris, 1877), p. 149.

they already enjoyed a measure of protection there.[10] Thus their chief concern was maintaining or retrieving their position in foreign markets. Obviously, import duties served no purpose in that endeavor, but trade treaties did, and, indeed, were indispensable for opening foreign markets and keeping them open. Once this was accomplished, however, success became a matter of lowering production costs and staying abreast of changing fashions (or developing new ones) in order to compete. For the silk manufacturers, this mainly involved technical adjustments—a shift in production from figured to plain silk and the adoption of power looms for the weaving of the latter.[11] It also involved keeping raw materials costs low through the free entry of raw silk, and in 1878 the head of the Union des marchands des soies, Lilienthal, led the defense of that policy against the Rhône silk growers' demands for renewed protection (in this instance, of course, defense of the weaving industry dovetailed nicely with the silk merchants' new interest in the Oriental silk trade).[12] For the manufacturers of blends, improvement of competitive position also involved technical change—power looms were first introduced in Tarare in 1878 in response to the crisis—but it centered on the reduction of import duties on the cotton yarns that constituted up to 80 percent (by weight) of the raw materials in cotton-silk blends. In testifying before the Chamber Tariff Commission in 1878, the leaders of the industry were unanimous in seeking such a reduction either through the lowering of the conventional duties in the trade treaties or by the extension of the temporary admission system to cotton yarn.[13] From the late 1870s

10. The only exception was the industry of Tarare. Not coincidentally, it alone among the industries of the region demanded increased protection for its fabrics in 1878.

11. Much of the foreign-made silk cloth competing with Lyons silk in France was a mechanically woven variety not yet produced in France. In response to this challenge, various silk merchants, led by Edouard Aynard, soon formed a society to promote the mechanization of Lyons's household weaving on the basis of electrical power (Report of the Fourth Section, Commission permanente des valeurs de douane, *Annales du commerce extérieur*, no. 87 [1876], p. 64; Permezel, "L'industrie lyonnaise de la soie," p. 169).

12. Lilienthal, *Journal officiel*, June 28, 1878, pp. 7121–7122.

13. See the testimony before the Chamber Tariff Commission of Thivel-Duvillard, Tezenas du Montcel, Françisque David, and Auguste Sévène (*Journal*

to the 1890s, the attack on the protection of cotton in general and the campaign to reduce import duties on cotton yarns in particular—led by Francisque David on behalf of the entire Rhône-Loire textile industry—became a major element in the free trade movement.

The membership of the Free Trade Association included representatives of other French weaving industries who exported much of their finished products, as did the Lyonnais and Stephanois, and thus wanted to preserve the trade treaties and who imported—or sought to import—foreign yarns and thus had an interest in reducing tariffs or establishing temporary admission of those items. Among these were Victor Crespin, who represented Calais and Saint-Pierre-lès-Calais, the centers of tulle manufacture in France, and Pierre Bertrand-Milcent, who presided over the production in and around Cambrai (Nord) of fine linen cloth for export.[14] In this context we should also mention the cotton

---

officiel, May 23, 1878, pp. 5611–5615; May 27, 1878, pp. 5823–5824; May 30, 1878, pp. 5999–6004; June 28, 1878, pp. 7120–7122). The temporary admission of cotton cloth (but not cotton yarn) had been instituted in 1861 for the benefit of the Alsatian cloth printing industry, but it was abolished in 1870 in one of the few concrete achievements of the protectionist campaign of the late 1860s. In 1872 the temporary admission of certain kinds of wool yarn was authorized for the shoelace industry of Saint-Chamond. However, the temporary admission of cotton yarn was not broached until the hearings of the Conseil supérieur du commerce in January 1877. In May 1877, it was debated before the Comité consultatif des arts et métiers—the *procès-verbaux* of which is found in AN F^{12} 5337—but no decision was reached.

14. Most of the 40–50 million francs worth of silk tulle and cotton tulle produced annually in Calais and Saint-Pierre was exported, thus guaranteeing the local industrialists' support for the trade treaties. In addition, the tulle producers saw the growth of cotton tulle exports being stunted by the high price of the thread they bought in Lille (high thread prices raised their production costs and put them at a disadvantage in the international market relative to English tulle makers), so in 1878 they pressed for the temporary admission of two- and three-strand cotton thread—against the vocal opposition of their "natural enemies," the Lille cotton spinners—in order to make foreign thread available or at least to force down the price of domestic thread (testimony of Victor Crespin, *Journal officiel*, May 30, 1878, pp. 6003–6004).

Bertrand-Milcent was motivated by similar concerns. While supporting continued protection in the home market of the linen he produced, he also demanded continuation of the trade treaties (half of his output was exported). Moreover, to enhance his ability to compete in the British and American markets with the mechanized linen industry of Ireland—and perhaps to avoid switching from hand loom weaving to power looms—he sought to reduce his production costs through

industry of Roanne (Loire), which was abandoning spinning in the 1870s in order to specialize in the mechanized weaving of vichy cloth using imported English and Swiss yarn, and the cloth printers of Rouen, who were seeking to reestablish temporary admissions on the cotton cloth they used.[15] Yet, however vocal these specialties were in promoting their interests, they all remained relatively small and uninfluential in tariff politics. Consequently, the only textile interests in the free trade camp that could begin to match the power and influence of the silk industry were in wool.

Stimulated by rising demand during the cotton shortage of the early sixties and aided by the influx of large supplies of cheap wool from Argentina and Australia, woolens had emerged as the largest and fastest growing textile industry in France by the 1870s.[16] Much of this growth centered in the production of combed wool and worsteds. Benefiting from the application of power looms to the weaving of wool and the invention of mechanical wool combing, this branch of the industry expanded its output for the domestic market at the expense of carded woolens after 1860. At the same time, because the quality of its products was high and because the trade treaties opened new markets, its exports increased. Indeed, so great was the increase in the exportation of worsteds that woolen cloth became France's

---

the temporary admission of cheap Belgian linen thread (testimony of Bertrand-Milcent, Conseil supérieur du commerce, *Admissions temporaires*, pp. 138–141; *Journal officiel*, July 17, 1878, pp. 7936–7937).

15. No one from Roanne joined the Free Trade Association in 1878 and, indeed, the Roanne Chamber of Commerce declared its support for tariff protection in 1877 (Sénat, *Enquête*, pp. 664–665). Yet leaders of Roanne's cotton industry—such as Charles Cherpin, deputy for the Loire—were conspicuously absent from the AIF in 1878, and in the course of the 1880s they became increasingly sympathetic to the demand for the temporary admission of cotton yarn voiced by the other weaving industries of the Loire. See the deposition of the Roanne Chamber of Commerce to the Conseil supérieur du commerce, 1890, in AN F¹² 6916.

On the Rouen cotton print industry, see the testimony of its leading spokesman, Alphonse Cordier, senator of the Seine-Inférieure, in the various inquiries of 1877–1878.

16. According to Markovitch ("L'industrie française," table 2), between the decades 1855–1864 and 1865–1874, wool combing grew at an average annual rate of 3.5 percent, wool spinning at a rate of 2.8 percent, and wool weaving at a rate of 2.6 percent. By contrast, the spinning and weaving of other fibers generally grew less than 2 percent annually in the same period.

foremost export by 1876, while the reexport of combed wool made wool France's fourth largest export.[17] In light of these developments, it is hardly surprising that certain centers of wool combing and worsted production became strong advocates of free trade in the 1850s and 1860s. The most important of these were Reims, France's largest center of mechanized wool weaving and long an exporter of its renowned merinos and cashmeres, and Fourmies, France's principal center for the spinning of combed wool and, like Reims, a center for the production of worsteds for export.[18]

For both Reims and Fourmies, production and exports were declining in the late 1870s because the worldwide depression lowered demand for high-quality woolens even as world capacity for their manufacture increased. Yet, because foreign markets remained indispensable to them and their products suffered little from outside competition in the home market (thanks to their quality and to existing import duties), both remained committed to the trade treaties and the other commercial policies of the Second Empire. Reflecting this situation, Léon Legrand of Fourmies and Jean-Simon Dauphinot (senator of the Marne, mayor of Reims, and president of its chamber of commerce) became leading members of the Free Trade Association and lobbied vigorously in the parliamentary hearings on the tariff in 1877–1878. So, too, did Gaston Grandgeorge, a spinner and weaver of combed wool at Guise (Aisne), and baron Auguste de Fourment, who operated three woolens mills in the Somme.[19]

17. The value of annual exports of woolen cloth rose from 224–236 million francs in 1867–1869 to a peak of 346 million francs in 1875 and remained at 316 million in 1876. The annual value of silk cloth exports fell from 423–452 million francs in 1867–1869 and a peak of 478 million in 1873 to 295.9 million in 1876 (*Tableau décennal*, I, xcix). While exports of all categories of woolen cloth increased, exports of merinos rose the most, from 1.3 million kilograms in 1868 to 4.56 million in 1874, and stood at 3.54 million in 1876. By contrast, export of common woolens rose from 3.4 million kilograms in 1868 to a peak of 5.7 million kilograms and stood at 4.4 million in 1876 (*Annales du commerce extérieur*, no. 102, *Exposé comparatif* [1867–1881], p. 169).

18. Fourmies had 600,000 spindles in 1878, versus 500,000 in Tourcoing, 324,000 in Sedan, 270,000 in Reims, and perhaps 247,000 in and around Elbeuf. Fourmies had 3,000 mechanical looms compared to 4,300 in Roubaix-Tourcoing and 7,162 in Reims (Claude Fohlen, *L'industrie textile au temps du Second Empire* [Paris, 1956], p. 465; *Annuaire statistique*, 1 [1878], 374–377; Sénat, *Enquête*, p. 270; Chamber Tariff Commission, *Procès-verbaux*, p. 300).

19. See the testimony of Léon Legrand, Sénat, *Enquête*, pp. 270–280, and

Of course, not all French woolens manufacturers (not even all manufacturers of combed wool and worsteds) supported free trade. Those of Roubaix-Tourcoing are a case in point. Once Lille's junior partner in the spinning of cotton in the Nord, Roubaix-Tourcoing had emerged as one of France's fastest growing industrial complexes in the 1860s on the strength of the mechanized combing and spinning of wool at Tourcoing and the mechanized weaving of worsteds and cotton-wool blends at Roubaix.[20] Because they exported much of their combed wool to England and much of their cloth to Spain and South America and imported their raw wool from Argentina via Dunkirk (in contrast to Reims, which still relied on wool grown in Champagne), the manufacturers of Roubaix-Tourcoing benefited from liberal trade policies. Logically, they should have defended such policies in 1878. However, because protectionism was so well ingrained in all segments of Nord enterprise (perhaps a response to the border location) and because many of the wool manufacturers of Roubaix, including Louis Motte-Bossut, were also involved in cotton spinning and were concerned with its protection, the leaders of the Roubaix-Tourcoing wool industry shunned the Free Trade Association. Indeed, seeing their exports fall and imports rise in 1876–1877, they took a protectionist tack in testifying before the Chamber Tariff Commission in 1878. Yet only Motte-Bossut went so far as to join the AIF. In the final analysis, the Roubaix-Tourcoing manufacturers wanted the best of both policies— protection of the home market and trade treaties to open foreign markets. Unwilling to support either free trade or protection exclusively, they stayed out of the fight over tariffs in the late 1870s.

Less equivocal on the tariff were the leaders of the old carded woolens industry of Sedan, Louviers, and Elbeuf.[21] Pressed by

---

Journal officiel, July 4, 1878, pp. 7521–7527; and Dauphinot, Sénat, *Enquête,* pp. 118–133, and Chamber Tariff Commission, *Procès-verbaux,* p. 302.

20. The manufacture of cotton-wool blends for women's clothing "had made Roubaix's fortune" in the 1840s and 1850s, according to one source (Wibaux-Florin dossier, AN F^{12} 5299). For an overview of Roubaix's rise, see Claude Fohlen, "Esquisse d'une révolution industrielle: Roubaix au XIXe siècle," *Revue du Nord,* 33 (1951), 92–103.

21. Aided by the influx of Alsatian capital, machinery, and labor from Bischwiller (Bas-Rhin) after 1871, Elbeuf converted to mechanized weaving (Georges

British competition, all favored increased protection in the 1870s, with the Elbeuvians doing so most vociferously. Elbeuf had exported much of its novelty weaves used in men's clothing to the United States and South America by way of England until 1875. Thereafter, Leeds and Huddersfield usurped those markets and even began encroaching on their domestic market. Coupled with growing competition at home from the worsteds of Roubaix and Reims (increasingly dependent on the French market after also having been bumped from some of their foreign markets by the British), this spelled depression. What had been for years a steady annual turnover of 90–95 million francs for Elbeuf had fallen to 75 million francs by 1877.[22] To compensate for this loss and to stem the downward trend, the Elbeuvians hoped to adapt the cheap combed wool of Roubaix to the manufacture of plain woolen cloth and thereby oust the more expensive cloth of the Hérault from the markets of southern France. At the same time, they sought to secure this potential market from all outside threats in the future through an increase in import duties. To obtain this increase, their representatives joined the AIF and testified before the Chamber Tariff Commission in 1878.[23]

Carded woolens was among those textile industries that did not depend primarily on foreign markets or were losing ground in foreign markets and believed—rightly or wrongly—that they could no longer depend on them and should henceforth look primarily to the domestic market. In line with this reorientation, these industries did not seek in commercial policy the means to improve their ability to compete abroad, but rather they sought to increase their hold on the home market by raising import duties (as compensation for the handicaps that put them at a disadvan-

Delahache, "De Bischwiller à Elbeuf," *Revue de Paris*, December 1, 1911, pp. 563–574). In 1875, the Seine-Inférieure had 3,969 power looms and was third behind the Nord and the Marne in this category. Still, in contrast to worsteds, the carded woolens industry depended mainly on hand looms. The Ardennes operated 5,500 hand looms and only 1,130 power looms in 1875; the Seine-Inférieure still had 5,537 hand looms in the same year (*Annuaire statistique*, 1 [1878], 374–381).

22. Testimony of Constant Flavigny, Sénat, *Enquête*, p. 249, and *Journal officiel*, June 29, 1878, pp. 7152–7154.

23. On this strategy, see Jules Maître to the minister of commerce, June 1882, in AN F[12] 4836.

tage in competing with foreigners at home). In addition to carded woolens, these industries included linen and cotton spinning and the weaving associated with them, silk floss spinning, and jute spinning and weaving.

The silk floss and jute industries were still relatively new and relatively small in the 1870s. Yet, because they were threatened by foreign competition, both played an important role in the protectionist movement in the persons of Emile Widmer, director of the S. A. de la filature de bourre de soie d'Amilly (Loiret), who became secretary of the AIF, and Charles Saint of Saint Frères (France's biggest producer of burlap bags), who served as a vice-president of the AIF. Launched in the 1820s to utilize the waste products of silk manufacturing, silk floss spinning had grown steadily in the 1850s and 1860s, and in 1870 it reached its maximum size—twelve firms and ninety thousand spindles. After 1870, however, the English and Swiss began spinning silk floss, and because their production costs were lower, they were soon underselling the French in their home market. By 1878, the French industry was down to sixty thousand spindles, and the surviving French producers—including Ernest Desouches of the Seine-Inférieure, Martelin of the Rhône, and especially Widmer—launched an appeal for higher import duties to prevent any further slippage.[24] Similar concerns underlay the protectionism of the jute industry. After 1845, when Anselm Bocquet and Robert Carmichael founded France's first jute spinning mill at Ailly-sur-Somme and the Saint brothers, manufacturers and wholesalers of linen bags, opened the first jute weaving mill nearby at Flixecourt (Somme), the jute industry had enjoyed steady growth and almost continuous prosperity for three decades, thanks to the rising demand for packing materials in an age of expanding commerce. Then, in the mid-1870s, the opening of new jute mills in Calcutta knocked Dundee, Scotland, out of the Indian market. Dundee, in turn, began to dump jute and burlap on the French and European markets at unprecedented low prices. Accordingly, the volume of jute yarns imported into France tripled in one year's time (72,600 kilograms in 1875 to 219,700 kilograms in 1876), and the importa-

24. Widmer et al., Sénat, *Enquête*, pp. 283–285; *Journal officiel*, June 28, 1878, pp. 7123–7126.

tion of burlap rose fivefold (379,000 kilograms to 1,968,000 kilograms) between 1875 and 1877.[25] To end this invasion, all twenty-six French jute producers—led by the oldest and largest, Saint Frères and Bocquet-Carmichael-Dewailly—pressed for a 40–50 percent increase in import duties in 1878.[26]

With government help to stop the takeover of the French market by foreign producers, France's silk floss and jute manufacturers could look forward to continued growth and prosperity. By contrast, the leaders of the linen industry faced a less certain future. To be sure, linen manufacture had expanded dramatically during the cotton famine of the early 1860s, especially at Lille— which had pioneered the mechanized spinning of flax and, by 1870, possessed six out of every seven linen spindles in France— and at nearby Armentières, where the mechanized weaving of linen cloth came to be concentrated. Linen remained France's third largest textile industry, rivaling cotton in the value of its output in the mid-seventies. By then, however, the industry was in the throes of a seemingly irreversible decline that had begun in 1867, when cotton reclaimed the customers lost in the early sixties, and had continued ever since. By 1878 the number of linen spindles in the Nord had declined from a high of 750,000 in 1867 to 500,000, and 50 of the 194 spinning mills operating ten years before had closed their doors.[27] Those who remained sought to assure their survival by winning prohibitive duties that would close French borders to all foreign linen—especially Belgian yarns—and thereby allow them to regulate production and set prices for a closed market through their cartel, the Comité linier du Nord. Of course, because linen was threatened by domestic cotton as much as by foreign linen,[28] such duties alone could not

25. *Tableau décennal*, I, 179 ff.; Depositions of Charles Saint, Sénat, *Enquête*, pp. 187–189, and *Journal officiel*, June 17, 1878, pp. 7040–7042.
26. See the petition in the Saint dossier, AN F[12] 5264.
27. Le Blan, Chamber Tariff Commission, *Procès-verbaux*, pp. 337–341.
28. Although linen yarn was still less expensive than cotton yarn in the 1870s, the fall in cotton prices was narrowing the gap and thus making the substitution of cotton for linen more likely. It was becoming increasingly difficult for linen to compete with cotton on the basis of prices because the production costs of linen were inherently higher than those of cotton. The spinning of flax required substantially more fuel and labor than cotton spinning (four workers per 220 spindles versus four workers per 2,000). Similarly, it was twice as expensive to

guarantee the industry's survival. At best, they would allow linen spinners, in the words of Alfred Aftalion, "to organize their decadence."[29] Still, these duties were necessary for the industry's strategy, and the linen spinners understandably gave them a high priority. To achieve them, five members of the Comité linier, including Julian and Paul LeBlan, Edouard Agache, and Gustave Dubar, joined the AIF and lobbied parliament. They were joined by linen producers from elsewhere in France such as Arthur and Léon Feray, who ran the linen spinning branch of their father's industrial complex at Essonnes (Seine-et-Oise), and Emile Magnier, whose Comptoir de l'industrie linière operated spinning mills in the Nord and Pas-de-Calais and weaving plants in the Sarthe and the Somme.

Although manufacturers of linen, jute, and silk floss all played important roles in the AIF, cotton was clearly the dominant textile industry in the protectionist movement in the 1870s and, indeed, was probably the most protectionistic industry in France ("the protectionists of coal and iron count for nothing alongside the cotton spinners," Isaac Pereire commented in 1877).[30] From the eighteenth century onward, the French cotton industry needed—or believed that it needed—high tariffs to secure its domestic markets against competition from the larger, more technically advanced cotton industry of Great Britain. Consequently, cotton spinners were in the forefront of the resistance to trade liberalization throughout the early nineteenth century, and after 1860 politicians tied to cotton spearheaded the attack on the trade treaties, which had substituted protective duties for prohibitory duties on imported cotton goods. In the mid-1870s rising imports and falling prices mobilized cotton on behalf of protection more than ever before.[31] Cotton spinners (Pouyer-Quertier,

---

weave linen as cotton (Jean Lambert-Dansette, *Origines et évolution d'une bourgeoisie: Quelques familles du patronat textile de Lille-Armentières* [Lille, 1954], p. 486).

29. Alfred Aftalion, *La crise de l'industrie linière et la concurrance victorieuse de l'industrie cotonnière* (Paris, 1904), p. 71.

30. Isaac Pereire, *Politique industrielle et commerciale: Budget des réformes* (Paris, 1877), p. 73.

31. The importation of unfinished cotton yarn rose from 1,952 tons in 1873 to 10,705 tons in 1876 and stood at 10,606 tons in 1877. The value of all imported

Waddington, Feray, and Claude) and representatives of cotton spinning districts (Méline and Pierre Legrand) organized the protectionist blocs in the Senate and Chamber after 1876, as previously discussed. And in 1878, when the AIF was formed, cotton manufacturers made up the large majority of its textile section (forty-eight of sixty members).

Some of these manufacturers represented the second-echelon spinning and weaving centers of northern and western France— Saint-Quentin, Amiens, Condé-sur-Noireau, Flers, Mayenne—all of which were declining because of their inability to compete with more efficient domestic and foreign producers. For example, the spinning industry of Saint-Quentin suffered a 26 percent reduction in its spindlage between 1865 and 1875 when the new water-powered mills of Switzerland displaced it as supplier of yarn to the rural weavers of Picardy. Similarly, the manufacturers of *articles d'Amiens*—cotton velvets and corduroy—lost their foreign customers to British competitors despite their belated switch from hand weaving to power looms, and in 1878 they faced an imminent British takeover of their domestic market as well.[32]

Rising foreign imports were also responsible for the decline of the weaving and spinning towns of lower Normandy and Mayenne, but only indirectly. "The importation of heavy yarns

cotton yarn, which fluctuated between 9 and 13 million francs during the crisis of 1867–1869, rose to 47.6 million francs in 1876. Likewise, the value of imported cotton cloth, which had been 18–24 million francs in 1867–1869, rose to 84.4 million francs in 1875 (*Tableau décennal*, I, xcv, 179 ff., II, 194 ff.). The official price of simple, unfinished cotton yarn fell from 5.05 francs per kilogram to 4.3 in 1876 and 3.55 by 1880. There were similar drops in prices of other cotton yarns and fabrics (*Annales du commerce extérieur, Valeurs arbitrées*, no. 89, pp. 483–486, 507–510; no. 101, pp. 89–92, 124–127). In line with this business trend, the number of cotton spindles in France declined from over 5 million in 1860–1865 to 4.69 million in 1877—the lowest number in the last quarter of the nineteenth century (by 1886, the number was back up to 5,124,140). At the same time, the number of hand looms was declining rapidly, from 78,037 in 1875 to 50,578 in 1878, as one would expect in an era of accelerating mechanization. More disturbing was the simultaneous, albeit temporary, dip in the number of power looms, from 62,537 (1873) to 59,107 (1877) (Statistique de la France, 2d ser., 19, *Résultats genéraux de l'enquête, 1861–65; Annuaire statistique*, 1 (1878), 374–377).

32. The value of British velours imports, which averaged 1.3 million francs in 1866–1871, was up to 6–7 million francs in 1875–1877 (Cosserat and Vulfran-Mollet, Sénat, *Enquête*, p. 218, 232–233; Fiquet and Motte-Bossut, *Journal officiel*, June 13, 1878, pp. 6632–6633).

and fabrics like those we produce has not been great enough to affect us directly," a spokesman for the Condé-sur-Noireau cotton industry wrote later, "but the importation of British, Swiss, and Belgian goods has hurt the spinners and weavers of the Nord, who have then been forced to produce goods similar to ours and thus have taken away our markets."[33] As a result of this "bumping" process, the weaving center of Flers (Orne), where 312 manufacturers employed 29,000 workers to operate 6,495 hand looms in 1860, had only 164 manufacturers employing 12,000 workers to operate 2,446 hand looms and 447 power looms in 1876. In the neighboring department of the Mayenne, the story was the same. One of the few cloth manufacturers to survive there, Gustave Denis of Fontaine-Daniel, did so only by despecializing. In place of the two basic fabrics he produced in 1860, Denis wove small quantities of some four dozen different fabrics—novelties for the rural market—in 1878.[34] This decline of the region's weaving industry natually had repercussions for the local spinning industry. Lower Normandy lost 42 percent of its cotton spindles between 1860 and 1880. Even though its principal spinning center, Condé-sur-Noireau, survived on a reduced scale through retrenchment and modernization, others of the area, such as Falaise, were forced out of cotton spinning entirely by the early 1880s.[35]

As part of their desperate struggle to survive, leaders of all these endangered cotton industries—Joly de Bammeville and Touron-Lemaire of Saint-Quentin, Cocquel of Amiens, Germain-Duforestel of Condé, Cabrol of Flers—joined the AIF and demanded higher import duties on cotton yarns and cloths in 1878. However, the most influential calls for increased protection emanated not from the small, declining centers of production but from the three largest—those of upper Normandy, the Nord, and the Vosges—each of which was expanding its plant in the 1870s.

33. Deposition of Chamber of Commerce of Condé-sur-Noireau to Conseil supérieur du commerce, 1890, AN F¹² 6917.
34. Cabrol, Comité industriel de Flers, Sénat, *Enquête*, p. 190; Gustave Denis, Chamber Tariff Commission, *Procès-verbaux*, p. 123.
35. Report of Germain-Duforestel, AN F¹² 6878; Gabriel Désert, "La modernisation de l'industrie falaisienne au XIXᵉ siècle," *Actes, Congrès des sociétés savantes, 1964* (Paris, 1965), II, 761–786.

The cotton industry of upper Normandy, located in and around Rouen in the departments of the Seine-Inférieure and the Eure, was France's oldest and largest. In the 1870s, as in past decades, it was also the most ardently protectionist branch of the French cotton industry (in 1878 it alone furnished seventeen members of the AIF). Founded by English entrepreneurs in the eighteenth century, Norman cotton had expanded rapidly under the high protection of the Restoration and July Monarchy. Yet, in the early 1850s, it had remained a dispersed, relatively backward, and essentially rural industry.[36] Only in the late fifties, under the pressure of internal competition, did modernization and consolidation begin. In a process heralded by Pouyer-Quertier's abandonment of water-driven mills in the Andelle valley and his opening of La Foudre at Petit-Quevilly in 1860, Norman cotton spinning was increasingly concentrated during the sixties in steam-powered mills in Rouen and in nearby towns, such as Bolbec and Le Havre, whose location on waterways or railroads gave them access to imported British coal. By the 1870s, power looms were added to existing spinning mills, and these towns had become weaving as well as spinning centers.[37] The leaders of this drive toward modernization, concentration, and integration— rather than the owners of the obsolete plants in the region—led the push for higher tariffs through the Syndicat des industries cotonnières de la Normandie, the Rouen Chamber of Commerce, and the AIF. In addition to Pouyer-Quertier and Richard Waddington, these included Henri Petit and Delamarre-Deboutteville of Rouen, Duret et fils of Brionne (the largest cotton spinners in the Eure), Edouard Davillier of Gisors, Desgênetais Frères and

36. In the mid-nineteenth century, mule jennies in the myriad water-driven mills dotting the tributaries of the lower Seine spun a coarse yarn that was dyed or bleached at Rouen and then woven by hand in the pays de Caux into shoddy *rouenneries* (weaves of colored yarn) or calicoes with which the cloth printers of Rouen produced cheap imitations of Alsatian prints for mass consumption (Fohlen, *L'industrie textile*, pp. 193–202; Guy Richard, "Du moulin banal au tissage mécanique: La noblesse dans l'industrie textile en Haute-Normandie dans la première moitié du XIXe siècle," *Revue d'histoire économique et sociale*, 46 [1968], 305–338, 506–549).
37. In the process, hand weaving in the hinterlands was killed off. The number of hand looms in the pays de Caux dropped from 60,000 in 1863 to 25,000 in 1877 (Cordier, Sénat, *Enquête*, p. 360).

Alfred Fauquet-Lemaitre of Bolbec, Octave Fauquet of Oissel, and Albert Courant and Ernest Siegfried of Le Havre.

Exactly why did the big cotton spinners of upper Normandy seek greater protection in 1878? Unlike their less advantaged colleagues in lower Normandy, none needed higher tariffs simply to survive (indeed, the expansion of the cotton industry of the Seine-Inférieure and Eure in the eighteen years since the advent of "free trade" had shown they could survive and even thrive in the absence of high protection). Rather, they wanted higher tariffs to provide an extra measure of security in the home market on the one hand, and, on the other, to correct the unfavorable turn business had taken in 1877–1878, which was "one of the worst years ever recorded," according to the year-end review of the Rouen Chamber of Commerce.[38] During 1878, the Rouen spinners lost their lucrative market for cotton yarn in eastern France to the British.[39] At the same time, their sales of yarn and cloth declined locally because the demand for the cheap calicoes printed in Rouen and for the traditional Norman specialty, *rouenneries,* was dwindling (neither was any longer à la mode at home, and neither could compete with less expensive English prints abroad, especially in the colonial market). To compensate for the decline of these traditional products, the Normans switched to the spinning of heavier yarns, which were then woven into coarse fabrics used in military clothing and upholstery (typical of this trend was Albert Courant's founding of a mill to produce cretonnes in Le Havre in 1875). Since the manufacture of these heavier yarns and fabrics required more cotton than the previous products did, the output (by volume) of the Norman cotton industry was rising in the late 1870s.[40] Yet, because the new goods commanded a lower price, the income and profits of the

38. Chamber of Commerce of Rouen, *Exposé sommaire des travaux pendant l'année 1878* (Rouen, 1879), p. 178.

39. In May, Pouyer-Quertier told the Chamber Tariff Commission (*Procès-verbaux,* p. 105): "The English have chased me from the Vosges. I once sold three million francs worth of numbers 22 and 29 cotton yarn in that region [yearly]; I now sell hardly any there."

40. Pouyer-Quertier's La Foudre turned out 1,620,000 kilograms of number 16 yarn in 1878, versus 918,000 kilograms of number 28 yarn in previous years (Pouyer-Quertier, Chamber Tariff Commission, *Procès-verbaux,* p. 105).

upper Norman cotton industry probably were declining in the late 1870s.

To reverse these trends was the Normans' first and foremost goal in seeking increased protection. Specifically, they believed that higher tariffs would reduce foreign competition in the home market and thus allow them to shift back to the more lucrative products they had recently abandoned or, at least, allow them to charge higher prices on their current products. Either way, the high profitability of their industry would be restored. Increased protection would also fit in nicely with the Normans' long-range business strategies. For some, these strategies involved expanding production to fill the gap left by the loss of Alsace and to take over the markets of less efficient domestic rivals (of course, with their switch to heavier yarns and cloth, the Rouen manufacturers were already doing this in lower Normandy). For others, the long-term plan was to reap maximum benefits from their existing plants for as long as possible, while preparing investments in other fields for the future. Pouyer-Quertier, for example, had already converted his textile firm into a joint-stock company (the Société anonyme des filatures et tissages Pouyer-Quertier), and in the 1870s he was devoting much of his time and money to new ventures such as the Compagnie française du télégraphe de Paris à New York. He and other cotton spinners were also pushing the development of Rouen as a port and entrepôt for Paris, which could only enhance the value of their real estate in the area.[41] The campaign for higher tariffs was thus one part of a larger effort to increase the stature of upper Normandy and the wealth of its cotton capitalists.

Norman cotton's oldest ally in the quest for tariff protection was the cotton industry of the Nord, centered at Lille and Roubaix. The steam-powered spinning of cotton had been introduced in the Nord around 1800, and, like the water-powered spinning in Normandy, it had grown rapidly under high protec-

41. On the conversion of Pouyer-Quertier's firm, see the note of June 13, 1891, by Georges Yver, the company's director, in AN F[12] 6878. On the Paris–New York cable company, see *Journal des chemins de fer*, April 5, 1879. On efforts to develop the port of Rouen, see letter of February 12, 1878, Chamber of Commerce of Rouen, *Exposé sommaire, 1878.*

tion in the first half of the nineteenth century. Like the Normans, the Nord cotton spinners assumed that their success depended on prohibitory import duties. Consequently, they led the opposition to the liberalization of tariff policy in the 1840s and 1850s, and in 1860 they vigorously protested the signing of the Anglo-French trade treaty, which they predicted would ruin them. To be sure, many did face a genuine crisis after 1860, when the British took over the supplying of fine yarn—a Nord specialty—to the weaving industries of the Lyonnais, especially that of Tarare. Yet those willing and able to change their specialty and modernize their plants survived the advent of free trade and even expanded. Indeed, instead of declining, the cotton spindlage of the Nord continued to increase after 1860, and by the mid-1870s the Nord possessed more cotton spindles than any other French department. In Roubaix, cotton spinning survived and expanded mainly as an adjunct to the burgeoning wool industry, producing yarn to be woven with wool in the cotton-wool blends. In the mid-1870s most of Roubaix's fourteen spinning mills and 240,000 spindles were directly or indirectly integrated with woolens production, such as in the Motte family enterprises.[42] In Lille, the hard times of the sixties thinned out the ranks of the cotton spinners. Many shifted to linen spinning during the cotton famine; many others went bankrupt in the collapse of the cotton market in 1866–1867. Whatever the reason, there were only twelve cotton spinners left in Lille by 1878, in contrast to forty-three in 1860. Those twelve, however, controlled considerably more spindles than did the forty-three of 1860 (one million versus 510,000), a reflection of their success in modernizing and adapting to new market conditions after 1860. According to Alfred Delesalle, the foremost spokesman for Lille cotton in these years, Lille cotton spinners spent over 30 million francs between 1860 and 1878 to install more powerful steam engines and to add new twisting spindles (by 1878, 400,000 of Lille's one million spindles were of

42. Louis Motte-Bossut had been Roubaix's leading cotton spinner until fire destroyed his plant in 1865. Then he shifted to worsted production. At the same time, however, he set up his sons, Léon and Georges, in cotton spinning and weaving. Meanwhile, his brother, Alfred, headed the family's wool combing, dyeing, and finishing works (Gaston Motte, *Les Motte* [Roubaix, 1952], pp. 53–98).

this type). This modernization allowed them to shift from the spinning of simple fine yarn to the manufacture of twisted yarn which was then marketed throughout France and Europe as sewing thread, a commodity in increasing demand because of the advent and spread of the sewing machine. Moreover, because Lille twisted thread could be given a silken appearance not found in any other thread through an exclusive glazing process invented by Alfred Thiriez in 1863, it was also in great demand among the tulle makers of Saint-Pierre and the ribbon makers of Saint-Etienne. Indeed, so great was the success of Lille's glazed twist that the Etablissements Thiriez, its leading producer, had become the largest *filature* in France—and in continental Europe—by 1880.[43]

Innovation, adaptation, and specialization in the 1860s thus brought great prosperity to the Nord cotton spinning industry in the early 1870s. In those years, the leaders of the industry probably supported tariff protection more out of a sense of tradition than out of any pressing need. It was only in the business slump after 1876 that the call for higher tariffs took on a sense of urgency. For Motte-Bossut, the problem at that time lay in the decline of the Amiens velours industry, to which he supplied cotton yarn, and his push for increased protection in 1878 thus focused on velours.[44] For the Lille cotton spinners, the problem lay in the depression of tulle and ribbon production, made worse by the rising competition of the English and Swiss, who, in the mid-1870s, had launched production of the glazed yarn that had previously been a monopoly of Lille. Thus, in 1878, the Lille spinners held unsold stocks of yarn representing eight months' production. In response to this glut, some began to cut working hours and reduce salaries. Most, however, believed that the best solution for their problems—and the basis of future prosperity and expansion—lay in higher tariffs. Led by Delesalle and Thiriez, the Lille cotton spinners joined the AIF and began to

43. On the development of Lille cotton spinning, 1860–1880, and especially on Thiriez's role in it, see the testimony of Alfred Delesalle, Chamber Tariff Commission, *Procès-verbaux*, pp. 182–185, and Lambert-Dansette, *Origines et évolution d'une bourgeoisie*, pp. 177–178.
44. Motte-Bossut, Sénat, *Enquête*, p. 181; *Journal officiel*, June 13, 1878, pp. 6632–6633.

demand import duties on cotton yarn sufficiently high not only to end competition in the domestic market for their current specialties—glazed thread and sewing thread—but also to allow them to recapture the sales of fine yarn to Tarare that they had lost to the English in the 1860s.[45] Thus the Nord cotton spinners, as well as those of upper Normandy, were seeking increased protection in 1878 not only to remedy a short-term crisis but also to help achieve their long-range goal of continued expansion.

In contrast to the cotton industries of Normandy and the Nord, which had been economically and politically important since the early 1800s, the cotton industry of the Vosges in eastern France— the third major cotton industry in the AIF in 1878—had come into its own only after 1870, when it underwent a revolutionary transformation and expansion unmatched in any other branch of French textiles in the late nineteenth century and, as a consequence, began to produce major protectionist spokesmen for the first time. The origins of this rise to prominence lay in development of the Vosges as a subsidiary of the Alsatian cotton industry before 1870. The immediate cause, however, was the conscious effort by local industrialists to make the Vosges the focal point of all cotton production in eastern France after the German annexation of Alsace in 1871.

The Alsatians had first introduced cotton spinning and weaving into the Vosges in the early nineteenth century in order to produce unfinished calicoes for the cloth printers of Mulhouse. As the cloth printing industry of Mulhouse prospered in the 1850s and 1860s, the cotton industry of the Vosges grew apace, aided by the building of a regional rail network and by the introduction of the Fourneyron water turbine, which allowed the department's streams to be harnessed at higher elevations than ever before.[46] But in 1870–1871 the Franco-Prussian War and the German takeover of Alsace permanently disrupted the symbiotic relationship between the cotton industries of Mulhouse and the Vosges and thus appeared to sound the death knell for both. After

45. Delesalle and Thiriez, Chamber Tariff Commission, *Procès-verbaux*, pp. 174–190.
46. Henri Boucher, "Industrie et commerce," in Léon Louis, ed., *Le département des Vosges*, v (Epinal, 1889), pp. 201–208.

January 1, 1873, when the collection of full customs duties commenced at the new Franco-German border, the German tariff virtually excluded Vosges calicoes from their principal market in Mulhouse. For its part, Mulhouse not only lost its main source of unfinished cloth but also found its prints shut out of a major market by French tariffs (import duties on finished textiles remained high in France even in the age of "free trade"). Yet what at first glance was an unmitigated disaster for all concerned soon proved to be an enormous windfall, at least for the Vosgians. Enticed by the opportunity of filling the gap in French textile production left by the loss of Alsace, which had possessed France's largest concentration of cotton spindles and power looms before 1870, and encouraged by the willingness of many Alsatians to migrate in order to preserve their French citizenship, the Syndicat cotonnier de l'Est shifted its seat from Mulhouse to Epinal (Vosges) in 1871 and began systematically to promote the transfer of the Alsatian cotton industry to the French side of the border.[47]

This unprecedented industrial development project unfolded on several levels in the 1870s. It involved, first, the modernization and expansion of spinning and weaving in the Vosges. Old water-powered spinning mills, such as Nicolas Claude's at Saulxures, were equipped with newer machinery from Alsace, and, more important, new steam-powered mills were built at lower elevations around Epinal and Remiremont, where coal was available by rail. As a result, the Vosges plant grew from 372,000 spindles and 14,000 looms in 1869 to 610,000 spindles and 24,000 looms ten years later. In a related development, the establishment of machine shops at Saint-Dié gave the Vosges the capacity to build and repair its own steam engines, looms, and spindles for the first

47. For a retrospective analysis of this project, see the report of August 19, 1879, Chamber of Commerce of the Vosges, *Extraits du registre des délibérations*, 4ᵉ cahier (Epinal, 1881). The effort to transfer all elements of the Alsatian industry to the Vosges gained momentum only after the failure in 1871–1872 of efforts by certain Alsatian and Vosgian industrialists, including Gustave Steinheil, deputy for the Vosges, to win modifications of the French tariff system that would have allowed the symbiosis of the Vosges and Haut-Rhin to continue. Pouyer-Quertier was finance minister at the time and undoubtedly played a role in blocking this maneuver in order to help the Normans replace Alsace in supplying yarn to Vosges weavers.

time. Meanwhile, a joint-stock company formed by both Vosgian and Alsatian industrialists in December 1871 launched the construction of a finishing plant at Thaon, near Epinal, to replace the, by then, inaccessible bleaching and dyeing works of the Haut-Rhin. Headed by Jules Favre of Epinal, the company obtained equipment and skilled manpower from the Alsatian firms of Gros-Roman (Wesserling) and Steinheil-Dieterlin (Rothau), recruited its first director, Armand Lederlin, from Rothau, and in 1875 opened the Blanchisseries et Teintureries de Thaon (BTT). The final step in the transfer of the Alsatian industry was taken in 1881, when another stock company founded by Claude brought the cotton printing of Cernay (Haut-Rhin) to the Vosges.[48]

Thus in the decade following the Franco-Prussian War, a dynamic new cotton industry had emerged in the Vosges. This industry, however, had certain flaws and problems. Because of its geographical location, the Vosges was at the mercy of French railroads both for its supply of raw cotton and coal and for the shipping of its finished products to markets in France, Italy, and Algeria. Throughout the seventies, the Vosges Chamber of Commerce vehemently protested the high freight rates which, it believed, restricted the growth of Vosges industry, and backed the construction of the Canal de l'Est in the hope that such competition would force down railroad charges—a hope fulfilled when the canal opened in 1883. A more difficult problem involved the basic structure of the Vosges cotton industry. The Vosges did not produce enough yarn in the 1870s to supply its looms. In fact, in 1878 some 50 percent of the yarns consumed in the department were imported from England, a fact that rankled the local cotton spinners no end (just as it rankled the Normans who had been knocked out of the Vosges by British competitors). The Vosges cotton spinners wanted to construct the 350,000 or so additional spindles needed to make the industry self-sufficient, but feared to

48. Report of March 6, 1876, Chamber of Commerce of the Vosges, *Extraits du registre des délibérations*, 3ᵉ cahier (Epinal, 1878); Report of the prefect of the Vosges, second quarter, 1875, AN F¹² 4548; Prefect of the Vosges to the minister of commerce, February 8, 1881, AN F¹² 4835; Armand Lederlin et al., *Monographie de l'industrie cotonnière* (Epinal, 1905), p. 34; Pierre Hoffmann and Jules Deboffe, *Cinquantes ans de travaux sur l'agriculture et sur l'horticulture* (Paris, n.d.), pp. 37–46.

do so until higher tariffs rendered them immune to foreign competition.[49] Thus, on their behalf, the chamber of commerce repeatedly demanded higher duties on cotton yarn in the 1870s,[50] as did the parliamentary representatives of the Vosges—Claude, Ferry, Méline—who came to the forefront of the protectionist blocs in the Senate and Chamber after 1876. For the same reason, the leading cotton manufacturers of the region joined the AIF in 1878. In addition to Claude, these included Louis-Alfred Ponnier, who operated the old Seillière family mills at Senones, Charles Laederich and Jules Favre of Epinal, Seitz of Granges, the Dietsch brothers of Saint-Dié, Alexandre-Schwartz of Remiremont, as well as Adolphe Noblot of Héricourt (Haute-Saône) and Scheurer-Sahler of Audincourt (Doubs).

In taking the lead in the quest for increased cotton protection, the cotton spinners of upper Normandy, the Nord, and the Vosges assumed the stance of their less fortunate colleagues in lower Normandy, Saint-Quentin, and elsewhere and argued that higher tariffs were a matter of life and death. In testifying before various parliamentary hearings, they repeatedly depicted their industry as handicapped by high costs for plant construction and machinery (relative to those borne by foreign producers) as well as by high taxes, high fuel and transport costs, and high labor costs (resulting from the low per capita productivity of French workers, not from a high wage scale). These handicaps, they argued, raised their production costs far above those of the English, Swiss, and German cotton industries and made competition with those industries in the domestic market impossible without "compensation"—that is, without import duties 40 to 50 percent above those in the existing conventional tariff.[51] This argument was

49. Jules Favre, Sénat, *Enquête*, p. 151; *L'industrie française*, August 29, 1878.
50. Reports of July 19, 1875, and March 6, 1876, Chamber of Commerce of the Vosges, *Extraits du registre des délibérations*, 3ᵉ cahier.
51. See Conseil supérieur du commerce, *Examen des tarifs de douanes* (Paris, 1876), and the depositions of the Syndicat des industries cotonnières de la Normandie, Chamber Tariff Commission, *Procès-verbaux*, pp. 54–123. In putting forth their demands for compensatory tariffs, the cotton spinners made much of the dramatic increase in the importation of cotton yarn in the 1870s. That increase, however, was more apparent than real because much of it stemmed from counting Alsatian production, which was French before 1871, in the import category after 1871. Thus imports of simple cotton yarn from Germany amounted to only 1,300

probably valid for the more backward and less advantaged cotton manufacturers in the protectionist front, but it was not really valid for the more modern and efficient manufacturers of Rouen, the Nord, and the Vosges. In all probability, the production costs of the latter were below, not above, those of their principal foreign competitors.[52] Thus talk of their inherent inferiority and need for compensation was a smokescreen. They needed higher tariffs, not to survive, but to achieve the more ambitious goals touched upon in the earlier discussion of each industry. In a nutshell, the cotton spinners of Rouen, the Nord, and the Vosges wanted to knock foreign competitors completely out of the French market with prohibitory duties, established in the name of compensation, and then to increase their share of the domestic market at the expense of weaker domestic producers as well as at the expense of foreigners. Ultimately they looked forward to dividing the French cotton yarn market among themselves, with the Nord producing fine yarns, the Vosges producing middle gauges, and upper Normandy producing heavy yarns.[53] Creation

---

kilograms in 1869 but jumped to 2.5 million kilograms in 1872 and to 6.26 million in 1876, and in most years they exceeded British imports of the same item (*Tableau décennal*, I, 179 ff.).

52. To document their relative inferiority and to underpin their demand for compensation, the cotton spinners put forth detailed computations showing that, on the average, it cost more to set up and to operate a cotton spindle in France than in England (see, for example, Georges Yver, *Tarifs de douanes: Mémoire pour servir à la détermination du tarif minimum des filés de coton jusqu'au no. 40* [Rouen, 1890]). The free traders disputed these figures. In a pamphlet published in 1880, Francisque David admitted that the base cost of setting up a spindle was higher in France than in England, but he also pointed out that, because the French ran their more expensive spindles more hours per week than did the English (seventy-two versus fifty-six), French operating and production costs per unit of finished product were actually lower than the English. Although "the expense per spindle in 11F05 in France, in contrast to 9F58 in England," he wrote, "the cost of spinning a kilogram of number 120 cotton [yarn] is fourteen centimes less in France than in England" (Francisque David, *Filature de coton: Prix comparatif du coût en France et en Angleterre de coton filés dans deux établissements semblables avec les mêmes machines et dans un même numéro* (Paris, 1880], p. 17). This differential in production costs, coupled with the transport costs on imported English yarn, meant that the major French cotton spinners could have held their own in the domestic market with less, instead of more, protection in the late 1870s, although perhaps not at as high a level of profit as they wanted.

53. This oligopolistic division of the market was already emerging de facto by 1878, as Nicolas Claude noted before the Chamber Tariff Commission, *Procès-verbaux*, p. 125.

of such an oligopoly—possible only after both external and internal competition was eliminated—would allow the cotton manufacturers of Rouen, the Nord, and the Vosges to continue to expand their plants (up to a point) and, more important, to keep operating those plants at maximum capacity with maximum profits for the foreseeable future.

Many of the lesser cotton producers eventually realized that the drive for protection would, in the end, mostly benefit the major producers. Yet, because they remained genuinely threatened by foreign competitors, they had no choice but to cooperate whole-heartedly with their stronger domestic rivals on the tariff question. (Once the threat of external competition was dispelled, however, they began to think about meeting the threat of internal competition through legislation curbing the "unfair business practices" of their fellow protectionists.[54]) Consequently, opposition to the big cotton spinners' plans for tariff reform came mainly from the independent weaving industries. The leaders of these industries understood not only that the call for compensatory duties on cotton yarn was really a call for prohibitory duties, but also that, if the cotton spinners succeeded in organizing the domestic yarn market, they would be able to take effective control of all domestic weaving and, in fact, to subordinate all textile production nationally to themselves.[55] Thus, it was not just to

54. By 1890, the Saint-Quentin Chamber of Commerce was blaming the decline of cotton spinning in the Aisne not only on foreign competition but also on the unfair competition of Vosges mills which were set up to "run day and night in defiance of . . . consideration . . . for the health of [their] employees." Therefore, while demanding higher tariffs "to make us the master of our own house and to arrest the invasion of foreign products," the chamber also realized that, for this to do Saint-Quentin cotton any good, it would be necessary "to equalize the fight between the various parts of France . . . by regulating work and by suppressing night labor" (response to the questionnaire of the Conseil supérieur du commerce, 1890, AN F^{12} 6418).

55. Francisque David later pointed out in his *Réponse à la brochure de M. Yver* (Saint-Etienne, 1891) that the cotton manufacturers of Normandy (and presumably those of the Vosges also) were seeking to subordinate independent weaving industries, such as Roanne's, to their own. Once foreign yarn had been excluded from the French market, David argued, Roanne would have to buy its yarn from the Normans and Vosgians and pay their price, thereby losing much of its ability to compete with Norman and Vosgian cloth on the basis of price. Indeed, Roanne would become a captive client, receiving only as much yarn as the cotton spinners wanted it to receive while serving as a convenient outlet for excess production, but

lower their production costs so that they could compete better abroad, but also to preserve their independence from the cotton spinners, that the weaving industries of Saint-Etienne, Tarare, and other towns opposed demands for the increased protection of cottons and pushed for the reduction of cotton duties.

Viewed in its immediate context, the fight over cotton duties was simply the product of the spinners' and weavers' efforts to cope with the economic slump of the late 1870s. Viewed in a broader context, however, it was part of a long-term struggle for survival in, and dominance of, the French textile industry—a struggle in which tariff policy had already played, and would continue to play, a major role. In contrast to mining and metallurgy, in which there was a sense of solidarity and a large measure of cooperation under the protectionist banner among natural economic enemies (such as the producers and consumers of coal or pig iron), solidarity and cooperation among the various branches of the textile industry was limited in the late 1870s. To be sure, the leading linen and cotton spinners, hoping to lay the groundwork for cartelization of their respective industries, cooperated through the AIF with producers of carded woolens, jute, and silk floss in seeking protection of all textiles and, indeed, the creation of a closed textiles market in France. At the same time, however, they continued to compete bitterly among themselves for domination of that market. More important, they confronted another alliance of textilists—the silk and silk blend manufacturers of the Loire and Rhône, the producers of combed wool and worsteds, and certain cotton and linen weavers—who denied the goal of national self-sufficiency in textile production and demanded freer trade (at least, for the semifinished goods they utilized) and maintenance of ties to foreign markets. This was a split of fundamental importance, not easily patched over, for it involved a battle for supremacy in France between two distinct

---

an outlet that could be eliminated if the health of Norman and Vosges cloth production so dictated. To complete this stranglehold on Roanne, the Vosgians were also seeking prohibitory duties on spinning equipment, to make it as hard as possible for the Roanne weavers to set up their own spinning mills and to keep them dependent on existing production. Thus, increased protection would only worsen a situation which, in David's eyes, was already producing "a rain of gold for [cotton] spinners" (David, *Réponse*, p. 4).

and divergent interest groups—the producers of high-quality finished textiles for the world market and the producers of lower-quality finished and semifinished textiles for the domestic and colonial markets. It was highly problematical that a tariff policy could be devised that would be equally acceptable to both groups. Thus, whereas the accommodation of interests was well advanced in mining and metallurgy in the late 1870s, it had scarcely begun in textiles.

The Fiscal Interest

In addition to mining, metallurgy, and textiles, there were other economically important industries that sent representatives to testify on tariff policy (mostly in a protectionist vein) before parliamentary commissions in 1877 and 1878. These included chemicals, raw sugar, paper, leather and hides, vegetable oil refining, and raw silk milling.[56] Yet none of these industries produced active members of the free trade and protectionist parties, and none produced politicians who played a major role in tariff politics.[57] Consequently, beyond the three clusters of private economic interests examined already, the interest that

56. Among the chemical manufacturers, Auguste Scheurer-Kestner sought to end import duties on the sulphuric acid that he manufactured at Thann (Haut-Rhin). Most other chemical producers—including Kuhlmann and Mayoussier of Saint-Gobain—sought increased protection (Chamber Tariff Commission, *Procès-verbaux*, pp. 527–545). So, too, did representatives of the leather industry, the paper industry, and silk milling and spinning (*Journal officiel*, May 23, 1878, pp. 5605–5610; January 29, 1879, pp. 632–637). The Comité centrale des fabricants de sucre defended the status quo against the demands of sugar refiners, such as Lebaudy, for tariff liberalization. Likewise, speaking on behalf of the Marseilles oil industry, Grandval demanded maintenance of the free entry of oleaginous seeds and the same duties on imported vegetable oils (*Journal officiel*, January 14, 1879, pp. 229–233; January 16, 1879, pp. 296–298).

57. This is not to say that these industries did not produce major politicians. Scheurer-Kestner, the Alsatian chemicals manufacturer, moved to Paris after 1871 and, as deputy, then senator, for the Seine, became an important political ally of Gambetta. Félix Faure, deputy for Le Havre, who spoke for the leather industry in 1878, eventually became president of the Republic. So, too, did Emile Loubet, deputy for the Drôme, who represented the silk millers of the Rhône valley in the 1878 tariff hearings. But, except for their participation in those hearings, none participated in tariff reform to the extent that Méline, Pouyer-Quertier, Say, and others did.

seemed to have the greatest stake in tariff reform was one that organized no lobbies and sent no spokesmen to parliamentary hearings. This was the French state—or, rather, the French fisc, embodied in the Ministry of Finance.

For most European states, import duties were a major source of revenue in the nineteenth century, and in the 1870s several governments undertook "tariff reform," not to aid their nation's industry or commerce, but to solve financial problems.[58] At one point, the French government was among these. In 1871 it faced a severe fiscal crisis. The treaty of Frankfurt, which ended the war with Prussia, required France to pay an indemnity of 5 billion francs, an unprecedented sum, which exceeded the combined French tax receipts for 1871 and 1872. To meet this extraordinary expenditure—and to make up for ordinary revenues lost during the war and occupation—the president of the new Third Republic, Thiers, had sought an increase in indirect taxes, especially import duties, in 1871–1873. But, as mentioned earlier, Thiers's efforts to raise tariffs were hampered by existing trade treaties and by domestic opposition, and they ultimately failed. Actually, a higher schedule of import duties was not needed to get France out of the red (which, in retrospect, lent credence to the charge that Thiers was only using the financial situation as a pretext for raising import duties for the benefit of certain French industries). The postwar boom in France pushed total tax receipts from 2.15 billion francs in 1871 to over 3 billion francs in 1875, and the simultaneous burgeoning of foreign trade brought with it a virtual doubling of revenues from import duties, even in the absence of an increase in the level of the duties.[59] Coupled with the successful efforts of the minister of finance, Léon Say, to put France back in the black by limiting expenditures to the level of

58. In Germany, Bismarck turned to tariff protection in the late 1870s to decrease the imperial government's dependence on contributions from the confederated German states; in Italy, the government renounced its trade treaties and legislated a higher tariff in 1878 in order to end its chronic budget deficits (W. O. Henderson, *The Rise of German Industrial Power, 1834–1914* (Berkeley, 1975), pp. 218–221; Frank J. Coppa, "The Italian Tariff and the Conflict between Agriculture and Industry: The Commercial Policy of Liberal Italy, 1860–1922," *Journal of Economic History*, 30 [1970], 744–746).

59. Revenue figures are presented in *Annuaire statistique*, 1 (1878), 533; *Annales du commerce extérieur*, no. 102, 176–177.

income, this growth of revenues effectively dispelled any notion that France required higher tariffs to maintain its solvency (on the contrary, France's fiscal performance in the mid-1870s seemed to verify what the Germans had accepted in setting up the Zollverein many years before—namely, that customs revenues could be maximized by keeping import duties low and by allowing trade to increase). However, given the emergence of the tariff reform issue in 1876–1877, independent of the fiscal question, the improvement in France's financial health did not end Finance's involvement in the making of tariff policy.

Where exactly did the Ministry of Finance stand on tariff reform in 1876–1878? Of course, that a free trader, Léon Say, headed Finance at this time did not mean that the ministry was willing to sacrifice existing tariff revenues to expand the free trade system. In the 1870s, Say's interest in fiscal and monetary integrity outweighed his commitment to the further liberalization of commercial policy (the same was true of most members of the commercial-financial elite). Therefore, in the Conseil supérieur du commerce's deliberations on a general tariff bill in 1876, Léon Amé, the general director of customs and the man responsible to Say for customs revenues, demanded the maintenance of the 1F20 duty on coal as a fiscal necessity, and he opposed the efforts of Fernand Raoul-Duval, Say's cousin, to get the council to abolish the duty.[60] Moreover, under Say's leadership, the ministry also sought to raise certain duties in the trade treaty negotiations with Italy the following year. As Amé informed Eugène Caillaux, the finance minister of the Seize Mai government, "M. Say had resolved to revise the tariff so as to obtain from it supplemental revenues of 16–18 million francs," and only after being told that this would require the revival of raw materials taxes had Say "contented himself with getting, through the doubling of the duty on vegetable oil, the additional nine million francs designated in the preliminary budget for 1878 as coming from customs

60. Conseil supérieur du commerce, *Examen des tarifs de douanes.* In the mid-seventies, the coal duty brought in over 9 million francs per year. Its importance as a source of revenue was exceeded only by the import duties on sugar, coffee, cacao, petroleum, and cotton cloth (the last of which became important only with the influx of British imports in the late 1870s). The breakdown of tariff revenues by commodity is in *Annales du commerce extérieur*, no. 102, 176–177.

duties."[61] At the same time, however, Amé insisted that, although individual duties might be raised for revenue purposes, no general move toward greater protection was warranted. "Our views [on tariff reform] approach those of the Italians," he told Caillaux, "with the difference that, even if we desire to raise some duties in the fiscal interest, we do not intend to proceed in this regard by a general measure, nor do we intend to seek additional protection for any national industry."[62]

The "fiscal interest" of the French government thus favored neither complete free trade nor complete protection but, rather, a measure of both. That is, the Ministry of Finance was on the side of free trade to the extent that it wanted importation of foreign products to continue and to increase. It was on the side of protection to the extent that it wanted such imports to bear a surcharge (as a source of revenue). In line with the latter consideration, Finance's interest in tariff reform focused primarily on a technical matter: the conversion of remaining *ad valorem* duties to specific duties, which would support the ministry's efforts to end customs fraud (the misrepresentation of the value of imported goods) and to streamline the collection of duties. Such a conversion would also guarantee that the government would continue to reap financial benefit from France's foreign trade, even when prices were falling because specific duties tied customs revenues to the volume of trade—which was rising in the 1870s—instead of to the value of trade, which was less certain in the face of the declining unit values of most imported commodities. This conversion turned out not to be controversial. Both protectionists and free traders supported it in 1876 and continued to support it through the subsequent vicissitudes of tariff reform.[63] Consequently, the Finance Ministry retired from active participation in

61. France. Ministère des Affaires Etrangères, Archives diplomatiques, *Négociations commerciales, Italie*, x (1876–1877), 130–133.

62. Ibid., p. 22 verso.

63. The conversion to specific duties did have a somewhat protectionist effect. Since specific duties remained constant, instead of fluctuating with prices, this meant that, in an era of falling prices, the import price (price at port of entry plus import duty) of goods entering France would fall more gradually than world prices in general, which in turn meant that domestic producers would get more of a buffer against falling world prices and more protection against foreign competition with specific duties than they would have gotten with *ad valorem* duties.

tariff politics, leaving the representation of the government's position to the Ministry of Commerce and Agriculture. As a result, fiscal considerations were largely eliminated from tariff politics. Henceforth the latter became almost exclusively a matter of rival businessmen (or their representatives) fighting among themselves to establish government policies congruous with their particular strategies for survival and expansion.

The Lines of Cleavage

In searching for the determinants of French tariff policy, we thus come back to the economic interests in the free trade and protectionist parties. What can we say, in summation, about the nature of these interests and about the nature of the conflict between them? How deep, how irreparable was the cleavage between free traders and protectionists? Looking at its broad contours, one could say that the conflict on the tariff was part of a struggle for supremacy between two mutually exclusive capitalist communities seeking to project French economic development in opposite directions. That is, the conflict can be seen as a battle between cosmopolitan commercial capitalists, striving to integrate France into the world economy, and nationalistic industrial capitalists, striving to make France economically self-sufficient. There is much truth in this picture, but it is also somewhat overdrawn. Most of the free traders and protectionists of 1878 were practical, self-interested businessmen little concerned with the fate of the French economy as a whole. Rather, they were concerned mostly with maximizing their own net incomes through the reduction of expenses and the elevation of gross receipts (the latter to be achieved by increasing the volume of their sales, the level of their prices, or both). Their interest in, and stand on, tariff policy was determined solely by the current effect of that policy on their profit maximization efforts and by the way that policy fitted in with their plans for the future development of their businesses.

The particular policies established in the 1860s and still in effect in the 1870s emphasized the opening of foreign markets for all French goods and the reduction of duties on raw materials, including certain semifinished or producer goods, imported into France. These policies naturally favored those involved in exportation (Bordeaux vintners, Reims worsted manufacturers, Lyons silk weavers) and those who bought staples abroad for sale in France (the import merchants of Paris, Lyons, and the seaports). Moreover, these policies were especially tailored to the needs of certain industries—the weaving industry of the Lyonnais, the engineering and construction industry of Paris—which imported semifinished raw materials and exports finished products (the trade treaties had secured low duties abroad on their exported finished goods in exchange for the lowering of French duties on the imported semifinished raw materials while leaving intact the protection of their finished goods in the home market). Representatives of these industries, along with the other beneficiaries of the policies of the Second Empire, formed the core of the free trade party in the 1870s. Obversely, the protectionist party in the seventies was made up of those who had been hurt by the policies of the sixties (or thought they had) or who believed they would be hurt by them in the future. These included manufacturers who cared little about increased access to foreign markets or who saw their foreign sales dwindling in the 1870s and expected to be dependent on the domestic market thereafter. Especially committed to the protectionist cause were the manufacturers of producer goods—cotton yarn, pig iron—whose protection had been sacrificed to the demands of the producers of finished consumer goods in the 1860s, but who, in the 1870s, still aspired to monopolize the supplying of their products to domestic finishing industries.

In the final analysis, then, the fight between free trade and protection was a fight between internationally oriented enterprises willing to sacrifice domestic producers to improve their own position in foreign markets and domestically oriented enterprises willing to sacrifice those in international trade for greater security for their protection at home. Obviously, the split between free traders and protectionists involved a genuine conflict of interest, yet reconciliation between the opposing sides was by no means impossible and, indeed, had already begun in mining and metallurgy with the formation of the AIF in 1878. It was feasible that, by formulation of a hybird policy, this reconciliation could be extended to include at least the moderates of both sides (that is, the free traders willing to settle for less than complete free trade and the protectionists willing to settle for less than absolute protection). The problem after 1878 was how to accomplish such a compromise. The previous strife over the tariff had encouraged interests to think in either-or terms. Consequently, the first phase of tariff reform, 1878–1882, became a straightforward contest between free trade and protection ending in a victory for the free traders. Only in the second, more prolonged phase of tariff reform, extending into the 1890s, did the mood change from one of confrontation to one of accommodation. It is this evolution of French tariff politics—from conflict in 1878–1882 to accommodation in the 1890s—that is the subject of the subsequent chapters of this study.

4

Free Trade's Pyrrhic Victory, 1878–1882

If tariff politics in late nineteenth-century France eventually produced a compromise policy that accommodated all major interests, the first round of tariff reform under the Third Republic, unfolding between 1878 and 1882, was characterized by incessant conflict (ultimately unresolved) between free traders and protectionists and by the struggle of various enterprises to survive and prosper amid the economic turbulence of the late 1870s. By 1878, tariff reform in France had come to center on two issues: the legislation of a new general tariff and the renegotiation of the trade treaties. Naturally, free traders and protectionists held opposing views and priorities on both. The protectionists considered the general tariff fundamental and inviolable; they could accept trade treaties only if they opened foreign markets to French products without reducing the schedule of French import duties in the general tariff, hardly a likely prospect. The free traders, however, considered trade treaties the essential element in French commercial policy and viewed the general tariff as merely a basis for the negotiation of a new conventional tariff. This basic disagreement on the relative purposes and importance of the general tariff and trade treaties, in turn, determined that the two sides followed different strategies in the politics of tariff reform. Concerned mainly with the legislation of the general tariff so vital to them, the protectionists first rejected the government's tariff bill as inadequate and then tried to ram their own version through parliament; thereafter they tried to frustrate all attempts to weaken the general tariff through commercial conventions. In contrast, the free traders bothered with the general tariff only to the extent of supporting the government bill as the lowest tariff realistically possible. They devoted most of their energy to renewal of the trade treaties in order to prevent implementation of any new general tariff and to preserve the commercial policy of Napoleon III. In other words, the making of the general tariff, detailed in the first three sections of this chapter, put the protectionists on the offensive and the free traders on the defensive. In the negotiation of the trade treaties, recounted in the fourth section, the roles were reversed.

Preliminaries: The Chamber Tariff Commission

On March 22, 1878, the thirty-three-member commission appointed by the Chamber of Deputies to study and report on the general tariff bill began its deliberations. As we have seen, the protectionists controlled this commission and installed Jules Ferry as its chairman,[1] and, although not fully stated at the time, they clearly hoped to obtain two results from its proceedings. First, because the government had failed to stipulate in its bill that the general tariff was a maximum subject to reductions in future trade treaties (even though that was obviously its intent), the protectionists sought to report the tariff out as an irreducible minimum which, if upheld by the rest of the parliament, would virtually destroy the government's chances of negotiation new trade treaties. Second, as a precaution against the failure of this first maneuver, the protectionists also sought the enactment of a schedule of duties so high that it would afford industry "suffi-

---

1. The usually reliable and perceptive correspondent of the *Echo du Nord* estimated that there were seventeen protectionists on the commission versus thirteen free traders; the other three—Charles Cherpin of the Loire, Albert Grévy of the Doubs, and Edmond Caze of the Haute-Garonne—were uncommitted (*Echo du Nord*, March 22, 1878).

cient" protection even if cut by a fourth or a half in subsequent trade treaties. Of course, in their estimation, the government's schedule could never serve this purpose even though, on a long list of items, its duties were 24 percent higher than those based on the existing conventional tariffs which the Conseil supérieur du commerce had recommended in 1876.[2] Consequently, the protectionists on the commission set out to formulate a new schedule and to gain its substitution for the government's when the full Chamber opened its debate on the bill. To acquire the information needed to justify the duties they wanted—and to give the business an air of objectivity—they supported the industrialists' long-standing demand for "no general tariff without an inquiry." Because the free trade minority on the commission also welcomed such a procedure as an opportunity to discredit protectionist arguments in public debate, the commission resolved almost unanimously to make a parliamentary inquiry on the tariff its first order of business.[3]

Following precedent, the commission requested written depositions from chambers of commerce and similar bodies before taking direct testimony. At the end of March it distributed a questionnaire asking French businessmen for their preferences on particular customs duties as well as their views on such matters as the conversion of *ad valorem* to specific duties, the renewal of trade treaties and the most-favored-nation clause, and the temporary admission system. Some fifty-eight chambers of commerce and consultative chambers responded between April and August.[4] Almost all favored substitution of specific duties for *ad valorem*

2. Article 4 of the government's bill raised the conventional duties 24 percent on chemicals, dyes, porcelain, glass, paper, leather, cutlery, hardware, and almost all textiles. Article 5 even stipulated that these duties could be raised an additional 50 percent on products of countries charging more than 20 percent *ad valorem* duties on French products (Projet du loi, *Journal officiel*, March 18, 1878, pp. 3036–3055).

3. The minutes of the tariff commission's closed deliberations are found in AN C 3223–3224, Chambre des députés, 2ᵉ législature (1877–1881), Douanes, Procès-verbaux, Commission relative à l'établissement du tarif général des douanes, 4 v. The published *Procès-verbaux* contains the inquest testimony, the subcommission reports, and the general report.

4. The twenty-nine responses received in April and May are found in AN C 3223; the twenty-nine received between June and August are in AN C 3224.

duties, but on the other issues they predictably split between free trade and protection. About half favored new trade treaties and continuation of temporary admissions; about half opposed them. Likewise, half favored the government version of the general tariff, while half wanted higher tariffs. Inconclusive at first glance, this poll actually indicated a trend toward protectionism since 1875 when, in a similar survey, a clear majority supported a low general tariff and renewal of trade treaties. Yet even the protectionists on the commission overlooked this trend; no one ever attempted the comprehensive analysis of the replies necessary to reveal it. With the depositions trickling in through the summer, such an analysis would have been feasible only in the fall. By then, however, the commission had long been preoccupied with its public hearings. The written depositions were apparently received and filed, then promptly forgotten. As in the Senate inquiry of 1877, they were no match for live testimony.

Between April 1878 and March 1879, the Chamber Tariff Commission conducted what its chairman later called "the most complete, the most practical, the best controlled, in a word, the most serious [inquiry] that has ever taken place."[5] Certainly it was one of the longest and most thorough parliamentary inquiries on an economic issue in nineteenth-century France. Most major industrial and commercial enterprises—including virtually every member of the AIF and the Free Trade Association—were represented in the hearings (the content of their testimony and their specific demands have been discussed in Chapters 2 and 3). Yet, for all their comprehensiveness and thoroughness, the hearings settled nothing concerning the formulation of the general tariff. Because they simultaneously demonstrated much sentiment for both higher and lower customs duties and both trust and distrust of trade treaties, the commission was no more united at their conclusion than at the start. At best, the hearings merely provided the free traders and protectionists with fresh ammunition—facts, figures, and opinions—for the real battle that lay ahead in the closed meetings of the tariff commission.

On March 17, 1879, the tariff commission resumed its deliberations under François Malézieux, a veteran protectionist from

5. François Malézieux, "Rapport général," *J des ec*, 4th ser., 9 (1880), 284.

Saint-Quentin who had just defeated the free trader Gustave Lebaudy for the chairmanship.[6] Faithful to the protectionists' strategy, Malézieux arranged the agenda so that the first item was to rule on whether or not conventional tariffs negotiated in trade treaties would be allowed to supersede the general tariff, that is, whether the general tariff was to be a minimum or maximum. The debate on this question consumed two weeks. On the protectionist side, Richard Waddington and Lucien Dautresme, deputies for Rouen and Elbeuf respectively, insisted that France have but one tariff—the general tariff—whereas the free traders, led by Paul Devès of the Hérault, defended the government's prerogative to formulate conventional tariffs in trade treaties. When it became apparent that the protectionists could not win outright repudiation of trade treaties, Waddington suggested that two duties be established on each item, a minimum duty applicable to the products of those countries linked to France by treaty and a maximum duty applicable to all the others. This plan was later incorporated in the Méline tariff of 1892. In 1879, however, it was still viewed with suspicion, and the commission rejected it on two occasions. Finally, on April 5, the commission passed a compromise resolution defining the new tariff as "neither a minimum tariff nor a maximum tariff, but one called simply the general tariff." The wording was obviously ambiguous and apparently resolved nothing, but in reality it concealed a major defeat for the protectionists for, in conferring with William Waddington and Tirard the same week concerning the prorogation of existing trade treaties, the commission recognized the government's right to open commercial negotiations once the general tariff was voted and thus accepted the eventual reduction of the general tariff by convention. Henceforth, despite the commission's resolution to the contrary, the general tariff was considered a maximum.[7]

6. Jules Ferry, who presided over most of the commission's inquiry, resigned the chairmanship in December 1878 to become minister of public instruction in the William Waddington cabinet. His successor, Pierre Tirard, served only until March 5, 1879, when he, too, resigned to enter the government as minister of commerce and agriculture.

7. Malézieux, "Rapport général," p. 286. In the summer of 1879 the question of proroguing the trade treaties proved to be as vexing for the protectionists on the tariff commission as was the general tariff itself. The government had renounced

Unable to achieve their primary goal—designation of the general tariff as a minimum—the protectionists turned to their second goal—establishment of as high a schedule of duties on manufactures as possible. Even before the minimum-versus-maximum issue was settled, they had launched their offensive on this matter in the deliberations of the two subcommissions—one for textiles and one for all other products—which were organized in March to prepare preliminary reports on the six hundred items and over one thousand separate duties encompassed in the general tariff. This offensive continued through July when the whole commission finished passing on the recommendations of the subcommissions. The work of the textile subcommission and particularly the handling of duties on cotton yarn indicate the character and ultimate success of this offensive. Cotton yarn was the most hotly contested item in the tariff, and a protectionist victory on it foreshadowed similar victories on other items.

Spokesmen for the protectionist cotton industry dominated the deliberations of the textile subcommission from start to finish. Led by Jules Méline, who served as reporter on all fabrics except silk,[8] they quickly focused attention on middle gauge (number 28) unfinished cotton yarn. Norman and Vosgian cotton spinners considered the government's recommended duty of 24F80 per 100

the treaties on December 31, 1878, so that they would expire the following December 31 and could thus be renegotiated on the basis of the new general tariff. When it became apparent that the new tariff would not be ready before the spring of 1880, the government decided to seek authorization to prorogue the old treaties until six months after the voting of the new tariff so that commercial relations would not fall under the old prohibitive tariff before new treaties could be prepared. Tirard submitted a bill to this effect in June. Although considered a formality by most, it met with stiff opposition from protectionists who feared that the bill would allow free traders to extend the old conventional duties indefinitely by delaying the completion of the general tariff. They were unable to block its passage, however, and trade treaty prorogation became law on August 4. True to the protectionists' forecast, this removed the urgency of finishing the general tariff before the end of the year, at least for the free traders, and the legislative process eventually dragged on until May 1881. See L'industrie française, June 16, 1879, July 24, 1879, August 7, 1879; André Daniel, ed., L'année politique: 1879 (Paris, 1880), p. 245.

8. Edouard Millaud of the Rhône was chosen to report on silks only after one thousand two hundred Lyons silk weavers protested the initial announcement that Méline would report on all textiles (Ernest Fournier de Flaix, "L'enquête industrielle et le projet du tarif général," J des ec, 4th ser., 9 [1880], 239).

kilograms on this item totally insufficient, so Méline, with help from Richard Waddington, set out to win approval of a much higher figure. Toward this end, he first played up all evidence of distress in the cotton industry and promoted the idea that French cotton manufacturers could not compete with British producers without compensatory duties. Then, in order to determine the "proper level" of compensation, Méline drew the subcommission into a close reexamination of the relative costs of English and French cotton production, which had already been thoroughly investigated in various government and parliamentary inquiries. Using figures presented by the Norman cotton syndicate which showed that it cost 50 to 100 percent more to spin number 28 cotton yarn in France than in England, Méline came up with 5F53 as the cost difference to set up and operate a cotton spindle in France and in England.[9] This figure, in turn, supposedly justified a compensatory duty of 30 francs on each 100 kilograms of number 28 yarn imported into France. Accepting the validity of these computations, the subcommission proceeded on April 4 to endorse a duty of 35 francs on numbers 25–30. This was below the 40 francs demanded by Norman spinners, but it equaled what Richard Waddington considered to be the minimum compensatory duty. Moreover, it was high enough so that, even if future trade treaties reduced it by one-seventh, the result would be the 30 franc duty that Méline demanded as minimal compensation.[10]

Believing that the conventional duty of 20 francs on number 28 yarn offered more than sufficient protection to French cotton

9. On behalf of the Conseil supérieur du commerce, Fernand Raoul-Duval calculated in 1876 that it cost only 3F78 more to set up a cotton spindle in France than in England and that the cost of spinning cotton was only 4 percent higher in France than in England, which seemed to show that the existing 20 franc duty provided more than sufficient protection to French producers. It is impossible to determine whether Méline's or Raoul-Duval's calculations were more accurate without reconstructing the costs of French and British manufacturers using data in company records. Evidence presented in the polemical literature—see especially Francisque David's pamphlets, discussed in Chapter 3—indicates that Raoul-Duval's figures are more valid (they are certainly more disinterested). Thus it is likely that Méline's figures were designed to achieve not just "compensation" but an excess of protection in line with the oligopolistic aspirations of the Vosges cotton spinners.

10. See the minutes of the textile subcommission in AN C 3223 and Méline's report on textiles in Chamber Tariff Commission, *Procès-verbaux*, pp. 957–981.

spinners and that approval of the government-recommended 24F80 duty in the general tariff would guarantee the maintenance of that 20 franc duty in future trade treaties, the free trade minority of the textile subcommission opposed the majority recommendation when it came before the full commission in mid-May. For over a week, the issue was hotly joined between Méline and Waddington, defending the subcommission's duty, and Edouard Millaud, Eugène Rouher, and Ernest Guillemin, who favored the government's duty. Of course, with the protectionists clearly in the majority, the outcome was a foregone conclusion. On May 21, the commission duly approved the 35 franc duty.[11] With that precedent set, Méline henceforth had his own way. In May and June, first the textile subcommission then the whole commission approved his recommendations on cotton cloth, linen, jute, silk floss, and woolens. On some items, particularly woolens, these duties coincided with those in the government bill, but most were substantially higher. Duties on some cotton tissues, for example, represented a 100 percent increase of the conventional tariff (versus a 24 percent increase in the government bill). In addition to raising the rates, the tariff commission approved more detailed classification systems for many yarns and fabrics: there was to be a separate duty for every five numbers of cotton yarn instead of one for every ten in the government version, and linen cloth was to be classified by weight per square meter as well as by number of threads. Thus the schedule of textile duties that emerged from the deliberations of the tariff commission by August was not just a revision of the government's schedule but a new schedule tailored to the specifications of the protectionist party.[12]

The protectionists did not control the other subcommission as completely as they controlled the textile subcommission. The chairman, Gustave Lebaudy, assigned several reports to free traders, or at least to nonprotectionists, who ignored the demands of the AIF. Consequently, on most items the duties initially

11. Procès-verbaux, Chamber Tariff Commission, AN C 3223.
12. See Appendix 2 for selected duties. For a comprehensive comparison of the duties recommended by the government and the tariff commission, see Jules Clère, *Les tarifs de douane: Tableaux comparatifs* (Paris, 1880).

recommended by the subcommission closely resembled those in the government's bill.[13] Yet, given their dominant position in the tariff commission as a whole, the protectionists were able to veto those recommendations of the Lebaudy subcommission that they found particularly noxious. Thus in July the commission rejected three reports—Lebaudy's on steel rails, Rouvier's on starch, and Prosper Dréo's on coal—that recommended duties below what the AIF thought sufficient. These three thereupon resigned their reporterships and were replaced by protectionists, who revised the reports to meet the demands of the AIF.[14] In response, the *Journal des économistes* denounced the tariff commission for completing its work "in a fever of duty-raising."[15]

In December 1879, the tariff commission finally submitted its version of the general tariff bill to the Chamber. In his supporting statement the commission chairman, Malézieux, characterized this bill as a moderate effort to establish a just equilibrium between French commerce and industry. "It is not a dike designed to block the entry of foreign products," he wrote, "but rather a dam constructed . . . to allow imports to enter in sufficient abundance to maintain a reasonable level of prices in the internal market and to stimulate and invigorate our industries but not [abundantly enough] to flood, stifle, or destroy them."[16] The liberal Ernest Fournier de Flaix, however, took a jaundiced view of the commission's work, characterizing it as an attempt to create "an artificial equality in the conditions and means of production of French and foreign industries . . . [and] to guarantee to the former their expenses and profits by means of a monopoly of

13. The locomotive and machinery manufacturers in the AIF had demanded a general tariff equal to twice the conventional tariff, while shipbuilders demanded an increase in their duties from 2 francs per ton to 8-12 francs per ton. The Lebaudy subcommission, however, concurred with the government in recommending a general tariff for those items equal to the old conventional tariff. Likewise, it ignored the demands of tinplate producers for more protection (the 130 franc conventional duty was to be the new general duty) and responded to the charcoal ironmakers' request for a tripling of the duty on iron wire by upping the government's recommendation from 60 to 80 francs.

14. The subcommission ultimately recommended a duty of 1F30 on coal and coke (versus 1F20 in the government bill), 7F50 on steel rails (versus 6 francs), and 6 francs on starch (versus 2 francs).

15. "Chronique économique," *J des ec*, 4th ser., 7 (1879), 163.

16. Malézieux, "Rapport général," p. 294.

internal consumption."[17] Unquestionably, the commission's bill bore the stamp of the protectionists, who, although failing to incorporate in it a clause prohibiting the negotiation of conventional tariffs, had succeeded in writing a schedule of duties reflecting the demands of most members of the AIF. But in the fall of 1879 they were quite uncertain of gaining legislative approval. Some protectionists still hoped that the government would substitute the commission's bill for its own before the Chamber debate started in order to avoid a floor fight. But with a free trader, Tirard, in the Commerce Ministry, such a hope was unrealistic. In January, Tirard insisted that the government would not modify its bill except to adopt the classification of cotton yarn recommended by the commission. Since the protectionists on the commission, especially Méline and Waddington, were equally devoted to their version of the general tariff, a showdown between the rival bills in the Chamber and Senate became inevitable. Actually, such a prospect surprised neither side. Since the summer of 1878, both free traders and protectionists had been working diligently to rally public support and to muster parliamentary votes.

Mobilizing Public Support

As the deliberations of the Chamber Tariff Commission revealed, by 1879 tariff reform in France had been reduced to a contest between the free trade program, calling for legislation of a moderate general tariff and negotiation of a new conventional tariff, and the protectionist program, calling for a stiff general tariff to be implemented if and when trade treaties were eliminated. Which program would win depended on how much support each side could muster in the government, the parliament, and the public at large. In pursuit of such support, both the Free Trade Association and the AIF began organizing rallies, conferences, and petitions in the summer and fall of 1878. Both subsequently increased their pressure on ministers and deputies and, more important, both attempted to win over the agricultural

17. Fournier de Flaix, "L'enquête industrielle," p. 239.

bloc, which would hold the deciding votes in the legislation of the general tariff and, later, in the ratification of the new trade treaties. Although these campaigns continued well into 1881, the critical period for both was the year and a half before the opening of parliamentary debates on the general tariff, especially the spring of 1879.

The free traders launched their campaign within weeks of the founding of their association in June 1878. At first, they intended to stage a series of demonstrations nationwide. By December, however, they had decided to limit their campaign to Paris, realizing that deputies and senators could be influenced there more efficiently than in their scattered home districts and realizing, too, that free traders could easily influence provincial opinion from Paris through such nationally circulated publications as the *Revue des deux mondes* and *L'économiste français* and through distribution of pamphlet literature in key towns.[18] Consequently, the free traders initially limited their public action to occasional banquets and conferences in the capital.[19] The most important of these was a meeting held on March 20, 1879, under the auspices of the Paris Chamber of Commerce, of some twenty chambers of commerce committed to trade treaty renewal. This convention was significant for two reasons. First, it completed the mobilization of free trade's supporters for the upcoming battle on tariffs and trade treaties. Second, because of its obvious success in influencing the government (the delegates to the conference had extracted a promise from Tirard that "the present regime, the regime of trade treaties, [would] be maintained"),[20] the free trade convention prompted the protectionists to accelerate their campaign in April and May.

Although they easily dominated the thirty-three-member Chamber Tariff Commission, the protectionists were at a disadvantage in the struggle to control the larger parliamentary and public arenas. They could match neither the free traders' aca-

18. According to *L'industrie française* (June 5, 1879), the free traders had mailed out some 120,000 pamphlets by May 1879, and thousands more had been distributed in France by the British Cobden Club.

19. The various actions of the free traders were reported in the *Journal des économistes* and *L'économiste français*.

20. Quoted by *La Liberté*, reprinted in *L'industrie française*, March 27, 1879.

demic credentials nor their position within the Parisian intelligentsia, and they could only envy their opponents' ability to influence ministers and lawmakers through such prestigious bodies as the Société d'économie politique.[21] In addition, the protectionists lacked the connections with the big Paris dailies that were vital in the molding of French public opinion. The free traders could count on the regular and enthusiastic support of the *Journal des débats*, *La République française*, and *La Liberté*, but the protectionists received regular support only from two lesser papers, *Le Soleil* and *La Télégraphe* (the latter founded in 1877 as "the organ of the Eastern cotton industry")[22] and sporadic backing from *Le Temps*, *Le Siècle*, and *Le XIXe Siècle*. Mostly they depended on provincial dailies—Gustave Dubar's *Echo du Nord* (Lille), Waddington and Dautresme's *Le Petit Rouennais*, Pouyer-Quertier's *La Nouvelliste de Rouen*, Méline's *Memorial des Vosges*, and Amédée Marteau's *Journal du Havre*—all of which were influential locally but none of which was read nationally. In sum, while the free traders were still insiders in Paris, the protectionists remained provincial outsiders.[23] For this reason, they had to assume a different style of campaigning. While the free traders staged sedate bourgeois gatherings in the capital, the protectionists set out to organize mass worker rallies and petitionings in their provincial strongholds in the hope that, in the age of universal male suffrage, the government would heed the party representing the most votes—or at least the one raising the most voices.

The protectionist agitation in the provinces unfolded in a number of locations between February and April 1879. In Lille,

21. In November 1878, Méline, Waddington, and other protectionists set out to balance the influence of the Société d'économie politique by forming the Société pour le progrès des sciences sociales in association with Paul Cauwès, the recently installed professor of political economy in the Paris law faculty, and other rising protectionist theorists holding similar chairs in the provincial law schools. Initially, however, this organization had little impact on policy making.

22. *L'industrie française*, May 26, 1881.

23. The committee of the AIF admitted in its report of April 2, 1879: "Nearly all of us live in the provinces [and] we can assemble and group ourselves only at infrequent intervals, at the price of great inconveniences. . . . It is a great disadvantage in the face of the constant presence and constant action of our adversaries [in Paris]" (*L'industrie française*, April 10, 1879).

Gustave Dubar formed a committee of foremen and managers which contacted various deputies and senators of the Nord and circulated a petition for higher customs duties among the workers. By April 10 this petition bore thirty thousand signatures, it was presented to President Jules Grévy at the Elysée Palace the following month. Meanwhile, the Amiens members of the AIF sponsored a similar petitioning and staged a similar demonstration before Eugène Spuller, prefect of the Somme. In the Vosges, meetings of industrialists, workers, and farmers had been held almost continuously since the previous fall, thanks to the efforts of Nicolas Claude. One of the largest, with seven hundred attending, took place on April 20 in Epinal. Nowhere were the protectionists more active than in Normandy. At Lisieux sixty workers and foremen demonstrated at the town hall; in the Orne the deputy Jules Gévelot led a group of workers before the prefect; at Flers the consultative chamber joined with a workers' committee to agitate for higher tariffs. In Rouen, at a workers' rally sponsored by *Le Petit Rouennais,* almost thirty thousand signatures were collected on a petition destined to be presented to the prime minister, William Waddington, by a delegation of foremen led by Dautresme and Richard Waddington.[24]

Taken together, all these demonstrations must have made a striking impression on the public, especially given the alarm with which working-class action of any kind was viewed in 1879. Indeed, Dufrenoy of *L'économiste français* reflected such feelings when he warned that "the protectionist agitation has taken the character of a veritable sedition and it is time people open their eyes to it. The agitators are no longer content to make speeches, petition, and exploit the crisis to persuade industrialists, merchants, and farmers; they are trying to unite with the workers [by telling them] that they are going to starve and that it is the fault of the treaties of commerce."[25] Yet for all the drama and notoriety of such rallies, they played a relatively minor role in the protectionist campaign. Like the free traders, the AIF sought

24. *Echo du Nord,* March 22 and 26, April 14, 1879; *Nouvelliste de Rouen,* March 29, 1879; *L'industrie française,* March 27–April 17, May 1–15, 1879.

25. Dufrenoy, "La dernière manifestation protectionniste," *L'économiste français,* May 10, 1879.

most of all to mobilize French businessmen, and its efforts along this line similarly culminated in a congress of chambers of commerce in Paris.

Planned during April by the leaders of the AIF, the protectionist congress convened on May 1 at the Grand Hotel in Paris with representatives of sixty-one or sixty-eight chambers of commerce—the estimate varied—along with senators, deputies, the officers of the AIF, and a "great number of Parisian *notabilités*" in attendance. *L'industrie française* boasted that "more than three hundred delegates coming from all points in France have taken part in this demonstration which is without precedent in the industrial and commercial history of our land. It is, in effect, the first time [since 1789] that our industrial centers and seaports, seconded in their efforts by agriculture and a large part of French trade [and] united by a common peril . . . have held grand assizes to make the nation's will heard."[26] Under the chairmanship of Pouyer-Quertier, who was reported to be picking up the tab for the conference, the delegates first approved a restatement of the AIF program calling for "effectively compensatory duties which [would] assure the existence of [French] industries," and then some two hundred of them presented this program to Tirard. Not surprisingly, they met with a cold reception. Standing firmly by the government's tariff bill, Tirard pulled no punches: "If your system prevails in the Chamber, it will not be my fault," he said, "for I will do my best to maintain the regime of commercial treaties which, you well know, I consider to be excellent."[27] His only concession was to promise to resign if the protectionists carried the day in parliament. *L'industrie française* thereupon bitterly complained that "M. Tirard, who received the demands of eighteen free trade chambers sympathetically, has taken no account of the wishes of the delegates of sixty-one protectionist chambers."[28] After a cordial but inconsequential audience with President Grévy, who had little power to influence economic policy, the delegates retired and the congress adjourned without visible success.

Even if the protectionist campaign in the spring of 1879 failed

26. *L'industrie française*, May 8, 1879.
27. Dufrenoy, "La dernière manifestation protectionniste."
28. *L'industrie française*, May 8, 1879.

to swing the government to the program of higher tariffs, it did succeed in mobilizing the traditional supporters of industrial protection. To sustain the interest of these supporters until the beginning of the general tariff debate, the AIF dispatched various spokesmen to the major industrial and commercial centers throughout the summer and fall. Breaking with the exclusively Parisian focus of its campaign, the Free Trade Association did likewise.[29] At the same time, however, both associations increasingly turned away from organizing and displaying their strength among their regular constituents and sought to win new support from the one group still largely uncommitted on the tariff: the agriculturalists. Indeed, for both free traders and protectionists, the appeal to the farmer had become the key phase in the mobilization of public opinion by the end of 1879.

The sixties had been a decade of unprecedented prosperity for the French farmer largely because the trade treaties, which had virtually ended the protection of agriculture, had also fostered a dramatic rise in the export of French foodstuffs, particularly to Great Britain. Consequently, the Société des agriculteurs had stood by the government in 1868–1870 when the protectionists mounted their initial assault on the treaties, agricultural publicists such as Edouard Lecouteux of the *Journal d'agriculture pratique* remained sympathetic to free trade in the seventies, and in 1878 the Free Trade Association believed it could still expect at least the tacit support of French agriculture. In August the association sent letters to all local agricultural committees requesting their participation in demonstrations in favor of the trade treaties, and in November, Eichthal and Fould confidently included commercial farming among the export industries they represented before the tariff commission.[30]

Such presumption was not entirely warranted, however, for in

29. Paul Aclocque, director of the Forges de l'Ariège and the future president of the AIF, spoke at Foix, Bolbec, and Toulouse; Pouyer-Quertier also spoke at Toulouse as well as before shipbuilders in Nantes and Bordeaux. For the Free Trade Association, Edgar Raoul-Duval and Octave Noël spoke at Bordeaux, Louviers, Saint-Etienne, and Lyons (*L'industrie française*, June 19, 1879; *L'économiste français*, June 20, 1879).

30. Courcelle-Seneuil, "La tactique protectionniste et la tactique libre-échangiste," *L'économiste français*, August 3, 1878, pp. 131–133; *Journal officiel*, November 28, 1878, pp. 11110–11112.

1878 French agriculture faced conditions far different from those of ten years before. Not yet in a full-blown crisis, it nevertheless was undergoing profound changes. In the North and West, a poor wheat harvest in 1878 led to a rise in grain importation from 4,641,000 hectoliters to 17 million. Imports were even greater the next year, when France suffered "one of the worst [harvests] in twenty years."[31] Simultaneously, livestock imports were rising in what some observers were already labeling the "invasion des biftecks."[32] In the South, phylloxera continued to ravage the vineyards of Languedoc, the silkworm blight worsened along the Rhône, and the madder cultivation of the Vaucluse approached extinction. More important than these natural disasters and short-term fluctuations, which many considered temporary and self-correcting, were the long-range structural changes, such as the worsening shortage of farm labor resulting from rural emigration in a stable population. Lecouteux repeatedly warned that high tariffs would not solve these problems.[33] Yet it was precisely by interesting the farmer in tariff protection as a cure for his ills that the industrialists hoped to gain his support on the general tariff. In the spring of 1879, while others in the AIF concentrated on arousing the industrial population, Pouyer-Quertier almost single-handedly launched a campaign designed—in the opinion of Michel Augé-Laribé—to foist the "false remedy" of protection on the unsuspecting French farmer.[34]

Pouyer-Quertier's plan was twofold. First, he sought to popularize protectionism in general within French agriculture. Then, once the farmers had been converted, he hoped to strike a bargain whereby they would back high duties on manufactures in return for industry's vote for protection of foodstuffs. Naturally, he did not aim his appeal at all farmers, certainly not at the subsistence farmers who still accounted for the largest portion of the rural

31. Jules Clavé, "La situation agricole en France," *Revue des deux mondes*, February 1, 1880, p. 614.
32. Paul Leroy-Beaulieu, "Le progrès de l'anarchie économique en Europe," *L'économiste français*, May 17, 1879.
33. Edouard Lecouteux, "L'agriculture et le gouvernement," *Journal d'agriculture pratique*, January 16, 1879.
34. Michel Augé-Laribé, *La politique agricole de la France, 1880–1940* (Paris, 1950), pp. 67–78.

population. Whatever their hardships, these peasants were economically isolated—that is, they were unaffected by foreign
imports because the French rail network remained incomplete—
and thus were unresponsive to tariff policy. Rather, his target was
the agricultural capitalists tied to the national and international
markets, specifically, the great landowners of the West and North
who supplied grain, meat, and dairy products to the cities of
northern France and England and who were already being hurt
by American competition, and, second, the phylloxera-ridden
winegrowers of the Midi, who were helplessly watching the
Italians and Spanish invade their domestic markets. Only these
agriculturalists were politically active; only they were accessible
through half-professional, half-political organizations like the
agricultural committees locally and the Société des agriculteurs
nationally.

Pouyer-Quertier first appealed, with little success, to the some
two hundred members of the Société des agriculteurs meeting in
Paris in February 1879.[35] Then he set out to spread the protectionist message to the other thirty-eight hundred members of this elite
organization. With the aid of two fellow Normans, Louis de
Douët, deputy for the Seine-Inférieure and president of the Le
Havre Agricultural Society, and Louis Estancelin, former deputy,
he drafted a program calling for the end of trade treaties and the
establishment of the highest schedule of agricultural duties in
twenty years.[36] On February 24, Douët submitted this program to
the Chamber Tariff Commission. That the commission ignored it
and eventually recommended the continuation of low duties on
foodstuffs of course complicated later efforts to forge an alliance
between protectionist industry and agriculture. In the meantime,
however, Pouyer-Quertier and his associates were more interested

35. At the urging of its general secretary, Lecouteux, the Société des agriculteurs
eschewed an outright endorsement of protection at this time and voted a vague
resolution calling for equal treatment of agriculture and industry in the general
tariff, calculation of customs duties with reference to economic conditions, and
commercial treaties based on reciprocity (*Journal d'agriculture pratique*, February 27, 1879, pp. 302–306).

36. Pouyer-Quertier proposed, for example, a 30 francs per head duty on bulls—
in contrast to 6 francs per head in the government bill—and a duty of 3 francs per
100 kilograms on wheat (*Journal d'agriculture pratique*, March 3, 1879, pp.
318–320).

in winning farmers to their program than in convincing industrialists of the need for agricultural protection. Consequently, Pouyer-Quertier concentrated on publicizing the program in dozens of farm towns during the spring while Estancelin won its endorsement by a national convention of agricultural committees which met in Paris on March 29. As a result, calls for higher tariffs poured into Paris from committees all over France.[37] Taking note, the free traders decided to counterattack. In late March they dispatched Fernand Raoul-Duval and Octave Noël to speak in areas still exporting agricultural produce, starting at Saint-Cyr-en-Vaudreuil near Louviers, and in April, Jules Simon addressed some four thousand winegrowers in Bordeaux at a rally organized by the Agricultural Society of the Gironde.[38]

The impact of these various appeals can be gauged through the resolutions voted by the general councils of agricultural departments in their spring sessions. Outright agricultural protection was favored in the Northwest, where councils, especially those of the Eure, the Nord, and the Seine-Infèrieure, were influenced by industrialists, and in the Southwest, by the councils of the Ariège and Cantal. Others, like the Aisne council, hedged by endorsing the vague program of the Société des agriculteurs. In the Center and the South most councils struck a balance between protectionism and free trade, calling for both compensatory duties and the renewal of trade treaties.[39] Thus French agriculture as a whole was not yet protectionist, but protectionism was becoming respectable, and certain commercial farmers, particularly the grain and livestock growers of the Atlantic littoral and the silk growers of the Rhône, had already converted.

Encouraged by this trend and hoping at last to forge a solid bond between industry and agriculture, Pouyer-Quertier returned to the national assembly of the Société des agriculteurs when it

37. For the propaganda campaign, see L'économiste français, April 5, 1879, pp. 416–418, and Journal d'agriculture pratique, April 3, 1879, pp. 456–457. For the demands and petitions, consult AN F[12] 2489.

38. L'économiste français, March 29, 1879; Journal d'agriculture pratique, May 1, 1879.

39. "Chronique agricole," Journal d'agriculture pratique, May 1, 1879, pp. 589–591.

met in Paris on February 2–5, 1880, at the outset of the Chamber's debate of the general tariff. For an hour and a half he harangued the members on the necessity of protection for both agriculture and industry. The president, the marquis de Dampierre, seemed only slightly more sympathetic than the year before, however. "Neither protectionism nor free trade is absolutely applicable to the complex situation of agriculture," he remarked. "We do not demand protection, but we wish no one to be protected to our detriment, within the country or without; if French industries obtain, in any form, protective duties, justice requires that agriculture, which is also an industry, participate in it equally, or that it receive considerable tax rebates to compensate for the protection afforded industry" (Dampierre was referring to the fact that the tariff commission had recommended high duties on industrials but rejected high duties for foodstuffs and that agriculture would thus obtain nothing by supporting the commission's schedule as it stood).[40] Heeding these words, the society again refused to ally directly with the AIF, but it did endorse the 10 percent *ad valorem* duty on all agricultural products which it had tabled the year before and thereby went on record for protection. Moreover, it left the door open for negotiations between deputies of the agrarian and industrial blocs in the Chamber in the weeks ahead.

The propaganda war that unfolded from the summer of 1878 to the winter of 1880 had thus yielded victories for both the free traders and the protectionists. Both groups had aroused strong support within the urban industrial populace. The free traders continued to hold the edge in official circles as the protectionists failed to win the government to their side. The protectionists, however, made significant inroads among the commercial farmers, who previously had favored free trade. Pouyer-Quertier and his colleagues had helped to create a nascent agricultural protectionism; if they could only convert it into parliamentary support for the tariff commission's version of the general tariff and into opposition to the trade treaties, the victory would be

40. *Journal d'agriculture pratique*, February 5, 1880, pp. 200–201.

theirs. If not, all the work of the tariff commission and the AIF would be rendered futile. Thus defined, the issue was to be finally settled in the deliberations of the Chamber of Deputies and the Senate between January 1880 and May 1882.

The Making of the General Tariff

The debate on the general tariff commenced in the Chamber of Deputies on January 30, 1880, amid considerable public sentiment for quick, decisive action. According to one correspondent, "Everyone sensed that the fortune and even the existence of the country was at stake."[41] The Chamber was not to be rushed, however, and it organized the debate in two stages as was customary in cases of major legislation. First there was a general discussion allowing advocates and opponents of the bill to present their views at length, ostensibly to enlighten the public and to convince uncommitted deputies. Then came the crucial stage, the debating and voting of the articles of the bill which in any tariff meant the examination of the schedule of duties item by item. Not surprisingly, the whole process dragged on for four months.

Pierre Tirard, the commerce minister, opened the general discussion. After summarizing French tariff history since Turgot from a liberal viewpoint and after praising the benefits of the 1860 trade treaties, he blasted the recommendations of the tariff commission, especially Méline's report on cottons, and thereby dispelled any remaining doubt that the government intended to stand by its version of the tariff. Méline responded on February 2 on behalf of "travail national" and the tariff commission. Citing the growth of imports since 1859 and reiterating the ills of the cotton industry, he defended the tariff commission's pessimistic outlook for the French economy and renewed its plea for high compensatory duties.[42] Thus at the outset Tirard and Méline dashed all lingering hope that the government and the tariff

41. *Echo du Nord*, February 1, 1880.
42. Chamber Tariff Commission, *Procès-verbaux*, pp. 1578–1611 (the transcript of the debate was bound with the transcript of the inquiry).

commission might reach an accommodation that would allow smooth passage of the tariff. It was to be a fight to the finish. Once this became clear, the general discussion degenerated into a sterile debating match in which various protectionist and free trade speakers rehashed all the familiar arguments and statistics already aired countless times in government hearings and in the press. The public and most deputies soon tired of the whole affair. They realized, of course, that the victor would be determined not by rhetoric within the Chamber but by the agitation, maneuvering, and bargaining for votes developing outside the Chamber. To understand the making of the general tariff, we thus must first examine this behind-the-scenes activity.

In January, protectionist and free trade lobbyists flocked to the capital from all over France in order to monitor and to influence the vote on the general tariff. "All who have an interest in [this] grave deliberation . . . are now represented in Paris," the *Echo du Nord* reported, "[and] on all sides arms are being furbished."[43] After making pro forma appeals to the newly installed Freycinet government, these lobbyists got down to the business of seeking out and organizing parliamentary support. At the Palais Bourbon "agitation [soon] reigned in the corridors,"[44] and in response to the external pressure three distinct blocs of deputies—one consisting of industrial protectionists, one of free traders, and one of agriculturalists—soon coalesced. Thus the stage was set for a potentially decisive breakthrough in tariff politics: the formation of an explicit alliance between industrial and agricultural protectionists in the Chamber.

In a caucus held on January 28, two hundred deputies representing predominantly agrarian districts agreed to seek approval of the 10 percent duty on farm products, later endorsed by the Société des agriculteurs, and to consider making a deal with the industrial bloc. Simultaneously the industrial protectionists,

43. *Echo du Nord*, February 2, 1880. Free traders from Bordeaux, Lyons, and Saint-Etienne took up residence in Paris for the duration of the debates while, on the protectionist side, textilists from Normandy, the Vosges, and the Nord, along with ironmasters from the Haute-Marne, met daily at AIF headquarters at the cité Rougemont.
44. *Echo du Nord*, February 1, 1880.

meeting in their caucus, voted "to seek common ground between industry and agriculture," and they selected ten of their number to confer with the farm bloc.[45] The negotiations began on January 31, and it was clear from the start that the tariff commission's schedule of duties would not, by itself, furnish a satisfactory basis for an agreement. The protectionists on the tariff commission had been cool toward the protection of foodstuffs, perhaps fearing the wrath of their urban and working-class constituents. As previously mentioned, they had rejected the high agricultural duties advocated in 1879 by Pouyer-Quertier, Douët, and Estancelin and had subsequently endorsed the low tariffs or exemptions recommended by the government, except on cattle, hogs, and sheep, for which they wrote slightly higher duties.[46] Thus the tariff commission's schedule was protectionist for industry, but not for agriculture, and as such the Société des agriculteurs refused to support it. Consequently, in February 1880, the industrial caucus finally realized what the tariff commission had never understood: it would have to concede higher duties to agriculture, particularly on livestock and raw silk, to win its support for the tariff commission's duties on manufactures. After two weeks of dickering on these points, it was announced that the two sides had agreed on "a kind of third project" on livestock and silkworm duties, substantially above all previous recommendations, and that, in return for the industrialists' support on these duties, the farm bloc was ready to vote for the tariff commission's schedule on everything else.[47]

If the agreement stood up, victory clearly would be within the protectionists' grasp. However, mistrust plagued the alliance from the first. In particular, there was some doubt within the agricultural caucus that the leaders of the tariff commission, Méline and Waddington, would honor the transaction, for they had not been party to its negotiation. To elicit a clear commitment from them, Emile Keller of Belfort issued an ultimatum on

45. *Echo du Nord,* January 29, 1880.

46. The tariff commission's report on agricultural products recommended 4 francs per head on cows, instead of 2 francs in the government bill, and 1F50 per head on hogs and sheep, instead of 50 centimes.

47. *Echo du Nord,* February 12, 1880.

February 14 during the general discussion in the Chamber: if the industrialists failed to back high tariffs for agriculture, he warned, agriculture would vote against high tariffs for industry. Waddington, however, remained evasive and ambiguous. In one breath he assured Keller that "if industry warrants moderate protection, logically agriculture does also. I do not hesitate to associate myself with the proposals of those more competent than I on this issue, particularly those representing agriculture in the Chamber." Yet in another breath he insisted that the tariff commission's schedule provided sufficient compensation for agriculture,[48] a contention the agriculture protectionists had already rejected. Thus the farm bloc remained dubious.

As relations between the agricultural and industrial deputies became strained, the free traders devised a plan to drive a wedge between them. On February 26, when the Chamber considered the procedure for voting the duties in the general tariff, one of the free trade leaders, Gustave Lebaudy, proposed that duties be voted under conditions of "urgency," that is, with only one reading, and that they be divided into four independent sections that would be voted separately and, once approved, sent directly to the Senate. The object of this motion—other than to save time—was to deny the industrial bloc the opportunity to retaliate on a second reading if the farm bloc refused to vote for their duties on the first reading. Conversely, it was precisely to preserve the indispensable element of accountability within the industry-agriculture alliance that Méline moved for two full readings. Gambetta, the president of the Chamber and a free trade sympathizer, argued that two readings would consume too much time, and he thereupon threw his support to Lebaudy's motion. The Chamber carried it by a wide margin on March 4. The decisive nature of the vote was discussed in the *Manchester Guardian*:

> This vote is the equivalent of a defeat for the protectionists . . . the first section of the law is that which concerns agricultural products. When this section is voted, it will be definitive and the farmers, discontented with the little they will have obtained, will vote against all the duties proposed for the other industries by the

48. *Journal officiel*, February 15, 1880, p. 1770.

protectionist majority of the tariff commission. The proposals of the commission will be rejected and those of the government will be adopted. This result would have been doubtful if "urgency" had not been voted, for the members favorable to cotton and iron would have *in extremis* made a deal with the agriculturists during the second deliberation.[49]

Uncannily, this prediction came true in the voting of duties which began March 11, with the exception that the industrialists, convinced of the duplicity of their allies and perhaps fearing that to vote duties on foodstuffs would ruin their political positions at home, betrayed the agricultural bloc on its duties before the latter could double-cross them on industrial tariffs. In the crucial vote on livestock, two amendments to raise duties on horses and oxen above the level in either version of the tariff were defeated when the industrial bloc failed to maintain discipline.[50] The Chamber subsequently adopted the tariff commission's recommendations on cattle and sheep, which were below what the agricultural bloc was demanding; on other livestock and on cereals the Chamber approved the government's recommendations. By March 22, when the voting of the agricultural section of the tariff was completed, the protectionist front in the Chamber was in ruins. "The pact which had been concluded between the farmers and the industrialists has been, in effect, dissolved," observed *Le Temps*. "Agriculture did not obtain the compensatory duties which it claimed; in all its essential demands . . . it has seen itself abandoned by its allies of old, forced to bow before the higher needs of feeding the public or before the vital interests of our largest national industries."[51] Unquestionably, the farm bloc agreed with Leroy-Beaulieu when he remarked that "the protectionist farmers have been the dupes of the protectionist manufacturers."[52]

49. Quoted in (and translated from) *L'industrie française*, March 18, 1880.
50. *Journal officiel*, March 12, 1880, pp. 2928–2929. Richard Waddington supported both amendments; Jules Méline and J.-B. Danelle-Bernardin backed the protectionist amendment on oxen but not the one on horses; and a large number of industrial protectionists, including Jules Ferry, Pierre Legrand, Lucien Dautresme, and François Malézieux, supported neither.
51. *Le Temps*, March 24, 1880.
52. Paul Leroy-Beaulieu, "La discussion sur le tarif des douanes: L'agriculture et la protection," *L'économiste français*, March 20, 1880, p. 343.

Unable to retrieve their losses in the Chamber, the agricultural deputies were nevertheless able to take revenge on their erstwhile allies in late April and May, when the Chamber took up the tariff commission's meticulously constructed schedule of duties on manufactures. Predictably, the Chamber quickly approved the government's recommendations on most of these items. When the duties closest to their hearts (or pocketbooks) came up for consideration, the protectionists delayed the vote—and the inevitable defeat—with interminable oratory that won little support in an increasingly hostile, or indifferent, Chamber. As one correspondent wrote, "When it came to manufactures, the discussion . . . was pursued before a thin, inattentive assembly, tired and almost disgusted at having to endure the complaints and pleas of the importunate beggars of protection."[53] Rarely did more than two hundred deputies attend these debates. Only a hundred showed up on May 28 for Dautresme's impassioned appeal for high duties on carded woolens to save the industry of Elbeuf, and in the discussion of cotton yarn—billed as the "grande bataille" of the entire tariff—as few as fifty heard the speeches of Méline, Waddington, and others which stretched over seven sessions between May 8 and May 22.[54] Nevertheless, when it came time to vote on these items, the Chamber always filled immediately and defeated the protectionists overwhelmingly. In frustration, *L'industrie française* denounced the Chamber for "reliev[ing] itself of all responsibility" and for "march[ing] with closed eyes . . . everywhere [the government] led it."[55] But Leroy-Beaulieu was probably on firmer ground when he traced the tariff commission's failure to its own overly ambitious, unrealistic goals:

> When a commission is named to examine a special bill which can gravely affect the situation of certain categories of persons, it is entirely natural that these interested persons display the greatest zeal and make all effort to enter the commission in a majority.

53. Charles Lavollée, "Le tarif des douanes devant le Sénat," *Revue des deux mondes*, November 15, 1880, p. 379.

54. *L'industrie française*, June 3, 1880; *Le Globe*, May 22, 1880; *L'économiste français*, May 22, 1880.

55. *L'industrie française*, May 13, 1880.

Usually they succeed. Rarely at the appointed hour is a cotton spinner, an ironmaster, or a landowner lacking who longs for the sliding scale or fears the invasion of foreign [products]. The word is passed around and all act with discipline in the choice of candidates and succeed in forming the majority of the commission. They then imagine they have won a great and decisive victory, but in this they are seriously mistaken. Once assembled, they become aroused [and] propose extravagant or ridiculous duties; a gulf opens around them, their exaggerations instruct the uninformed or indifferent, and when they come to the public discussion, they are astonished to find themselves in a weak minority. Such is the fate of most commissions affecting national interests.[56]

The free traders, of course, did not have their way on all the voting. They sustained defeats on amendments to abolish the duty on coal and to lower the duties on petroleum and fine cotton yarn below the level recommended by the government (the latter constituted yet another defeat for the Rhône-Loire blend makers). But by June 4, when the voting ended, the free traders had clearly achieved their principal goal: on every industrial tariff, the government had defeated the tariff commission. Moreover, they won an additional victory on the last day when the Chamber— with Tirard's blessing—struck out the article granting the commerce minister the option of imposing a 50 percent tariff surcharge on the products of any country not extending its most favorable tariffs to France. Thus, reviewing the Chamber's handling of the general tariff, *La Liberté* waxed enthusiastic: "If all the interests which demand new tax reductions are not yet satisfied, still the principle of our economic policy is definitely consecrated, and the foundations on which it rests are henceforth unshakable."[57] Actually, such a statement was premature, for the general tariff had yet to pass the Senate, and in May 1880, even as they were being routed in the Chamber, the protectionists were making plans to recoup their losses there.

In the Senate the protectionists repeated, on a smaller scale and in a shorter period of time, the strategy and tactics they had

56. *Journal des débats*, May 12, 1880.
57. *La Liberté*, June 6, 1880.

employed in the Chamber. First they captured a majority of the places on the commission selected to review and report on the tariff as it was sent over from the Chamber. With eleven of the eighteen seats, they easily installed Feray as chairman and Pouyer-Quertier as general reporter. Moreover, they monopolized the key reports: Gustave Denis, the Mayenne spinner, was to report on textiles; Louis Robert-Dehault, an ironmaster and mayor of Saint-Dizier, was to report on metals; Auguste-Joseph Paris, senator for the Pas-de-Calais, was to report on agriculture. Although no formal inquest was planned, the commission decided to accept depositions from select witnesses. In keeping with Feray and Pouyer-Quertier's desire to placate and again ally with the farm bloc, the first and only testimony was presented by Estancelin and a contingent of agricultural protectionists.[58] After hearing them, the commission settled into closed deliberations on a schedule of duties to be presented to the Senate as an alternative to the government's schedule.

Meanwhile, outside the Senate the protectionists began new agitation in favor of an industry-agriculture front. At the Grand Hotel, Estancelin presided over a second congress of agricultural committees, where he denounced Tirard as "a minister *against* agriculture, not a minister *of* agriculture, whose ignorance of the farm issue has no equal and never will have."[59] At Estancelin's urging, the congress sent out some six thousand questionnaires on the tariff in a quasi-plebiscite which *La République française* denounced as "quite simply an act of the coalition of certain big landowners and certain big industrialists to increase at once the rents of farms and the revenues of spinning mills artificially."[60] Simultaneously, the AIF renewed its campaign by calling a second congress of chambers of commerce for May 1 in Paris. Unlike the previous year, Estancelin and representatives of agriculture attended the congress, and the dominant theme to the speeches was no longer industrial solidarity, but rather industrial-agricultural cooperation. With AIF leaders characterizing industry and agriculture as "two sisters" owing each other

58. *L'industrie française*, May 13, 1880.
59. *L'économiste français*, May 8, 1880, p. 573.
60. *La République française*, June 7, 1880.

reciprocal aid, the congress went on record for high duties on agricultural products as well as on manufactures.[61]

In the face of these developments, *La République française* warned that France was "in the presence of a coalition which, unable to succeed in the Chamber, is trying to form again in the Senate," and that consequently the work of the Chamber was menaced with "complete destruction."[62] The government apparently took this threat seriously. At the end of April it had dispatched Léon Say to England as temporary ambassador in order to negotiate, on the basis of the tariffs just voted in the Chamber, a preliminary convention that would render any subsequent protectionist victory in the Senate meaningless. Throughout May, Say worked under a cloak of secrecy. Then on June 1 he announced at the Lord Mayor's banquet in London that, although the French government had signed no formal treaty, it was seeking one and might concede lower duties in the process. "I have the impression," he told his British audience, "and it is supported by the facts, that our two countries will soon renew the treaties of 1860, ameliorating them in a liberal sense."[63] Quick on the heels of this revelation, Say's *Journal des débats,* in its editions of June 10 and 11, dropped heavy hints that the preliminaries of a new treaty had indeed been signed and had even been forwarded to the House of Commons by William Gladstone. This had not actually happened,[64] but the reports outraged the protectionist majority of the Senate tariff commission. With the 1877 negotiations with England fresh in his mind, the commission chairman, Feray, rushed to demand an explanation from Charles de Freycinet, the minister of foreign affairs. On June 14, Freycinet and Tirard denied before the commission that any convention had actually been signed and presented the correspondence of Say and Lord Granville, the British foreign secretary, to prove it. The next day, Feray put a parliamentary

61. *L'industrie française,* May 6 and July 22, 1880.

62. *La République française,* June 6, 1880.

63. Quoted in *L'industrie française,* June 10, 1880.

64. Although Say conferred with Gladstone, Granville, and Charles Dilke repeatedly between May 11 and June 7, formal action did not go beyond the exchange of memoranda. See MAE, Négociations commerciales, Grande-Bretagne, 27 (1880), especially nos. 48–51 (Léon Say, "Note pour le ministre").

question to the government on whether lower duties on iron, coal, and textiles had been offered to the British; Freycinet assured him no such offer had been made and virtually promised that no treaties would be negotiated before the completion of the general tariff.[65] For practical purposes, the case was closed. The government's maneuver had failed, and the Senate commission resumed its work unimpeded.

The commission spent the rest of the year drafting a schedule of duties which by and large recapitulated the schedule previously recommended by the Chamber Tariff Commission, but with one crucial difference. On some sixty farm products for which the Chamber commission's proposed duties had been insufficient to seal the pact between industry and agriculture, the Senate commission recommended higher duties. For livestock it endorsed the duties put forth by Pouyer-Quertier and his Norman associates in 1879. These included 30 francs per head on bulls, against 6 francs per head in both the government and Chamber Tariff Commission versions; 20 francs per head on cows, against 4 francs voted by the Chamber; 5 francs per head on sheep, against 50 centimes recommended by the government and 1F50 voted by the Chamber.[66] Obviously these duties were every bit as protective as those proposed for industrial products and, although no formal caucuses were formed and no formal agreements were made, it was widely assumed that "the deal was on" between industrialists and agriculturists in the Senate on the basis of the commission's recommendations.

The Senate opened its discussion of the general tariff on February 15, 1881; four days later, the debate of and voting on the articles commenced. The voting procedure was identical to that followed in the Chamber: there was to be only one reading under the stipulations of "urgency." For that reason, the industrial-agricultural alliance again failed to hold up, despite the efforts of the protectionists on the tariff commission. This time the agricultural bloc administered the double-cross after the industrialists had faithfully voted for the commission's high duties on livestock and foodstuffs and had thereby allowed them to carry. As before,

65. *Echo du Nord*, June 16–17, 1880; *L'industrie française*, June 10–24, 1880.
66. *L'économiste français*, January 1, 1881.

when textiles were debated, the Chamber emptied; when it was time to vote, the agriculturists reappeared only to vote down the commission's recommendations and to approve the government's. A gleeful *République française* colorfully described this second disintegration of the protectionist front: "Taken as a whole, the campaign presented two distinct phases: the agricultural battle and the battle of textiles. In the first, the protectionist army gave its all; in the second, the agriculturists imitated the Saxons at Leipzig and deserted with arms and baggage, leaving the [cotton] spinners to disengage themselves from the enemy on their own."[67]

The high duties the agricultural bloc had won by treachery were not destined to stand up, however. The Senate's version of the tariff, completed on March 25, went back to the Chamber, where the tariff commission, frustrated in its efforts to win protection for industry, saw no need to uphold the Senate's duties on livestock. After a week of deliberation it proposed a compromise between the livestock duties voted in the Chamber and those voted in the Senate, placing the duty on bulls at 15 francs a head, versus 30 francs in the Senate and 6 francs in the Chamber; the duty on sheep at 3 francs, versus 5 francs and 1.5 francs; the duty on cows at 8 francs, versus 20 francs and 4 francs. This represented duties of only 2 to 3 percent *ad valorem*. On April 2, the Chamber voted this compromise without debate; a week later, on recommendation of the Feray commission, the Senate followed suit.[68] On May 8, 1881, the general tariff law was promulgated and the four-year struggle between free traders and protectionists over its legislation was at an end.

In the final analysis, what had each party gained or lost on the general tariff? The AIF and its parliamentary allies had staked the most on the general tariff and had lost the most. Except for the shipbuilders, who had won subsidies in the separate merchant marine law completed in January 1881, the members of the AIF had nothing to show for their efforts. Neither the demands put forward by industrialists in the tariff hearings of 1878 nor the duties recommended by the Chamber Tariff Commission in 1879

67. *La République française*, March 28, 1881.

68. "Chronique agricole," *Journal d'agriculture pratique*, April 7, 1881, p. 457; *L'économiste français*, April 9, 1881, pp. 447–448, and April 16, 1881, p. 482.

were reflected in the new law. Rather, for manufactures, the general tariff was the old conventional tariff—converted from *ad valorem* to specific duties and raised 24 percent—just as the government had proposed in 1878. For this defeat the protectionists tended to blame themselves. "The industrial world has crumbled into dust," moaned *L'industrie française*. "Isolation is the rule and the sentiment of common interest seems to have failed completely."[69] Nevertheless, despite such harsh self-criticism, the AIF survived and looked toward recouping its losses by blocking the negotiation and ratification of new trade treaties.

In contrast to the industrial protectionists, the agricultural blocs of the Chamber and then Senate had joined the protectionist movement late, and the with less than complete commitment, yet they did not come away empty-handed in the making of the general tariff. Their victory in the Senate gained higher duties on livestock. To be sure, livestock, as well as all other agricultural products, was still protected much less than manufactures, but the law stipulated that no agricultural duties could be altered in the new trade treaties. Thus for agriculture, in contrast to the situation for manufactures, the new general tariff was automatically the conventional tariff; it could not be lowered. Moreover, since they were to remain outside the trade treaties, the agricultural duties would be of no fixed duration, but rather could—and would—be raised whenever the agricultural protectionists gathered sufficient parliamentary support.

Despite these limited successes of the farm bloc, the real winners in the fight on the general tariff were the free traders, who had had the least to gain, but also the least to lose, in the whole affair. Because of their own diligence and the inability of the industrial and agricultural protectionists to cooperate, the free traders won approval of the government's version of the general tariff and thereby cleared the way for the trade negotiations that would reaffirm and extend the commercial regime of 1860. As a result, in May 1881, the France of international commerce appeared very close to triumphing over the France of national industry.

69. *L'industrie française*, March 31, 1881.

The Trade Treaties of 1882

When the general tariff held the national spotlight between 1877 and 1881, the old trade treaties lived on precariously, and the question of when they would be renegotiated, if at all, and on what basis, remained unanswered. Originally they were to have been renegotiated in 1877. In that year, however, the Seize Mai crisis interrupted the talks with the British, and the controversial treaty concluded with Italy fell victim to the protectionist resurgence in the Chamber. For the time being, the original treaties thus remained in effect. On December 31, 1878, the French government formally renounced all these trade treaties in accordance with the formula for renegotiation devised in 1873. Since all would expire one year hence, it was presumed that new negotiations would begin at once. But problems arose in the spring of 1879 when the Waddington government promised the tariff commission that all negotiations would await completion of the general tariff and when, soon after, it became clear that this could not occur before the next year. Because France would have faced commercial chaos if the expiration of the treaties had allowed the old, prohibitive general tariff to go into effect, the parliament authorized the government in August 1879 to extend the renounced treaties six months beyond the promulgation of the general tariff in order to accommodate the negotiation of new treaties. Thereafter the ground rules for these negotiations gradually took shape. First, during the debate of the general tariff in March 1880, the Chamber defeated two attempts to restrict the terms of future trade treaties. The government thus was able to bargain freely in the upcoming talks. Exactly when these talks would begin, however, remained uncertain. The parliamentary repudiation of Léon Say's mission to London in June 1880 graphically demonstrated the futility of any attempt to open negotiations before the promulgation of the general tariff. Only after May 8, 1881, when the general tariff finally became law, was the government in a position to undertake negotiations without fear of parliamentary interference. Consequently, only then were the terms of the negotiations finally clarified by the Conseil supérieur du commerce. Meeting in mid-May, the council first rejected a last-ditch effort by cotton spinners, led by Richard Waddington, to have cotton duties excluded from any new trade treaties, and then it recommended that the old conventional tariff (that is, the new general tariff reduced by 19 percent) serve as the basis of French proposals in the upcoming trade talks. In turn, the issue of time and place for the negotiations was quickly resolved: formal talks were to open with the British in London on May 26.[70]

The government's firm commitment to the system of commercial conventions throughout this period of uncertainty, its unfaltering resolve to negotiate new treaties at the first opportunity, and the actual commencement of negotiations can all be attributed to the influence of the free traders. It was their publicity campaign, especially in 1879, that had kept support for the treaties alive. More important, throughout these years they maintained their stewardship of the three cabinet posts—finance, commerce, and foreign affairs—that were most responsible for commercial policy. As leaders of the commercial-financial elite of France, they alone seemed to possess the expertise these jobs required. Consequently, even though an avowed protectionist, Jules Ferry, headed the government in May 1881, Pierre Tirard still held the Commerce Ministry, as he had throughout the two-year battle on the general tariff, and thus a free trader was in position to dominate the forthcoming trade talks. Moreover, Tirard could expect support from the foreign minister, Jules Barthélemy Saint-Hilaire, a Parisian sympathetic to the needs of international commerce,[71] and from the various officials of the Commerce and Finance Ministries who had helped to formulate and administer France's liberal trade policies in the previous two decades and who, in 1881, formed the core of the French negotiat-

---

70. For the background to the trade negotiations, see Léon Amé, "Négociations commerciales avec l'Angleterre," *J des ec*, 4th ser., 18 (1882), 34, and AN F^{12} 6416, Traités de commerce, Rapports aux Sénat et Chambre. For the action of the Conseil supérieur du commerce in May 1881, see *L'industrie française*, May 12 and 19, 1881.

71. Barthélemy Saint-Hilaire was a former Saint-Simonian who, as a member of a parliamentary study commission, had participated in the planning of the Suez canal (*DPF*, I, 185–186).

ing team. Most notable of these was Léon Amé, the former director of customs, whom the protectionists viewed as "one of the most determined adversaries of national production, a man who has expressed a special hatred for the French cotton industry."[72] With such men in charge of making commercial policy, the free traders believed that, once negotiations began, nothing could prevent the renewal of the trade treaties, and as a measure of their confidence they disbanded the Free Trade Association in June 1881.[73] Yet the triumph of the free traders was far from certain in the summer of 1881. Only after surmounting numerous obstacles—including the failure of negotiations with England and a concerted protectionist campaign to block ratification of treaties with other countries—did the government succeed in extending the liberal trade system of the Second Empire.

Negotiations with the British dominated the early months of the French drive for new trade treaties. Tirard and his associates gave priority to a treaty with Great Britain because it remained France's chief trading partner in 1881 and was particularly vital to members of the free trade party as a source of imports and a market for exports.[74] Moreover, the treaty with England was the oldest of the commercial conventions and was rightly considered the crucial link in the chain of commercial alliances. Yet, despite Tirard's eagerness to conclude a treaty, he did not feel at liberty to give the British overly generous terms. He was constrained—at least informally—by the guidelines voted by the Conseil supérieur du commerce in June which stipulated that cotton duties should not be offered below those in the 1860 convention.[75] In

72. *L'industrie française*, June 2, 1881.

73. As the association's secretary, Octave Noël, explained in his final report (*J des ec*, 4th ser., 15 [1881], 299), "The voting of the general tariff, in view of which our association was created, and the opening of the first negotiations for the renewal of the treaties naturally puts an end to our mission, and the association, as it has been instituted, no longer has an immediate *raison d'être*. Its principal task has been accomplished."

74. In 1869, France's trade with England was worth 1,453,000 francs, almost equal to the total value of its trade with its three next largest partners—Belgium, Italy, and the Zollverein. In 1909 trade with England still exceeded trade with either Belgium or Germany by 55 percent (Emile Levasseur, *Histoire du commerce de la France*, 2 vols. [Paris, 1911–1912], II, 779).

75. Conseil supérieur du commerce, *Examen du tarif des fils de cotons* (Paris, 1881), p. 298. This ruling was a major blow to the Rhône-Loire blends manufac-

addition, Tirard was acutely aware of the growing parliamentary strength of the protectionists, and he hesitated to offer the British too much for fear that any treaty containing broad concessions would not be ratified.[76] Consequently, although Tirard was willing to give the British the duties they wanted on metals and machinery, he balked at meeting their demands on textiles. Specifically, he offered to reduce French import duties on woolen yarn 20 to 30 percent and duties on woolen cloth 16 percent, but not the 50 percent the British were asking. Similarly, on cotton yarn, thread, and cloth, he offered to reduce the new general tariff only 10 to 20 percent (thus making the new conventional tariff up to 10 percent higher than the old one), while the British insisted on cotton duties 10 percent below those in the 1860 convention. Unwilling to accept these terms, the British broke off negotiations on June 30.[77]

The French free traders blamed Tirard and the French negotiators for the breakdown in the talks with England. "Our government has been both fickle and obstinate in this affair," wrote Leroy-Beaulieu; "it has lacked both economic perspicacity and political flexibility."[78] Such judgments were hardly warranted, however, for the real source of the deadlock lay in the unrealisti-

---

turers, and, to mollify them, the council recommended the extension of temporary admissions to all cotton thread employed in the manufacture of blended cloth to be exported.

76. As early as September 1880, Tirard had informed the British that "our sincere desire is to continue with our overseas neighbors the friendly relations that have been so profitable to our country from an economic as well as a political point of view. But . . . it can not be forgotten that our treaties must be submitted to the ratification of parliament, and . . . it must be admitted that even the principle of trade treaties will be vigorously combated there. It is thus necessary not to augment the difficulties arising in the discussions by giving our adversaries the chance to argue that we have imposed needless sacrifices on them. . . . This is not the time to propose for ratification any treaty containing reductions of tariffs. We would experience a certain defeat" (MAE, Négociations commerciales, Grande-Bretagne, 27 [1880], pp. 110–112).

77. For Tirard's offer and the British response, see MAE, *Documents diplomatiques, négociations commerciales entre la France et la Grande Bretagne, août 1880–fevrier 1882* (Paris, 1882), pp. 59–62. The *procès-verbaux* of the formal talks were published as MAE, *Documents diplomatiques: Conférences pour le renouvellement des traités de commerce entre la France et la Grande-Bretagne, mai 1881–janvier 1882* (Paris, 1882).

78. *L'économiste français*, August 27, 1881, pp. 253–255.

cally high goals of the British. Since 1860 many British industrialists—the Manchester cotton masters in particular—had come to believe that trade treaties in general benefited them less than they benefited the French and that simple most-favored-nation conventions might serve their needs better. Consequently, in 1881 they pressured the government to conclude a treaty only on their terms. As Gladstone told the French ambassador in July, "The true opinion of England would be much more opposed than favorable to the conclusion of any treaty which was less liberal than that of 1860."[79] In short, because the treaty was not essential to them politically or commercially, the British decided to eschew compromise and to go for all or nothing. This attitude, in turn, led directly to the stalemate in the talks during the summer and fall. For, once the British had determined that Tirard was not going to improve his offer, they began to stall—focusing attention on the prorogation of the existing treaty for this purpose in July and August—in the hope that the French elections scheduled for late August would bring in negotiators willing to grant them further concessions. To be sure, it was a long shot, but it seemed to pay off. The Republican Union's decisive victory at the polls on August 21 virtually assured that its leader, Léon Gambetta, would head the next government. Gambetta, of course, was made to British order. He was not only a free trader, but also an Anglophile who on frequent trips to London had become a close friend of Dilke, the leader of the British negotiators, and who had often served as an unofficial escort for the Prince of Wales in Paris.[80] Thus, as the *Manchester Guardian* confessed in October, the British resumed the trade negotiations in September with no intention of bargaining seriously until Gambetta came to power.[81]

79. Challemel-Lacour to Barthélemy Saint-Hilaire, July 28, 1881, *Documents diplomatiques, France–Grande Bretagne, 1880–1882*, p. 62. Gladstone was speaking for the Association of British Chambers of Commerce which had just gone on record against any new treaties that did not improve on previous treaties (MAE, Négociations commerciales, Grande-Bretagne, 31 (1881), 130.

80. In the fall of 1881, the prince accompanied the British negotiators to Paris and, on November 5, he and Dilke dined with Gambetta at the Moulin Rouge (*Echo du Nord*, November 7, 1881).

81. *L'industrie française*, October 6, 1881. The French free traders were less sanguine about the advent of Gambetta. He supported low tariffs to assure low

When Ferry finally resigned in November on the Tunisian question and Gambetta launched his "Grande Ministère" with Maurice Rouvier of the Free Trade Association in Commerce, the British prepared to accept what they anticipated would be generous terms. Yet even the Gambetta government, which the *Echo du Nord* called "the most free trade ever,"[82] did not feel free to go to any lengths to conclude treaties, especially in the face of growing agitation in protectionist textile districts.[83] Consequently, in negotiating with the British in January, Rouvier went beyond previous French offers, but he did not go as far as the British expected. In the realm of textile duties—the only remaining bone of contention—he offered substantially lower duties on the first two classes of unfinished cotton cloth, but he refused to cut duties on all classes of the commodity. Likewise, on woolen cloth and cotton-wool blends, he offered several new reductions, but duties as a whole remained well above what the British were demanding.[84]

When Tirard returned to the Commerce Ministry on January 30, after the unexpected fall of the Gambetta government on constitutional revision, he stood by Rouvier's proposals. In a memorandum of February 11, Tirard informed the British that "in maintaining M. Rouvier's propositions, the French government has [already] greatly surpassed the limits set by parliament in the discussion of the general tariff . . . [and] it is difficult to go any further. Therefore, these propositions must be considered our last, absolutely definitive word."[85] Even in the face of this ultimatum, the British would not accept France's terms. On February 15, Lord Granville, the British foreign secretary, virtu-

---

prices on the foodstuffs, textiles, and other items consumed by his middle- and working-class followers but was little concerned with promoting the specific business interests in the free trade party. Thus most free traders considered him naive and quixotic on economic policy and probably agreed with the protectionist commentator who chided him for supporting free trade "without knowing why" (*Le Soleil*'s Bernard, quoted in *L'industrie française*, September 15, 1881).

82. *Echo du Nord*, January 31, 1882.

83. See the petitions filed in MAE, Négociations commerciales, Grande-Bretagne, 31, 127–148.

84. Rouvier memorandum, January 25, 1882, *Documents diplomatiques, France–Grande Bretagne, 1880–1882*, pp. 98–103.

85. Tirard note, February 11, 1882, ibid., pp. 105–110.

ally broke off the talks by instructing Lord Lyons, the British ambassador in Paris, to request a simple most-favored-nation convention through which England could benefit from any conventional tariff emerging from France's other trade negotiations. Two weeks later the Chamber of Deputies approved such a convention without discussion. The Anglo-French treaty of commerce was dead.

The failure to reach an agreement with the British and the subsequent demise of the Anglo-French treaty cannot be ascribed merely to the "protectionist revival in France," as Arthur L. Dunham asserts.[86] To be sure, the free traders who conducted the talks for France were sensitive to the protectionists' strength in the Chamber and Senate and, for the sake of political expediency, they limited their concessions in order to ensure ratification of the treaty. Nevertheless, they offered a schedule of duties which, with a few exceptions, was equal to or below that of 1860. The British, on the other hand, would accept nothing short of a 20 percent reduction of the former duties in the belief that they could always get the status quo through the most-favored-nation convention in combination with the treaties France had just signed with other countries (Belgium in particular). Of course, the success of this strategy—as well as the future of Anglo-French trade and, indeed, the future of the liberal trade system—depended on those treaties being approved by the French parliament. Precisely for that reason, the question of ratification took on special significance in the spring of 1882.

Between October 1881 and February 1882—while public attention focused on the negotiations with England—France signed trade treaties with seven continental countries: Belgium, Italy, the Netherlands, Portugal, Sweden-Norway, Spain, and Switzerland.[87] Of these, the treaties with the nonindustrial or semi-

86. Arthur L. Dunham, *The Anglo-French Treaty of Commerce of 1860* (Ann Arbor, 1930), pp. 345–348. Dunham presents an account of the Anglo-French negotiations, based on British published documents, which is clearly slanted toward the British.

87. The *procès-verbaux* of the negotiations with these countries were published in various "yellow books." See, for example, *Livre jaune* no. 75: MAE., *Traité de commerce conclu entre la France et l'Italie, le 3 Novembre 1881. Texte et procès-*

industrial nations of Europe were relatively uncontroversial because they entailed no major concessions in French industrial tariffs. The treaty with the Netherlands, for example, simply renewed previous conventions whereby the Dutch, who had few industries to protect, admitted French manufactures almost duty-free without requiring correspondingly low duties from France. The treaties with Spain, Portugal, and Sweden-Norway opened foreign markets to French products in exchange for the maintenance of low French import duties on agricultural products and industrial raw materials such as wax, palm oil, and wine exported by Spain and Portugal, and copper, iron ore, and paper pulp exported by Sweden.[88] To be sure, the treaty with Italy did involve the lowering of French duties on some manufactures (citric acid, glass, gloves). Mainly, however, it facilitated continued export of French manufactures (textiles and hardware) in exchange for continued importation of Italian agricultural products (olive oil and wine), and it came under fire from French protectionists in December only because it happened to be the first treaty to come up for ratification, not because it posed any particular threat to domestic French industry.

The real threat to French industry was posed by the negotiations with France's industrialized neighbors, Switzerland and Belgium. The Swiss had greatly expanded their production of textiles in the 1870s, and their cottons, silks, silk floss, and blends were competing successfully with the French in foreign markets by 1881. In the trade negotiations that opened in Paris in the fall of that year, they hoped to gain greater access to the French domestic market for these items as well. Fortunately for the French manufacturers, however, the Swiss proved unwilling to make reciprocal reductions in their industrial tariffs to gain such access. Because they insisted that the French accept their high

verbaux des conférences (Paris, 1881). In addition to these trade treaties, conventions with Russia, Austria-Hungary, and the Ottoman Empire remained in effect, and, of course, through the most-favored-nation clause in the Treaty of Frankfurt, Germany continued to enjoy the best available terms of trade.

88. For a brief description of the negotiation and terms of these treaties, see Léon Amé, "Négociations commerciales de la France avec la Belgique, l'Italie, la Suisse, l'Espagne, le Portugal, la Suède et la Norwège, et les Pays-Bas," *J des ec*, 4th ser., 18 (1882), 343–369.

general tariff on manufactures as the conventional tariff, their demand for lower French duties on textiles lost its force. Ultimately each side agreed to apply to the other the conventional duties on manufactures worked out in other treaties. Thus, although the negotiations were still difficult and protracted because of a controversy over duties on French wines, they produced a treaty that was much less controversial than it might have been. Signed on February 23, 1882, it was ratified without discussion in April.[89]

The treaty with Belgium, concluded on October 31, 1881, had the most serious implications for the French home market and spawned the greatest controversy. Although it naturally included a few items pertaining to Franco-Belgian trade exclusively,[90] its most significant feature was a schedule of industrial tariffs which, as the first to be negotiated, was eventually incorporated into the other treaties and would be applicable to England and Germany as well through the mechanism of the most-favored-nation clause. Because Belgium exported the same things to France as England did—textiles, machinery, metals, and coal—and thus naturally asked for the same concessions, this schedule of duties closely resembled the British demands. Specifically, the French insisted on a higher conventional duty than before on some categories of cotton cloth, as they did with the British, but on most tissues and yarns, various kinds of machinery, and iron and steel, they conceded import duties that were equal to or lower than the previous ones. The duty on pig iron was reduced from 20 to 15 francs per ton, the duty on bar iron was reduced from 60 to 50 francs per ton, and the duty on steel bars was reduced from 11F25 to 9 francs. The duty on tinplate was lowered from 130

---

89. Ibid., pp. 351–353; Drumel's report to the Chamber of Deputies, AN F12 6416; MAE, *Traité de commerce et conventions annexes entre la France et la Suisse conclus le 23 février 1882. Texte et procès-verbaux des conférences* (Paris, 1882).

90. In exchange for lower Belgian duties on wine, cotton cloth, jewelry, clocks, pottery, and other items, France ended its *surtaxe d'entrepôt* on coffee, timber, and other products imported through Belgian ports, reduced its duties on refined sugar, and extended the agreement of October 18, 1873, prohibiting the trafficking in customs permits for flour which had once served to subsidize Dunkirk flour exporters and Marseilles grain importers (Amé, "Négociations," pp. 344–346). See also MAE, *Négociations pour la conclusion d'une traité de commerce entre la France et la Belgique, septembre-octobre 1881* (Paris, 1881).

francs to 120 francs. Among textiles, France extended its existing conventional duties on simple cotton yarn, jute yarn, and most linen cloth; it reduced duties on two- and three-strand cotton thread, linen yarn, and woolen yarns.[91] In short, the conventional duties embodied in the Belgian treaty, if ratified, would single-handedly extend the liberal tariff system of the Second Empire and render the general tariff of 1881 inapplicable to any country in Europe. Because all this represented a clear threat to the interests of the industrial protectionists and denied all they had worked for in the previous twenty years, they mounted a campaign to block its ratification—and the ratification of all the other treaties—in November 1881. Simultaneously, the free traders began working just as earnestly toward the opposite goal. The inevitable parliamentary clash came first in December, when the Italian treaty was before the Chamber, and then in March, when the Belgian treaty came before the Chamber and the Italian treaty came before the Senate.

The protectionist campaign commenced at the annual meeting of the AIF in Paris on November 17. There the members present approved a resolution calling for the immediate discussion and rejection by parliament of the treaties with Belgium and Italy, and they selected a delegation, headed by the AIF president, Alexandre Jullien, to press this demand on the Chamber of Deputies.[92] Meanwhile, other members raised a hue and cry in the provinces. An assembly of linen manufacturers in Lille denounced the terms on linen in the Belgian treaty, and the Lille Chamber of Commerce sent a protest to members of the Chamber commission on the treaties objecting to the 20 percent reduction in yarn duties. In December a group of Roubaix manufacturers led by Aimé Delfosse protested the lower duties on woolens and wool blends, while spokesmen for both the woolens industry and the metallurgy interests of the Northeast lobbied around Rouvier in Paris. Finally, as the ratification of treaties was being debated in late March, the AIF staged another major congress of chambers

91. *L'économiste français*, November 19, 1881, pp. 628–629. Figures taken from the conventional tariff as published in the *Bulletin de statistique et de législation comparée*, 11 (1882-1), 514–541.
92. *L'industrie française* and *Echo du Nord*, November 17, 1881.

of commerce in Paris which demanded no diminution of the duties in the general tariff and, provided the treaties were not ratified, the formulation of a minimum tariff to be implemented through most-favored-nation conventions.[93]

While the protectionists agitated in public, the free traders took command of the situation where it mattered—in the parliamentary commissions that reported on ratification of the treaties and in the actual debate and voting on ratification. To be sure, the twenty-one-man commission on the treaties, selected by the Chamber in early November, included protectionists as well as free traders, and neither bloc held a majority. Nevertheless, the free trader Gustave Lebaudy won the chairmanship and succeeded in swinging the independent members of the commission to the free trade side. The commission quickly recommended ratification of the Italian treaty, the first submitted to it. On December 9, the Chamber of Deputies as a whole considered this treaty and, after nominal debate, voted ratification overwhelmingly. Despite the oratory of Méline and others, the protectionists could muster only eighty-four "no" votes, primarily because, with duties on farm products exempted from the treaty, agricultural deputies could approve measures that facilitated the importation of manufactures (and thereby lowered the domestic prices on those items) without fear of exposing agriculture to similar treatment. In any case, the protectionists in the Chamber again tried to block ratification in the case of the Belgian treaty, but again failed. The treaty commission quickly recommended passage, and on March 25, after a perfunctory debate, the full Chamber complied.[94]

Meanwhile, the Senate was taking up the treaty with Italy. The protectionists were in a strong position in the eighteen-member Senate treaty commission formed in January, and they succeeded in electing François Viellard-Migeon of Belfort, head of the Morvillars ironworks, as chairman and Gustave Denis as secretary. However, the free traders on the commission, led by Millaud

---

93. *Echo du Nord,* November 25–December 13, 1881; *L'industrie française,* December 15, 1881, January 5 and April 6, 1882.

94. On the work of the Chamber treaty commission, see AN F^{12} 6416; for the parliamentary debate, see *Journal des débats,* December 10, 1881; *L'industrie française,* December 15, 1881, and March 30, 1882.

of the Rhône, Dauphinot of Reims, and Gaston Bazille of the Hérault, succeeded in installing Teisserenc de Bort, the commerce minister in Simon's cabinet, as reporter. Teisserenc's strong endorsement of the treaty apparently won over two independent members previously in opposition, for the commission, initially reported to be divided ten to eight against ratification, ended up by approving the treaty by the same numbers.[95] In the debate in the full Senate on March 28, the protectionists vainly tried to reverse this defeat by proposing that the Senate substitute a legislated minimum tariff for the negotiated conventional tariff. When sentiment for such a move began to rise in the course of discussion, Tirard quickly called in the prime minister, Freycinet, to shore up support. The government carried the day, 165 to 95.[96]

The free traders' victories in the Chamber on the Belgian treaty and in the Senate on the Italian treaty foreshadowed similar victories on all the others. By May 11, both the Chamber and the Senate had ratified all the treaties, and the new conventional tariff went into effect on May 15. Through the perseverance of its leaders in the government and in parliament, the free trade party had at last won the extension of the liberal tariff system. To be sure, the new conventional tariff was not ideal from the free traders' point of view: on some one hundred items the duties were higher than before, and another three hundred items, mostly foodstuffs, remained under the general tariff. On the other hand, such crucial duties as those on cotton yarn remained at their previous level, and duties on some 140 items were lower than before, making the average of all duties some 20 percent below the general tariff (in other words, comparable to the old conventional tariff).[97] Moreover, the continuation of the temporary admissions system under the terms of the general tariff law held out the prospect to some importers of circumventing even these duties. Thus, on the whole, Léon Amé was justified in characterizing the tariff reform completed in 1882 as "a new and probably definitive consecration of the work of 1860."[98]

95. Report of the Senate treaty commission, March 22, 1882, AN F[12] 6416.
96. *L'industrie française*, March 30, 1882.
97. See Appendix 2 for a comparison of the new conventional duties and the old conventional duties.
98. Amé, "Négociations," p. 366.

Yet the free traders of France considered the "consecration" of the status quo a poor substitute for continued liberalization of the tariff. They were particularly disappointed by the government's failure to conclude a trade treaty with England. Indeed, throughout the spring of 1882, Leroy-Beaulieu pushed incessantly for new negotiations with the British; the same demand was issued by a congress of free trade chambers of commerce which met in Paris the first week in May.[99] Despite these efforts, however, negotiations did not reopen, and the advent of Pierre Legrand of Lille, a "resolute protectionist," in the Commerce Ministry in August dispelled any lingering hopes that they would ever reopen. "The presence of M. Pierre Legrand at the Ministry of Commerce," wrote *L'industrie française*, "is a sure guarantee that nothing will be attempted against [the will of] our centers of manufacturing . . . [his appointment] signifies the maintenance of the status quo on customs duties and the abandonment of any notion of renewing the commercial negotiations with England."[100] Indeed, even though Legrand served as commerce minister only six months, his tenure of office effectively broke the momentum of the tariff liberalization drive. As many people sensed at the time, the period of the Gambetta and Freycinet governments in the winter and spring of 1882 had offered the last real opportunity to move France toward freer trade under the Third Republic, and the free traders had been able to capitalize on it only to a limited extent.

The free traders were thus gloomy in victory. The protectionists, by contrast, were optimistic in defeat, for they saw several encouraging signs in the events of 1881 and 1882. They particularly noted that their political strength had intimidated Tirard and his negotiators and forced them to limit the concessions they offered in the negotiations. In this manner their pressure had contributed to the breakdown of the talks with England. They were especially happy about this, not because it ended British competition in France—actually under the most-favored-nation convention, Anglo-French trade continued as before—but because it indicated that things would go their way more and more in the future. Thus, in contrast to its bitterness and cynicism the

99. *L'industrie française,* May 11, 1882.
100. *L'industrie française,* August 10, 1882.

previous year, when the protectionists were defeated on the general tariff, *L'industrie française* took a hopeful stance in the spring of 1882, declaring that the doctrine of protection that had not prevailed this time "would certainly triumph in ten years, at the expiration of the treaties just concluded."[101] Similarly, in statements later in the year, Jules Méline reaffirmed his faith in protectionism and reasserted that, with strong organization and hard work, it would be only a matter of time until the AIF could reverse the policies set in 1881 and 1882.[102] In the short run, events did vindicate these convictions in that the resurgence of protectionism dominated the 1880s. Yet the long-term lesson to be learned from the first round of tariff reform was that there could never again be a clear-cut victory for either side and that, sooner or later, free traders and protectionists would have to come to terms. Pierre Tirard's metamorphosis from committed free trader to circumspect compromiser—from idealist to realist—during his tenure in the Ministry of Commerce, 1879–1882, foreshadowed a trend among all leaders of the Third Republic in the following decade away from commitment to either free trade or protection and toward concern for accommodation and conciliation in the matter of the tariff.

101. *L'industrie française,* May 18, 1882.
102. See Méline's speeches in Remiremont and Paris in *L'industrie française,* October 26 and December 14, 1882.

5

Compromise and Conciliation, 1883–1900

In 1882 the free traders won a Pyrrhic victory that they were not able to duplicate in subsequent warfare over tariff policy. As the depression continued and as the commitment to free trade waned at home and abroad in the late 1880s, the momentum soon passed to the protectionists. In 1892, true to Méline's earlier forecasts, France abandoned the trade treaties, legislated a stern two-tiered tariff (the Méline tariff), and revised or eliminated most other elements of the liberal trade policy in operation since the 1860s. These actions, however, did not mean that France returned to high protection on the pre-1860 scale, as is often asserted. Rather, the commercial policy that emerged in the 1890s represented a compromise between the demands of the free traders and the demands of the protectionists. As such it was consistent with the growing tendency in late nineteenth-century France to accommodate all major economic interests for the sake of the survival and stability of the capitalist system. Indeed, the compromise on the tariff was an indispensable part of that accommodation and can be appreciated only in relation to it. For this reason, the present chapter will first survey tariff politics, 1883–1900, emphasizing the progress, triumphs, and eventual "taming" of the protectionist offensive. Then it will turn to the more important task of placing those politics and the resultant policy in the context of interest accommodation. Finally, the conclusion will relate both the making of tariff policy and the accommodation of interests to the broader economic and political developments unfolding in France at the turn of the century.[1]

Compromise: The Méline Tariff and Beyond

Despite the setback of 1881–1882, the offensive launched by the protectionists in the late 1870s gained ground rapidly in the course of the eighties thanks to developments on various levels. First, the shift toward protectionism continued elsewhere in Europe, epitomized by Italy's renunciation of its trade treaty with France in 1886 and its subsequent legislation of a high protective tariff. This trend naturally undercut France's ability to maintain a liberal trade policy (in response to Italy's action, for example, the French had no recourse but to apply their general tariff to Italian imports, which in turn helped to precipitate a vicious tariff war). It also undercut France's desire to maintain a liberal trade policy because, as tariffs rose elsewhere, it became less and less likely that keeping France's import duties low would serve to open foreign markets to French exports (and even free traders in France considered free trade without reciprocity foolhardy).[2] Thus, as protectionism waxed abroad, the French government's

1. Because the tariff politics of 1883–1900 merely presented variations on themes well defined in the earlier phase of tariff reform and because the men and interests involved in tariff politics after 1882 were substantially the same as those involved before 1882, the account of those politics here need not be as full as the account of the earlier phase. Descriptions and analyses of the making of the Méline tariff already are available, which is not the case for the tariff of 1881. See Eugene O. Golob, *The Méline Tariff* (New York, 1944), and Jürgen Hilsheimer, "Interessengruppen und Zollpolitik in Frankreich: Die Auseinandersetzungen um die Aufstellung des Zolltarifs von 1892," Ph.D. dissertation, Heidelberg, 1973. An abstract and critique of the latter is found in Pierre Barral, "Les groupes de pression et le tarif douanier français de 1892," *Revue d'histoire économique et sociale*, 52 (1974), 421–426.

2. On the return to protection in Europe and its impact on French policy, see, among others, Walter Bennett Harvey, *Tariffs and International Relations in Europe, 1860–1914* (Chicago, 1938); Charles Augier, *La France et les traités de commerce: Etude sur les tarifs des douanes de la France et de l'étranger* (Paris, 1906); and Auguste Devers (Arnauné), "La politique commerciale de la France depuis 1860," *Schriften des Verein für Socialpolitik*, 51 (1892), 127–208.

commitment to low tariffs at home inevitably waned. It also waned because of the changing leadership in key ministries. During the 1880s, provincial politicians, increasingly at home in Paris and increasingly in control of the parliamentary system, were acceding to cabinet posts with growing frequency. Since these included protectionists as well as free traders (in contrast to the previously dominant Parisians, who, by definition, were all free traders), this trend on balance benefited the cause of protection. Specifically, it meant that in the 1880s protectionists finally broke the free traders' long-standing monopoly of economic policy-making positions. After falling to a protectionist, Pierre Legrand, for the first time in 1882, the Commerce Ministry was held alternately by free traders (Tirard, Rouvier, Edouard Lockroy) and protectionists (Legrand, Dautresme) until a true middle-of-the-roader, Jules Roche, took the position in 1890. Similarly, the Ministry of Agriculture, created by Gambetta in 1881 and held at first by free traders (Paul Devès, François de Mahy), was held mainly by protectionists after Méline acceded to the post in 1883.

Although changes in trade policy abroad and in the power structure at home improved the protectionists' position and undercut the free traders' position in the 1880s, what gave the protectionist message particular force and opened the way for a concerted attack on France's liberal tariff regime was the continuing depression in industry and agriculture. In industry, the 1880s, like the late 1870s, were a period of declining prices, stagnating production, and contracting profits, especially in metallurgy.[3]

3. For the big metallurgical firms, the crisis stemmed mainly from the cutback in railroad building when the Freycinet plan was phased out in 1883. State rail orders, which amounted to 195,582 tons in 1883, declined to 19,377 tons by 1885 (Yasuo Gonjo, "Le 'plan Freycinet,' 1878–1882: Un aspect de la 'grande depression' économique en France," *Revue historique*, 248 [1972], p. 76). Orders by the Northern railway dropped from 22,000 tons to 10,000 tons between 1882 and 1886 (François Caron,. *Histoire de l'exploitation d'un grand réseau: La Compagnie du chemin de fer du Nord, 1846–1937* [Paris, 1973], p. 336). As a consequence, steel rail prices, which had momentarily stabilized at 216–218 francs per ton in 1878–1880 during the Freycinet plan boom, resumed their long-term decline, dropping to 120 francs by 1888 (Jean Fourastié, *Documents pour l'histoire et la théorie des prix*, I [Paris, 1958], 122 ff.). Steel companies—83 percent of whose production consisted of steel rails—sank into a period of profitless production (Jean Bouvier et al., *Le mouvement du profit en France au XIXe siècle: Matériaux et études* [Paris, 1965], pp. 411–430).

This slump could not be blamed simply on rising foreign competition, as the slump of the late 1870s had been,[4] but mining, metallurgical, and textile interests still looked to higher tariffs (although not exclusively to tariffs) to solve their problems. Consequently, the representatives of these industries persevered in their search for protection. Instead of disbanding after the tariff reform of 1881–1882 (as the Free Trade Association had done), the AIF formalized its organization, regularized its meetings, and set out to broaden its appeal, as was indicated in the change in the title of its official organ from *L'industrie française* to *Travail national* in 1884. More important, it set out to ally with the agricultural protectionists, whose emergence in large numbers in the 1880s was the depression's chief contribution to the transformation of tariff politics.

As we saw in the last chapter, French agriculture was already in the throes of a multifaceted crisis in the late 1870s, and because that crisis involved a dramatic increase in the importation of foreign foodstuffs (which was, in turn, the by-product of improvements in overseas transport and the opening of farmlands in North and South America), the resurgence of agricultural protectionism in France had begun in 1880 during the debate on the general tariff. Subsequently, the crisis deepened and the conversion of French farmers from free trade to protection accelerated. Though not again reaching the level of 1879, grain and flour imports remained high in the early 1880s, and this, coupled with the recovery of domestic production following the crop failures of 1878–1879, drove grain prices steadily downward, from 22 francs per hectoliter in 1881 to 16 francs in 1885.[5] Producers of most other foodstuffs suffered similar price falls. Accordingly, the Société des agriculteurs soon abandoned the moderate stand on the tariff it had maintained in 1878–1881. In November 1884, it

4. For most commodities the level of foreign imports in the 1880s was below the level of the 1870s. For example, the value of iron and steel imports, which rose from 13–15 million francs in the mid-1870s to a peak of 27 million francs in 1882, was down to 7–8 million francs by the late 1880s. Likewise, the value of imported cotton cloth, which amounted to 84 million francs in 1875, was only 41 million francs in 1888 (*Annales du commerce extérieur*, no. 120, pp. 34–37; *Tableau décennal*, I, 179 ff.; II, 194 ff.).

5. *Annuaire statistique*, 13 (1890), 503.

organized the first of a series of national agricultural conventions to rally all French farmers—large and small—to a program of higher tariffs on livestock and grain (it was unwittingly aided in this effort by the extension of rural roads and railroads, begun in 1881, which brought more and more peasant farmers into the national market economy in the course of the eighties and thereby sensitized them to the tariff issue by exposing them to the effects of foreign competition for the first time). The mobilization of grain and meat producers in the cause of protection was soon matched by the mobilization of Midi winegrowers. Although wine prices remained stable in the 1880s, the winegrowers of southern France could no longer produce enough to supply their markets—or to maintain their incomes—because of the progressive spread of the phylloxera blight. As a result, what had been a trickle of foreign wine imports in the 1870s became a flood by the 1880s, posing a threat to the Midi winegrowers equal to that of the phylloxera. Consequently, in 1887 they formed the Syndicat des viticulteurs to push for higher duties on imported wine and, more immediately, to fight the government's efforts to renegotiate the recently renounced trade treaty with Italy, under which the Italians had sent to France wine valued at 89.7 million francs—nearly one-fifth of France's imports—in 1886.[6]

With the protectionist mood holding firm in industry and increasing in agriculture, parliamentary representatives of each soon overcame the mutual suspicion that prevented their cooperation during the general tariff debate in 1880–1881, and in the mid-1880s they launched a coordinated assault on the existing tariff policies.[7] First, in December 1884, they undercut the free trade regime for colonies, dating from 1866, by attaching a rider to the budget bill that required the assimilation of Algerian tariffs to those of metropolitan France (this reform was particularly coveted by metallurgists competing with foreigners in the supply-

6. On wine imports, see ibid., p. 505. On the founding of the winegrowers' syndicate, see Hilsheimer, "Interessengruppen und Zollpolitik," p. 95.

7. A crucial step in bringing the agricultural and industrial protectionists together was taken in 1884 by Jules Méline, who, in his second year as minister of agriculture, endorsed high duties on farm products—reversing his previous position—and thereby swung industrial protectionists behind the protection of agriculture for the first time (Nicole Heber-Suffren-Lévèque, "Méline, ministre de l'agriculture, 1883–1885," *Annales de l'Est*, 5th ser., 16 [1964], 359).

ing of rails to North Africa). In 1887, tariff assimilation was
applied to Indochina as well.[8] Meanwhile, in 1885 and again in
1887, the protectionist bloc won new increases in the duties on
livestock and grain, which were exempt from the trade treaties.
The duty on oxen, for example, was raised from 15 francs per
head to 38 francs; the duty on cows was raised from 8 francs to 20
francs and that on calves from 1F50 to 8 francs; on sheep it was
raised from 2 to 5 francs. Most striking, the duty on wheat was
raised eightfold, from a token 60 centimes per 100 kilograms to 5
francs. At the same time, beyond parliament, the winegrowers
won a comparable victory when the government ended efforts to
conclude a new trade treaty with Italy and imposed "war tariffs"
on imported Italian wine which soon reduced the value of those
imports from a peak of 97.3 million francs in 1887 to a mere 1.3
million francs in 1890.[9]

To consolidate these gains and, more important, to eliminate
the trade treaties once and for all and to replace the existing
general and conventional tariffs with a much higher schedule of
duties, the AIF and the Société des agriculteurs agreed in 1888 to
work closely together in the upcoming parliamentary review of
the tariff system. The next year they commenced their agitation in
earnest during the election of the Chamber of Deputies. The tariff
question did not dominate this election any more than it had
dominated the elections of 1877 or 1881.[10] Nevertheless, in 1889
the protectionists pressured candidates more systematically than

8. Arthur Girault, *The Colonial Tariff Policy of France* (Oxford, 1916), pp. 81–133.

9. Golob, *The Méline Tariff*, pp. 152–159; *Annales du commerce extérieur*, no. 120, p. 130.

10. In any given election under the Third Republic—including that of 1889—the small size of French electoral districts made it unlikely that both free trade and protectionist interests would be strong in any one district. More likely, all candidates in a given district—whether of the Left or the Right—would be in agreement on the tariff, favoring either free trade or protection according to what interests dominated the area. Thus the tariff question tended to pit one region against another instead of dividing voters within a particular district, and thus it rarely became an electoral issue (although, in the national context, it was surely as important as those things that *were* electoral issues). For a discussion of the protectionists' inability to make the tariff an electoral issue in 1877, see Michael S. Smith, "Free Trade, Protection, and Tariff Reform: Commerce and Industry in French Politics, 1868–1882," Ph.D. dissertation, Cornell University, 1972, pp. 188–194.

ever before, and they succeeded in extracting pledges of support from many winning candidates. Then they made good on these pledges by organizing formal blocs in the Chamber during the fall legislative session. By December 5, a unified Left-Right agricultural bloc of three to four hundred deputies had come into being under the presidency of Méline. Simultaneously, Wadding-ton and Dautresme formed an industrial bloc, the "groupe du travail national."[11] Together these protectionist blocs engi-neered the creation of a permanent tariff commission, which was to serve as their vehicle for the protectionist revision of the tariff.[12]

The protectionists did not have to depend on this body as much as they first thought because, in contrast to the earlier round of tariff reform in which the government was resolutely liberal, events in 1890 led to the formation of a government amenable to increased protection. In March, various opponents of the Tirard cabinet put it in the minority on a vote in the Senate concerning ongoing commercial negotiations with the Ottoman Empire. This did not represent a formal vote of no confidence, but Tirard, well known by then for having "tender skin" on economic questions,[13] decided to resign anyway. He was succeeded by Charles de Freycinet who, ever sensitive to the drift of opinion in parliament and in the public at large, vowed at the outset to cooperate with the protectionists in the upcoming tariff reform.[14] He received strong backing from the Conseil supérieur du com-merce et de l'industrie and the Conseil supérieur de l'agriculture, which had already been commissioned to conduct inquiries on

11. Hilsheimer, "Interessengruppen und Zollpolitik," pp. 175–176; *Le travail national*, December 8, 1889.

12. The permanent Chamber Tariff Commission first met in January 1890, with Méline presiding. According to Augustin Hamon and Georges Bachot (*La France politique et sociale: Année 1890*, 2 vols. [Paris, 1891], I, 40), its membership consisted of eight free traders, eight free traders "in principle" who were nonethe-less "disposed to vote certain duties," ten moderate protectionists, and twenty-nine "protectionnistes irréducibles."

13. Charles de Freycinet, *Souvenirs, 1878–1893*, 4th ed. (Paris, 1913), p. 435.

14. Freycinet's ministerial declaration stated that "the country has affirmed its wish to revise the basis of its tariff system . . . it demands, after a thoughtful study, more effective protection for agriculture and national enterprise [*travail*]. The government adheres to this thought without reservation" (*Journal officiel, Débats parlementaires*, Chambre des députés, March 18, 1890, p. 563 [quoted in Golob, *The Méline Tariff*, p. 173, and Barral, "Les groupes de pression,"; p. 425]).

the tariff question and to draw up recommendations. In polling interested parties, both councils discovered a strong shift toward protectionism since the tariff reform of a decade earlier. Consequently, both proposed that the existing legislated general tariff and the negotiated conventional tariff be replaced by two legislated tariffs—a maximum and a minimum (the latter to be applied to countries giving France their best terms)—with duties in both pegged substantially above those in the existing general and conventional tariffs. With minor changes, the government incorporated these recommendations in the tariff bill it submitted to the Chamber in October 1890.[15]

By proposing a protectionist tariff bill, the government virtually precluded at the outset any further liberalization of the French tariff system. To be sure, there were still men in France who desired such a liberalization and, after years of inactivity, they mobilized inside and outside parliament in 1890–1891. In particular, "comités de défense" appeared in the seaports and in various centers of wool, silk, and wine production. Their actions in turn were coordinated through a central committee headed by Georges Berger, deputy for the Seine, who had gilt-edged free trade credentials (he was a brother-in-law of Gustave Roy, the Paris importer, and was also tied by marriage to the Cruse family, Bordeaux wine exporters). Berger also participated in a free trade parliamentary caucus—the "groupe industriel, commercial, et maritime"—along with Edouard Lockroy of Paris, Edouard Aynard of Lyons, Jules Charles-Roux of Marseilles, and David Raynal of Bordeaux.[16] Because of the government's stance on tariff reform and the protectionists' domination of the Chamber

15. On the inquiry of the Conseil supérieur du commerce, see AN F^{12} 6367, 6418, 6916, and 6917, and Conseil supérieur du commerce et de l'industrie, *Enquête sur le régime douanier. Questionnaire. Analyse sommaire des réponses* (Paris, 1890). For its deliberations and recommendations, see Conseil supérieur, *Enquête sur le régime douanier. Examen des tarifs de douane*, 2 vols. (Paris, 1890). No comparable files or published proceedings are available for the Conseil supérieur de l'agriculture. For discussions of its work, drawn from press accounts, see Golob, *The Méline Tariff*, pp. 147–157, and Hilsheimer, "Interessengruppen und Zollpolitik," pp. 250–263. For the tariff bill, see *Journal officiel, Documents parlementaires*, Chambre des députés, 1890, session extraordinaire, pp. 1 ff.

16. On Berger, see Gustave Roy, *Souvenirs, 1823–1906* (Nancy, 1906); on the free trade bloc, Hilsheimer, "Interessengruppen und Zollpolitik," pp. 184–198.

Tariff Commission, however, these free traders lacked the leverage in 1890 and 1891 that they had had in 1878–1882. Despite their prominence and eloquence in the tariff debates that unfolded in the Chamber between April and July 1890 and in the Senate during November and December, they were unable to split the agricultural and industrial protectionists, as they had done in 1880, and thus they failed to control the outcome.

That the free traders did not dominate the tariff reform of 1890–1891 did not mean that the protectionists had their way completely. Though not a majority in parliament, the free traders represented powerful interests. Recognizing this, the Freycinet government did not aim solely at satisfying the demands of industry and agriculture for more protection, but sought to find a tariff acceptable to all interested parties, free trade and protectionist alike. The commerce minister, Jules Roche, made this policy clear in his introduction to the government's tariff bill. "We have not thought it wise," he wrote, "to pass abruptly from one extreme to the other in the matter of economic policy. [Rather] we think it possible to give satisfaction to the complaints raised against the present regime without renouncing the essential advantages that that regime assures."[17] As a result, the government was willing to preserve the conventional tariff in the form of a legislatively determined minimum tariff (over the protests of the Société des agriculteurs). It also meant that, while raising duties on many items in both the general and conventional (minimum) tariff, it was willing to raise them only so far. Indeed, although the government's recommended duties were identical to those of the AIF and Société des agriculteurs on some items (wheat and other grains, most textiles, and most metals), on other items (wine, livestock, domestically produced raw fibers, hemp yarn and tissues, strings and cords, heavy cotton yarn, iron wire, and others), the government's recommendations were substantially below the protectionists'. The protectionists on the tariff commission were thus forced to draft an alternate schedule of duties and to seek its substitution for the government's schedule in a parliamentary floor fight, just as in 1880. But, also as in 1880, their

17. *Journal officiel, Documents parlementaires,* Chambre des députés, 1890, session extraordinaire, p. 1.

success was limited. They won increases on some foodstuffs against government opposition, but they had to compromise on duties on manufactures and industrial raw materials. How this compromise was achieved is perhaps best revealed in the handling of duties on cotton yarn, which had long been a major point of conflict between free traders and protectionists in France.

In 1882 the cloth manufacturers of the Loire and Rhône and the tulle makers of Calais, who favored free entry of cotton yarn, had won a major victory over French cotton spinners when, through ratification of the trade treaties, parliament maintained the existing duties on most cotton yarn and actually lowered the duties on twisted yarn. Shortly afterward, these "free traders" won an additional victory when the government honored a recommendation of the Conseil supérieur du commerce and decreed the temporary admission of fine cotton yarns (those numbered above 50)—that is, these were exempt from all import duties if used in the manufacture of cloth for export. Indeed, in 1885, they almost won extension of the temporary admission system to all other cotton yarns as well; only through a concerted effort in parliament, backed by grass-roots protests, did the cotton spinners block such a move.[18] In any case, it was to end these recently established duty-free admissions of fine cotton yarn and to set a minimum duty on all cotton yarns well above that of 1882 that cotton spinners remained active in the AIF in the 1880s and, through their positions on the Conseil supérieur du commerce and the Chamber Tariff Commission, took charge of the drafting of the new tariff in 1890. Instituting high protection of cotton yarns nevertheless proved to be an exceedingly difficult undertaking.

In the Conseil supérieur, the reporter on textiles was the Mayenne cotton manufacturer, Gustave Denis. Although a resolute protectionist, Denis found that he had to contend with—and eventually come to terms with—representatives of Loire-Rhône weaving on the council who were demanding lower duties on cotton yarns. Consequently, he ended up recommending a schedule of duties on cotton yarn, later incorporated in the govern-

18. On the entire controversy on temporary admission of cotton yarn, consult AN F¹² 6954.

ment tariff bill, which was higher than the existing schedule but well below what Méline and the Chamber Tariff Commission deemed necessary in 1879 and well below what cotton spinners were demanding in 1890, and it is not surprising that the Chamber's subcommission on textiles, led by Richard Wadding-ton, challenged this recommendation and formulated a more protective substitute schedule.[19] Of even greater concern to the protectionists was the clause placed in the bill by Roche to placate weaving interests which extended the policy of temporary admis-sion to all cotton yarn, not just those above number 50. Leading cotton spinners viewed the defeat of this clause as so vital that Méline, the chairman of the Chamber Tariff Commission, and Pierre Legrand, its reporter on textiles, persuaded their colleagues on the commission to set aside Waddington's substitute duties and to accept the government's schedule in order better to focus their attack on temporary admissions (Méline believed that it was preferable to have moderately protective duties without tempor-ary admissions than high duties with temporary admissions; more to the point, he feared that the voting of high duties on cotton yarn would persuade many deputies that the weavers' demands for temporary admissions were justified and would thereby virtually guarantee the approval of such a policy).[20] Thus, when the debate on cotton yarn opened in the Chamber on July 9, the tariff commission eschewed a floor fight with the government over the schedule of duties, such as had occurred in 1880. A fight over temporary admissions, however, became all but inevitable.

The debate began with an effort by extreme cotton protection-ists, led by Jules Delafosse of Vire (Calvados) and Louis Ricard of Rouen, to substitute Waddington's recommendations on the lower numbers of cotton yarn for the government's (Wadding-

19. For example, on number 28 unfinished yarn, the bellwether of French cotton tariffs, the subcommission recommended a minimum duty of 32 francs per quintal, versus the 25 franc duty recommended by the government and the 20 franc duty in the existing conventional tariff (AN C 5464, Chambre des députés, Commission générale des douanes, Procès-verbaux des séances, vol. IV, session of December 23, 1890).

20. Méline to Chamber, Journal officiel, Débats parlementaires, July 9, 1891, p. 1710.

ton himself had moved over to the Senate by this time). With help from Méline and moderate protectionists, the government easily defeated this motion and thereupon won preliminary approval of its schedule of duties. But the short-lived government-protectionist front broke up when Roche strongly endorsed an expanded temporary admissions system and, with the support of the free trade bloc, secured its passage. Having supported the government's duties only on the condition that temporary admissions would be eliminated, Méline now called for the rejection of those duties in the final vote on the schedule of duties and temporary admissions together. Consequently, the duties and temporary admissions, already approved separately, were defeated as a package. Tiring of the controversy, the Chamber approved a motion maintaining the status quo on cotton yarn duties (that is, the existing conventional duties were to become the minimum duties and temporary admission was to continue for yarns above number 50).[21] For the moment, the cotton spinners were back where they had started and, if anyone had achieved a victory, it was the Loire-Rhône "free traders." Incensed by this outcome, Delafosse spoke for all representatives of cotton spinning districts when he threatened to withdraw his support for increased duties on other commodities in retaliation and thereby shatter the protectionist alliance:

> For two months we have voted considerable increases in duties for the benefit of all industries; these increases will weigh heavily on spinning, yet it alone—being the most endangered of all industries—will not attain its due level of compensation. Consequently, when the general tariff returns from the Senate, we must closely reexamine the proposed duties. For my part, I pledge to reject all new duties for other industries, which I have previously supported, and I will keep my word![22]

But the protectionists remained united, for in December the Senate worked out a settlement on yarn duties acceptable to Delafosse and the cotton spinners as well as to the yarn-importing

21. Ibid., July 9, 1891, pp. 1688–1710; July 11, 1891, pp. 1735–1760.
22. Ibid., July 11, 1891, p. 1760, quoted in André Daniel, ed., *L'année politique: 1891* (Paris, 1892), p. 188.

weavers. By the terms of this settlement duties were raised on the lower gauges of cotton yarns—particularly numbers 20–40—which were most threatened by foreign competition.[23] On number 28 unfinished yarn, for example, the duty was set at 28 francs per quintal, which split the difference between the government's recommendation and the textile subcommission's. The cotton spinners also got the revocation of temporary admissions on cotton yarn. On the other hand, the weaving interests were accommodated by the setting of minimum duties on yarns numbered above 40 at only 10 francs more than the old conventional duty, which represented an average hike of 15 percent (by contrast, the duty on number 28 constituted a 40 percent increase). More important, in lieu of the abolished temporary admission system, which had applied only to high gauges of yarn, a procedure was established to reimburse cloth manufacturers 60 percent of the duties on all gauges of imported yarns used in exported cloth and to reimburse them up to 100 percent in the case of exported lace, tulle, and muslins.[24] In this way the government's goal of striking a balance among interests on yarn duties—a goal even shared by Méline and the Chamber Tariff Commission—was ultimately achieved.

The compromise on cotton yarn was not unique. In the making of the Méline tariff, similar compromises were struck on linen and hemp yarn, textile machinery, and many other manufactures.[25] The spirit of compromise was also seen on the issue of

23. Waddington estimated that 96 percent of all cotton yarns imported into France were numbered below 60 and that fully 57 percent were in the 20s (AN C 5464, Chambre des députés, Commission générale des douanes, Procès-verbaux des séances, vol. IV).

24. See the terms of the final tariff law in *Bulletin de statistique et de législation comparée,* 31 (1891-I), 12 ff.

25. On lower and middle gauges of linen and hemp yarn, parliament approved a moderate increase in duties, but it rejected the even higher duties recommended by the Chamber Tariff Commission for hemp. Moreover, on the higher gauges of both, it voted the status quo (that is, the old conventional duty became the minimum duty) against the wishes of both the government and the tariff commission. In the realm of textile machinery, the government recommended a minimum duty of 10 francs per quintal—the existing conventional duty—on looms for specialty weaving. The Chamber Tariff Commission recommended a much higher duty: 27 francs. The compromise solution called for a duty of 5 francs on tulle and lace looms, 27 francs on knitting and hosiery looms (based on a

industrial raw materials. The Méline tariff maintained the free entry of raw silk and cocoons, flax, hemp, wool, and oleaginous seeds, despite the vigorous protests of the domestic producers of those commodities. But in compensation, subsidies were granted to silk, hemp, and flax growers, while wool raisers were expected to benefit from higher duties on imported sheep. Similarly, the domestic milling and food processing industry was compensated for the raising of wheat duties in 1887 by the maintenance of temporary admission of wheat (temporary admissions were continued on most items previously eligible except, of course, cotton yarn). Moreover, in many cases where import duties were raised in the late 1880s or in 1892, the effects on domestic importers were eventually mitigated by the negotiation and ratification of trade conventions that reduced many of France's minimum duties below the level set in the Méline tariff (this was possible because in May 1891 the protectionists failed in their bid to insert a clause in the new tariff law expressly forbidding the negotiation of conventional duties below the legislation minimum). Specifically, in negotiating most-favored-nation agreements with Russia (1893), Switzerland (1895, 1905), and Italy (1898), France lowered its minimum duties on petroleum, silk cloth and yarn, milk, cheese, wine, various kinds of machinery, and other items. When extended to other nations by the action of the most-favored-nation clause, these new "consolidated" duties came to constitute, in all but name, a new conventional tariff.[26]

In the final analysis, then, the tariff system that emerged out of all the committee hearings, parliamentary debates, and international negotiations of the 1890s was a cross between free trade and protection. The hybrid nature of the tariff was reflected in its structure: the minimum-maximum system in essence combined the protectionists' general tariff and the free traders' conventional tariff. It was reflected even more in the schedule of duties. The Méline tariff effected an overall shift toward protection relative to the conventional duties in operation from 1860 to 1892 but did

comparison of the final tariff [ibid.] and the recommendations of the government and tariff commission [*Journal officiel, Documents parlementaires*, 1891, ii, 895 ff.]).

26. Augier, *La France et les traités de commerce*, pp. 68–81.

not entail an increase in all duties. Duties on foodstuffs, cotton and linen textiles, and machinery and other sophisticated metallurgical products were raised, but those on coal and coke, iron and steel, woolen and silk textiles, and many other manufactures remained the same. Some—those on rolled steel and iron, for example—were lowered.[27] By and large, the new schedule of duties struck a balance between what the protectionists wanted (and what was in effect before 1860) and what the free traders wanted (or what was in effect, 1860–1892). In other words, despite the apparent rise of the protectionists and the apparent decline of the free traders in the 1880s and early 1890s, the second and definitive stage of tariff reform under the Third Republic ended in compromise, not in a one-sided protectionist victory. To understand why this happened and why the compromise took the form it took, the making of the Méline tariff must be viewed in the larger context of the accommodation of interests. For just as the tariff reform of 1878–1882 makes sense only when seen as part of the battle among various interests for advantage and preferment, the compromise policy of the 1890s makes sense only when seen as part of an effort to reconcile all interests in the name of economic stability and political solidarity.

The Interests Accommodated

While the battle between doctrinaire free traders and protectionists dominated the French business scene in the late nineteenth century, the idea was emerging (or reemerging) that lawmakers and government officials should eschew excessive concern with economic doctrines and turn their attention to devising policies that would promote, balance, and reconcile—in a word, accommodate—all major economic interests in France. This idea found expression as early as 1860 in J. du Mesnil-Marigny's tract, *Les protectionnistes et les libre-échangistes conciliés*. It also surfaced in the deliberations of chambers of commerce, such as those of Saint-Etienne and Marseilles, which included representatives of both free trade interests and protec-

27. To compare the duties of 1892 with those in previous tariffs, consult Appendix 2.

tionist interests and thus sought a middle way in tariff policy to assure domestic tranquillity. Indeed, in the 1870s the Saint-Etienne Chamber of Commerce believed it had already found in the existing tariff policy the basis for reconciling the conflicting interests within its jurisdiction, and, in describing its local situation to the Chamber Tariff Commission in 1878, it previewed the pattern, and even more the spirit, of accommodation that took hold nationally later on:

> At Saint-Etienne [the reporter, Jules Euverte, wrote] coal, iron, steel, arms—none of which could live without compensatory duties—are juxtaposed to ribbon, velvet, passementerie, laces, elastics, etc., which defy all competition and demand only the freedom to reach the whole world. With such diverse interests present, one might well expect permanent conflict here . . . [but] under the influence of the idea of conciliation we have found, after a time of trial, a meeting ground where all can be assured of a tolerable economic situation.
> Those on one side have understood that it is necessary to renounce any notion of exaggerated protection and that it is necessary to facilitate exchange by all means; they have unreservedly rallied to the treaties of commerce of 1860. Those on the other side, recognizing that certain industries are closely tied to natural conditions impossible to modify and that they can survive only in the shelter of compensatory duties, have accepted the necessity of such duties. The treaties of 1860 have thus become the basis for an accommodation.[28]

Many other interests did not find "a basis for accommodation" in the treaties of the 1860s and, in any case, the voices of those calling for accommodation were effectively drowned out by the continued squabbling between free traders and protectionists in the sixties and seventies. In the late 1880s, however, they began to find an audience among the political leaders of the Third Republic. This interest in an accommodation was perhaps a by-product of the depression and the attendant social and political unrest in France (manifested most clearly in the Boulanger phenomenon), which seemed to demonstrate the need to concil-

28. Report of the Saint-Etienne Chamber of Commerce, March 24, 1878, AN C 3224.

iate as many economic interests as possible to assure maximum support for the bourgeois Republic and the capitalist system. But, whatever the origins of the rising concern for the accommodation of interests, it is clear that the achievement of such an accommodation had become an explicit government objective by 1890, when Jules Roche acceded to the Ministry of Commerce.

Roche set out to create an economic policy—and particularly a tariff policy—that would balance the demands of all interests and maintain a mixed economy in France.[29] His search for compromise, conciliation, and equilibration was aided by the give-and-take of interests in the parliamentary arena (aptly demonstrated in the working out of import duties on cotton yarn) and also by the growing willingness of both free trade and protectionist spokesmen to set aside economic dogma to promote and preserve specific interests. For example, in seeking election as deputy for the Hérault in 1889, Paul Leroy-Beaulieu abandoned his strict adherence to free trade and called for greater protection of the Midi wine industry. Likewise, Maurice Rouvier called for higher duties on olive oil, and Georges Berger, leader of the commercial bloc in parliament, supported protection of electrical appliances.[30] On the other side, Jules Méline departed from his ultraprotectionist position in late 1892 when he supported negotiating duties below the legislated minimum on some items in order to preserve French trade with Switzerland.[31] As a result of all these developments, the accommodation of interests, which had begun in the 1870s in some industries (mining and metallurgy)

29. Roche spelled out his intentions in a speech at Marseilles on October 9, 1891: "For us, the words protection and free trade have no magical powers which allow us to dispense with the study of the facts themselves. To be sure, we are constrained in all cases to protect and encourage national enterprise, but we have never thought there was only one way to attain that end—that is, through the establishment of elevated customs duties on all products without distinction. . . . [Instead] we have resigned outselves in advance to attaining, in many cases, only compromise solutions, happy if we succeed . . . in holding a balance among the diverse interests for which we are responsible" (Chamber of Commerce of Marseilles, *Compte-rendu des travaux pour l'année 1891* [Marseilles, 1892], p. 369).

30. Hilsheimer, "Interessengruppen und Zollpolitik," p. 95; Golob, *The Méline Tariff*, p. 191.

31. AN C 5465, Commission générale des douanes, Procès-verbaux des séances, vol. ix (December 1891–November 1892).

and in some regions (the Loire), became general in the early 1890s and was ultimately institutionalized in the Méline tariff. How this tariff served to accommodate all interests has been partially revealed in the previous section, but can be elucidated more fully by examining the main divisions of the French economy—agriculture, industry, commerce, and finance—as they stood in the last decade of the nineteenth century.

In French agriculture, the accommodation of interests centered on a return to protection. Duties raised piecemeal in 1885 and 1887 were confirmed and consolidated in the Méline tariff, then raised higher in the late 1890s and in the tariff of 1910. Of course, protection did not cure all of agriculture's ills: prices on foodstuffs remained low in the 1890s, and prices on wine, which had been high in the 1880s, fell drastically in the late 1890s when domestic production increased. Moreover, it is problematical to what extent protection was responsible for the eventual general recovery of French agriculture in the early twentieth century.[32] But tariffs probably did serve one vital function: the reduction or containment of foreign imports. The average annual value of grain imports, which stood at 365 million francs in the 1880s, fell to 333 million in the 1890s (295 million if 1898 is omitted) and 159 million in 1900–1909. Similarly, the value of wine imports declined from 392 million francs in the eighties to 125 million after 1900. The value of livestock imports, which peaked at 187 million francs in 1883, fell to 64 million francs in 1891 and to 26 million in 1900.[33] This meant that, whatever its internal problems, French agriculture did not suffer the fate of British agriculture, which was virtually destroyed in this period by the influx of cheap foodstuffs from the New World. Agriculture survived as a major sector of the French economy and this in turn had crucial social implications (the survival of the French peasantry) and equally crucial political implications (the maintenance of peas-

32. For a discussion of the agricultural recovery, see Pierre Barral, *Les agrariens français de Méline à Pisani* (Paris, 1968), pp. 93–98.
33. The figures on grain and wine imports are computed from data in Golob, *The Méline Tariff*, pp. 68, 236. The figures on livestock imports are taken from *Annales du commerce extérieur*, no. 120, pp. 30–31; no. 129, pp. 56–57.

ant support for the Republic), which will be mentioned in the conclusion. For now we need only to note further that there were limits to the protection offered agriculture. While duties on foodstuffs were raised, duties on industrial raw materials (wool, flax, oil seeds) were rejected. This selective compliance with agriculture's demands in turn reflected the government's and parliament's desire to accommodate industry as well as agriculture. We can get a more precise view of this second level of accommodation by looking at those industries most interested in tariff policy—mining, metallurgy, and textiles.

As we saw in Chapter 2, the mining and metallurgical firms in the AIF worked out a program of economic reforms acceptable to all among them in 1878. This program included the continuation of existing import duties on coal, pig iron, and most basic forms of iron and steel (including rails) and the raising of duties on specialized forms of iron, such as tinplate and fine iron wire, and on most metallurgical manufactures. The program did not prescribe a policy on temporary admission of pig iron since that remained in dispute among AIF members, but it did demand improvement and enlargement of the French transportation system and the reduction of railroad freight rates. In seeking implementation of this program between 1878 and 1882, the colliers and metallurgists were only partially successful. To be sure, they were given the Freycinet plan, which promised to solve their transport problems even as it provided increased demand for their products. But they received no relief on freight rates and relatively little consideration on tariff policy. The tariff reform of 1881–1882 maintained the 1F20 duty on coal, as requested, but it reduced duties on pig iron (from 20 francs per ton to 15), on iron and steel rails (from 60 to 50 francs per ton), and on tinplate (from 130 francs to 120), and existing duties were maintained on many items for which higher duties were demanded, such as iron wire.

Thus, in sum, the economic policy making of 1878–1882 only began the process of accommodating mining and metallurgy, but it did establish a pattern of accommodation. This pattern was characterized first by a tendency to promote basic industries by

means other than tariffs (while reserving tariffs for highly finished goods), and second by a tendency to accommodate the
largest and/or most politically influential industries at the
expense of smaller, less influential industries. Once established,
this pattern can be discerned in all subsequent tariff reform. At
the same time, the tendency to favor export industries over
domestically oriented industries—which was dominant in
1860–1882—declined in the 1880s and 1890s and was replaced by a
greater effort to accommodate all industries, whether export-
oriented or not.

The accommodation of the coal industry after 1882 centered on
the producers of the Nord and Pas-de-Calais, who were increasingly dominating the national market,[34] and, in line with their
demands, it consisted mainly of modifications in transport and
railroad policy. Specifically, the Compagnie du Nord steadily
reduced its freight rates on northern coal in the 1880s, while by
contrast the P-L-M continued to charge the southern colliers
considerably higher rates. Just as important, it established with
neighboring railroads a low joint rate that facilitated the marketing of Nord coal in other parts of France, especially in the rapidly
growing metallurgy centers of Lorraine.[35] As a result, Nord's
share of the coal market in eastern France rose rapidly at the
expense of the Belgians in the 1890s, and it became increasingly
clear that import duties on coal were not needed to extend
markets or raise price levels.[36] Indeed, as the colliers realized even
in 1878, raising duties would have been politically counterpro-
ductive. Therefore, in 1891 they were content to see the existing
nominal duties on coal and coke continued. As in the past these
duties served primarily as a subsidy, as icing on the cake of
production and profits which, even without the duties, would

34. Total French coal production did not quite double between 1878 and 1900,
but the production of the Nord–Pas-de-Calais coalfield tripled. Thus its percentage of the French total rose from 40 percent in 1878 to 60 percent in the early
1900s. For the statistics, see Marcel Gillet, *Les charbonnages du nord de la France
au XIXe siècle* (Paris, 1973), pp. 471, 478–479.

35. Caron, *Histoire de l'exploitation*, pp. 368, 409.

36. After slumping in the late 1870s and 1880s, prices on Nord coal rose again in
the 1890s although they would not return to the level of the early 1870s until the
twentieth century (Gillet, *Les charbonnages du nord*, pp. 478–479).

have expanded in the 1890s because of the economic recovery in general and the expansion of metallurgy in particular.[37]

Just as the accommodation on coal focused primarily on the Nord–Pas-de-Calais branch of the industry, so, too, the accommodation of metallurgy focused primarily, but not exclusively, on the pig iron and steel producers of the North and Northeast. This followed naturally from the sudden shift in French metallurgy's center of gravity in the 1880s when the introduction of the Thomas-Gilchrist basic steel process made possible the efficient utilization of Lorraine iron ore and Pas-de-Calais coal in steel-making for the first time. Iron and steel production grew by leaps and bounds throughout the eighties and nineties in the Nord, Pas-de-Calais, Ardennes, and especially the Meurthe-et-Moselle. Already France's largest pig iron producer in 1880, the Meurthe-et-Moselle expanded its output in the next twenty years, from 538,132 tons to 1,669,189 tons. Just as important, the department's pig iron producers added steel mills to their blast furnaces (seen in the founding of the Aciéries de Longwy by Adelsward and Labbé in 1881), and steelmakers from elsewhere, such as the Schneiders of Le Creusot, set up new plants in the department to utilize the newly available ores. Consequently, the Meurthe-et-Moselle's steel output—an insignificant 1,497 tons in 1880—rose to 41,265 tons by 1887 and 271,405 tons (largest in France) by 1900.[38] The department of the Nord—already France's second

37. For similar reasons, the southern colliers, though not favored in railroad policy as were the northern colliers and not expanding production at their rate, if at all, continued to sell—at favorable prices—as much coal as they could or would produce. Thus they had no more need for a stringent tariff than did the Nord–Pas-de-Calais colliers, although they did have reason to complain about the nonapplication of the existing tariff (in the 1880s, Graffin of the declining Grand'-combe mine protested that British coal could be unloaded directly from British to French ships in Marseilles harbor without paying the 1F20 duty, which helped to cut the colliers of the Gard out of that segment of the Marseilles market; see "Voeu formulé au Conseil général du Gard sur les moyens propres à conjurer la crise industrielle dans le bassin houille du Gard," AN F¹² 6848B).

38. These and subsequent statistics on the growth of iron and steel are taken from *Annuaire statistique*, 6 (1883), 314–317, and 21 (1901), 202–205. The growth of the Lorraine steel industry, well reflected in the figures for the Meurthe-et-Moselle, is equally well shown by statistics available for the Aciéries de Longwy. This firm increased the number of its employees from 793 in 1880 to 2,573 in 1894 and 5,959 by 1910; its pig iron production rose from 110,000 tons in 1888 to 300,000 by 1910; its output of steel ingots rose from 85,000 tons in 1893 to 255,000

largest pig iron producer and foremost iron producer in 1880—also became a center of steelmaking in the 1880s. Steel production there rose from 43,245 tons in 1880 to 87,664 tons in 1887 and 239,789 tons (second only to the Meurthe-et-Moselle) in 1900.

While the metallurgy of the North and Northeast expanded, the once dominant pig iron and steel centers of the Massif Central were unable to keep pace. Prevented from competing with Lorraine in a period of declining demand by the relatively high cost of its fuel and ore, the pig iron production of the Allier, Saône-et-Loire, Loire, Rhône, Ardèche, and Gard fell from 607,700 tons (34 percent of French production) in 1880 to 244,400 tons (17 percent) in 1887. The steel production of the region suffered a comparable decline. Indeed, in the Loire, which had produced more steel than any other department as late as 1880, virtually all Bessemer converters were extinguished by 1887, and Terrenoire, once France's largest producer of Bessemer steel, was in bankruptcy. Some firms of the area did, of course, survive and even expand in the 1880s and 1890s by shifting their pig iron and steel production to areas of cheaper coal and ore (in 1881 Marine steelworks began producing pig iron and steel with Spanish ore and English coal near Bayonne while Le Creusot invaded Lorraine) and by converting their facilities in the Massif Central to specialized, labor-intensive production such as the manufacture of steel plate, armaments, bicycles, and automobiles (Holtzer et Cie and the Aciéries de France in the Loire specialized in casting automobile parts, whereas Le Creusot in the Saône-et-Loire and Châtillon-Commentry in the Allier moved into arms production). Indeed, as these firms made the transition to high-quality manufacturing, the value of Loire's steel production would again rise to the highest in France by 1900, while the Saône-et-Loire's would be fourth largest. Still, the volume of that production would be insignificant compared to that of the Nord and the Meurthe-et-Moselle. There remained little doubt by the 1890s that the future of French metallurgy lay in the North and Northeast rather than the Center and the South.[39]

in 1910; and its annual turnover increased from 7 million francs in 1888 to 48 million francs by 1910 (Dreux dossier, AN F^{12} 8577).

39. On the development of the metallurgy of the Massif Central—especially that of the Loire—see L. Babu, "L'industrie métallurgique dans la région de Saint-

The shifting economic balance of power in French metallurgy soon altered the focus of government and parliamentary efforts to accommodate metallurgical interests, as was demonstrated by the revision of the temporary admissions policy for pig iron in 1888. As we saw earlier, the temporary duty-free admission of pig iron, which also entailed considerable permanent duty-free admissions along France's northern border through the trafficking in customs permits, had long pitted the *fonte* producers of the Meurthe-et-Moselle and the Nord, who naturally opposed the practice, against the iron and steelmakers of the Massif Central and certain northern metallurgical manufacturers, who benefited from it. In 1877 the government had ruled in favor of the latter interests when the Conseil supérieur du commerce, instead of requiring the reexportation of imported pig iron (*admissions temporaires à l'identique*), endorsed continuation of the policy of *admissions temporaires à l'équivalent*, which allowed the Massif Central producers, exporting goods made with domestic pig iron, to redeem at a profit permits purchased from northern manufacturers who had used them to bring in Belgian and Luxembourg *fontes*.[40] This did not really resolve the issue, however. With the depression idling twenty-one of their fifty-four blast furnaces in the mid-eighties, the Meurthe-et-Moselle *fonte* makers soon intensified their drive to have temporary admissions tightened up or eliminated.

In 1885, Arthur Mézières, deputy for Longwy, interpellated the government on this matter. Then, in 1886–1887, it was again brought before the Conseil consultatif des arts et manufactures and the Conseil supérieur du commerce. Terrenoire's director, Alexandre Jullien, appeared before both forums to defend the existing system, by which his declining firm received a modest bonus on exports. Jullien accused the Lorraine ironmakers of seeking a policy "which would render them masters of pig iron production in France," and he argued that the country would

Etienne," *Annales des mines*, 9th ser., 15 (1899-1), 421–462. See also Comité des forges de France, *La sidérurgie française, 1864–1914* (Paris, n.d.), pp. 115–166; François Crouzet, "Remarques sur l'industrie des armaments en France: Du milieu du XIXᵉ siècle à 1914," *Revue historique*, 251 (1974), 409–422.

40. Conseil supérieur du commerce, *Admissions temporaires* (Paris, 1877), p. 59.

gain more by favoring *fonte* users than by favoring *fonte* producers.[41] There was truth in Jullien's words, but, in light of the changing structure of French metallurgy, they carried little weight. Councillors who had seen the need to support Loire metallurgy on this question in 1877 saw with equal clarity the need to help Lorraine metallurgy ten years later. Consequently, both the Conseil consultatif and the Conseil supérieur voted to impose *transport a l'usine* ("transport to the plant") on temporarily admitted pig iron (that is, they voted to convert *admissions temporaires à l'équivalent* to *admissions temporaires à l'identique*).[42] To be sure, in acting upon these resolutions, the government struck the inevitable compromise. In January 1888, it decreed *transport à l'usine* on *fontes d'affinage* (pig iron to be refined into steel) but not on *fonte de moulage* (pig iron to be cast).[43] But this was really a minor modification meant to accommodate Pont-à-Mousson which supplemented its own pig iron production with Luxembourg *fonte* in the casting of iron pipe. It did not measurably lessen the economic impact of the council's decision—an impact epitomized by Terrenoire's failure in 1888 and by the sextupling of Longwy's profits between 1889 and 1892.[44] Nor did it alter the underlying political meaning of the council's recommendations: henceforth the government would never again promote the industries of the Massif Central at the expense of those of the North and Northeast. On the contrary, if forced to choose, it would support the latter over the former.

The accommodation of Nord-Lorraine metallurgy that began with the revision of the temporary admissions system in 1888 continued with the passage of the Méline tariff. Since they imported most of the coal and coke used in their smelters and converters, the Meurthe-et-Moselle metallurgists benefited from the Méline tariff's maintenance of low duties on those commodities (actually, they had demanded free trade for coal in 1878, so their acceptance of the 1F20 duty in 1891 was something of a

41. Address to the Conseil consultatif des arts et manufactures, AN F[12] 5337.

42. Conseil supérieur du commerce, *Admissions temporaires des fontes* (Paris, 1887).

43. Comité des forges, *La sidérurgie française*, p. 426.

44. Profits of the Aciéries de Longwy rose from 471,000 francs in 1889 to 3,042,375 francs in 1892 (Dreux dossier, AN F[12] 8577).

concession to industrial solidarity). The new tariff benefited the Nord-Lorraine metallurgists in other ways as well. In the 1890s many of them were coming to realize that their future prosperity might depend as much on exports as on domestic sales and that, to gain access to foreign markets, they would have to give up high import duties on their own products. As the Nancy Chamber of Commerce put it in 1890, "To obtain acceptable conditions in neighboring countries for the entry of our products, we must be ready to make concessions."[45] Thus, although the Nord-Lorraine metallurgists desired a measure of protection on the pig iron, iron, and steel they produced, they did not want import duties so high as to invite retaliation against their exports by foreign countries (besides, given their technical superiority, such duties were unnecessary to maintain their control of the domestic market). In the final analysis, the Méline tariff's maintenance of existing duties on basic forms of iron and steel served their purposes nicely.

If the Méline tariff paradoxically accommodated the interests of the Nord-Lorraine iron and steelmakers by not raising certain duties, it more predictably accommodated other branches of French metallurgy by giving them an added measure of protection. This was the case, for example, with metallurgical manufacturers such as J. J. Farcot and Batignolles, which were granted higher duties on steam engines, boilers, pumps, and the like in 1891 (while, at the same time, they benefited from continued low duties on basic iron and steel). It was also the case with the steelmakers of the Loire. Having just been forced out of basic iron and steel production by internal competition, these metallurgists were moving into production of axles, wheels, firearms, and various "pièces detachées," and in compensation they received higher duties on all these items. Likewise, the charcoal iron and steel producers of the Ardennes, Haute-Marne, and Doubs— denied special consideration in 1881–1882—were granted a new, high duty on fine tool steel plus significant increases in duties on iron and steel wire to counter the continuing Swedish threat. Finally, the tinplate producers, although not granted the broad

45. Deposition of the Chamber of Commerce of Nancy, AN F^{12} 6916.

increases demanded in 1878, did get more protection for the thin gauges of tinplate used in canning. Thus the message emerging from the second round of tariff reform was clear: henceforth the government would support all reasonably modern, viable metallurgical industries, not just those oriented to exports. No enterprise capable of surviving internal competition was to be sacrificed to foreign competitors in order to promote the exports of another enterprise, just as no enterprise dependent on foreign markets was to be denied those markets simply to promote the inordinate growth of domestic enterprises. While necessarily giving first consideration to the largest sectors of French metallurgy, the government nonetheless sought to accommodate all sectors, and the growth and prosperity manifested throughout the industry in the 1890s and 1900s seemed to confirm the wisdom and success of this intention.

In textiles, as in metallurgy, France departed in the 1890s from its previous policy of favoring export industries over domestically oriented industries and sought instead to accommodate all major industries. Also as in metallurgy, the search for accommodation did not simply result in a blanket increase in tariff protection but in the formulation of a mulitfaceted, hybrid policy. To be sure, this policy did include a significant increase in protection for cotton, linen, and jute manufacturers. But it accommodated silk and woolens producers through the maintenance of existing duties and the negotiation of trade conventions to keep foreign markets open. And, as we have seen, for producers of blends it provided loopholes in the application of cotton yarn duties to protect their access to foreign yarns. Moreover, to all textiles it offered low duties on imported coal, the expansion of the colonial market, and the free entry of raw materials. In other words, the new policy contained something for everyone. Indeed, the Méline tariff represented the government's commitment to establish the necessary, if not the sufficient, conditions for the survival and growth of all major textile industries, inasmuch as tariffs and related policies could accomplish this goal, and, under this policy, most textile industries did survive and prosper in the 1890s. If, in the last analysis, the protectionist industries benefited more from this policy than the free trade industries and fared better economically, they did so not from preferment but because the aid a government could give to domestically oriented industries was bound to be more efficacious, in an age of rising protectionism, than the aid it could give to export industries. (The French government could offer domestic industries positive support against foreign competitors with protective tariffs, but the government's dependence on tariff revenues kept it from recycling customs duties in the form of export subsidies; thus it could offer only the indirect aid of reducing barriers to foreign markets; in competing in those markets, French exporters were necessarily on their own.) In addition, the relatively greater success of protectionist textiles in the 1890s can also be traced to changing styles, changing technology, growing internal competition in home markets, and growing foreign competition in foreign markets—problems over which no tariff policy, however well designed, could exercise much control.

Thus in the silk-based textile industry of Lyons and Saint-Etienne, the slump that began in the late 1870s continued through the 1880s and into the 1890s despite the industry's victory in the tariff reform of 1881–1882, despite the expansion of temporary admissions of yarn in 1883, and despite the voting of continued protection of silk cloth and continued free entry of cocoons and raw silk, along with subsidies for silk spinning, in 1891.[46] Obviously, a favorable tariff policy by itself could not offset the serious problems the industry faced in the late nineteenth century—changing fashions and declining demand at home and abroad, growing competition from Milan in the silk trade, and growing competition from the Swiss and Germans in marketing silk manufactures in Europe and elsewhere. Only when conditions changed in some of these areas did Lyons recover. Specifically, as styles changed again in its favor, as the general economic recovery raised demand for luxury goods, and as technological modernization—such as the switch from hand

46. The bonuses on silk spinning did make a difference: the importation of cocoons, which fell from 1,961,445 kilograms in 1881 to 163,130 kilograms in 1890, had risen back to 1,278,481 kilograms by 1893. But meanwhile the value of exported silks, which had fallen from 301.2 million francs in 1883 to 210 million in 1887, stagnated at 220–245 million in the early 1890s (*Annales du commerce extérieur*, no. 120, pp. 91–93; no. 129, p. 97).

looms to power looms and the electrification of ribbon weaving—improved its position vis-à-vis foreign competitors, the Lyons industry experienced a rise in the value of its silk cloth exports, from around 200 million francs in the late 1880s to 278 million francs in 1899 (the highest level since 1883).[47] Of course this did not mean that the Lyonnais returned to the level of production of the early 1870s or regained the virtual monopoly in supplying silks and ribbons to Europe and America that had supported that level of production (the rise of silk industries elsewhere made such a recovery impossible). But it did mean that, with continued government aid in protecting the home market and in gaining as favorable a position in foreign markets as possible, the main branches of the Lyonnais industry—Saint-Etienne ribbon, Lyons plain and figured silks, Tarare blends—were able to stabilize their production and exports at the relatively high levels of the early 1880s by the turn of the century.

In woolens the government also sought to accommodate all major producers in the making of tariff policy in the 1890s, but as in silk this did not necessarily guarantee the success of all producers. The export-minded worsted industry of Reims, for example, lost business abroad in the 1880s, despite the renewal of the trade treaties in 1882, and at best only held its own in the following decade as the general economic malaise, the rise of worsted industries abroad, and the imposition of protective duties abroad all conspired to limit its share of the world market. As a consequence, it reduced the size of its plant and cut back production.[48] At the same time, the domestically oriented woolens industry of Elbeuf suffered a decline in output even though the high level of woolens imports, which had drawn the Elbeuvians into the AIF in 1878, decreased in the 1880s.[49] The primary cause

47. The recovery is best seen in decennal averages of silk export values (in millions of francs): 430 (1867–1876), 251 (1877–1886), 243 (1887–1896), 280 (1897–1906) (Emile Levasseur, *Histoire du commerce de la France*, 2 vols. [Paris, 1911–1912], ii, 760–763).

48. Figures in the *Annuaire statistique* indicate that, during the 1880s alone, the Reims plant contracted from 299,886 spindles to 210,000; from 8,540 power looms to 8,100; and from 1,619 hand looms to 310.

49. The value of woolen cloth imports rose through the 1870s and the early 1880s to a peak of 91.8 million francs in 1883 and then declined to 66.9 million

of this decline—and a secondary cause of Reims's troubles—was growing competition from the Roubaix-Tourcoing woolens and worsted industry. Instead of relying on tariff policy, this industry had long concentrated on upgrading its technology, on developing its sources of raw materials, and on getting maximum advantage from its location and resources.[50] The result was continuous expansion through the last quarter of the nineteenth century. Indeed, in the course of the 1880s and 1890s, Roubaix-Tourcoing became the largest center of wool combing in the world, accounting almost single-handedly for a jump in the value of France's wool exports from 103 million francs a year in 1877–1886 to 225 million francs a year in 1897–1906. Building on the foundation provided by wool combing, it also concentrated much of France's wool spinning and weaving in its mills at the expense of older centers such as Fourmies, Sedan, Louviers, and of course Reims and Elbeuf.[51] Thus, even as the government and parliament sought to tailor French tariff policy to the needs and circumstances of all sectors of the woolens industry, the decline of free trade Reims and protectionist Elbeuf and the rise of Roubaix-Tourcoing seemed to show that those industries which depended too much on trade policy—whether free trade or protection—would inevitably fall prey to those which emphasized technological excellence and entrepreneurial daring.

If tariff policy played only a secondary role in the successes and failures of the silk and woolens industries in the 1880s and 1890s, it played a primary role in the development of the jute and burlap industry of the Somme, the linen industry of Lille, and the cotton industry of the Nord, the Vosges, and Rouen, all of which had been frustrated by the tariff reform of 1878–1882 but won major increases in protection under the Méline tariff. Specifically, the

francs by 1890 and to 38.3 million by 1898 (*Annales du commerce extérieur*, no. 120, pp. 34–37; no. 129, pp. 46–47).

50. The Tourcoing Chamber of Commerce gave particular credit for the success of the local woolens industry to "the considerable effort taken to found counting houses in Australia, La Plata, Algeria, etc.—that is, in all centers for the production of the raw material—in order to eliminate the middlemen and to buy wool on the best possible terms" (deposition to the Conseil supérieur du commerce, 1890, AN F^{12} 6916).

51. Emile Levasseur, *Questions ouvrières et industrielles sous le Troisième République* (Paris, 1907), pp. 100–107.

jute industry gained virtually prohibitory duties on yarn and cloth, which abruptly cut off imports from its chief rival, Dundee, Scotland, in the 1890s and ended a long slide in prices.[52] Subsequently, the Saint brothers of the Somme, who as leaders of the AIF had forecast the imminent demise of their industry in 1878, were able to expand the spinning and weaving capacity of their plant at Flixecourt, and by the end of the nineties they had achieved a level of production three to four times that of 1878.[53] Increased tariffs were equally important for Lille linen manufacturers in the 1890s. Since the 1870s, French linen consumption had contracted continuously as the popularity of cotton rose, and French linen production had fallen accordingly. However, the decline was not experienced by all producers uniformly but only by the dispersed, unmechanized rural producers, such as those of the Mayenne, who lacked good sources of cheap flax and fuel. Possessing relatively modern equipment and a good supply of coal and flax, the Lille industry was able to keep its plant stable at five hundred thousand spindles even as the size of the national linen plant contracted. Indeed, by the 1890s Lille's five hundred thousand spindles constituted practically the entire French linen spinning capacity. To protect from foreign competition what thus amounted to a national monopoly in linen manufacture, the Lillois demanded and eventually won increases of 20 to 30 percent in import duties on linen yarns and even greater increases in linen cloth duties. Buttressed by such duties, the linen spinners were able by 1900 to form a cartel to set prices and production quotas for the whole industry and to dispel once and for all the specter of competition from the domestic market. In this way, tariff reform

52. The value of burlap bags and cloth imported from Great Britain fell from 3.4 million francs in 1891 to 700,000 francs in 1893 and 500,000 francs in 1899; the value of total imports of woven jute fell from 4.5 million francs (1891) to 670,000 (1899) and spun jute imports fell from 269,000 francs (1891) to 19,000 francs (1900) (*Annales du commerce extérieur*, no. 129, pp. 46–47, 124). Prices on spun jute fell from 80 centimes per kilogram (1880–1881) to 67 centimes in 1890, then rebounded to 80 centimes by 1899 (*Annales du commerce extérieur, Valeurs arbitrées*, no. 101 [1880–1881]; 1890–1891; 1899–1900).

53. In 1878 Saint Frères produced 24,500 kilos of yarn and 24,000 sacks a day and did business worth 15,882,655 francs for the year. In 1900, it produced 120,000 kilos of jute and hemp yarn and 84,000 sacks a day and did business worth 39,207,403 francs (Saint dossier, AN F[12] 5264).

guaranteed at least a modest prosperity for those who continued to produce linen in the 1890s and 1900s, although naturally it could do nothing to prevent linen's lingering death at the hands of rival textiles.[54]

In cotton as in jute and linen, increased protection was often crucial in allowing industries to survive and prosper amid growing foreign and domestic competition in the 1890s. For example, Saint-Quentin, unable to continue spinning cotton in the face of competition from Lille, nonetheless found a safe and stable niche within the national cotton industry by specializing in the manufacture of embroidered muslin curtains after import duties on these items were raised to a prohibitory level in 1892.[55] Even more important, increased protection under the Méline tariff allowed the ambitious and aggressive cotton spinners of Lille, Rouen, and the Vosges to take control of the domestic yarn market and eventually to cartelize production for it. Of course, as noted earlier, the import duties that these spinners obtained in 1891 were not as high as they wanted (that is, they were not inherently prohibitory). Since they were fixed specific duties rather than *ad valorem* duties, however, they came to represent an ever greater proportion of the value of imported yarns as prices fell in the 1890s. Indeed, by 1899 prices were sufficiently low that these duties equaled 40 percent of the cost of production—de facto a prohibitory rate—and the importation of cotton yarns soon dwindled, from 10,651 tons in 1891 to 2,330 tons in 1899,[56] despite the provisions for refunding 60 percent of the duties on yarns reexported in finished cloth.

In these circumstances the domestic cotton spinners—or rather those of Lille, Rouen, and the Vosges, who, by that time, had concentrated most of French cotton spinning in their own hands at the expense of less efficient producers—could at last make good on their goals of the 1870s. First they expanded their plants to

54. Alfred Aftalion, "Les kartells dans la région du nord de la France: Les kartells à formes simples dans les filatures de coton et de lin, 1899-1907," *Revue économique international*, 4 (1908), 144-165.

55. "Note traitant des effets du tarif minimum proposé par le gouvernement français sur nos exportations en France," MAE, Négociations commerciales, Belgique, 9 (1891-1901), 20-44.

56. *Annales du commerce extérieur*, no. 129, pp. 46-47.

serve the now captive home market: the number of cotton spindles in France rose from 5 million in the late 1880s to 7 million by 1907, of which 2.3 million were in the Vosges, 2.2 million were in the Nord, and 1.75 million were in Normandy.[57] Then they formed cartels—the Comité français de la filature de coton in 1899 and the Congrès de l'industrie cotonnière française in 1904—in order to fix prices and set production quotas, and within this cartelized framework they virtually eliminated competition by having each of the major centers specialize in a separate branch of production.[58] Lille specialized in spinning fine yarn, which constituted 60 percent of all French yarns, and in making sewing thread. It supplied the former to the clothmakers of Saint-Quentin, Troyes, and Tarare (having at last recovered these markets from the English), and the latter to the expanding French garment industry. Meanwhile, the Vosges, having completed the plant expansion begun in the 1870s, spun middle gauges of yarn which were woven into cloth locally and then dyed or printed at the BTT works at Thaon. The finished calicoes were marketed throughout France and, after tariff assimilation, in the various colonies, especially Algeria. Finally, Rouen, having enlarged and modernized its mills and having concentrated most of Norman cotton spinning and weaving within its boundaries, prospered by producing heavy yarns and coarse cloth for the rural French and colonial markets.[59]

Of course, not all sectors of French cotton were able to benefit from the tariff reform of the 1890s and from other measures designed to promote the textile industry. For example, the small cotton towns of Picardy, lower Normandy, and western France—spared from foreign competition by the Méline tariff—nonetheless succumbed to internal competition from the "Big Three" by the early twentieth century. At the same time, Roanne, whose mechanized cotton industry thrived in the 1880s by weaving

57. Paul Mairet, *La crise de l'industrie cotonnière, 1901–1905* (Dijon, 1906), p. 27.

58. Aftalion, "Les kartells dans la région du nord de la France," pp. 107–143.

59. R. B. Forrester, *The Cotton Industry of France* (Manchester, 1921), pp. 12–16, 33; Armand Lederlin et al., *Monographie de l'industrie cotonnière* (Epinal, 1905); J. R. Levainville, *Rouen: Etude d'une agglomeration urbaine* (Paris, 1913), pp. 217, 363–364.

vichy cloth with imported English and Swiss yarns, suffered in the 1890s, not because of the return to protection of cotton yarns, since provisions were made in exempt cloth exporters like the Roannais from those duties, but because Spain raised its duties on Vichy cloth in retaliation for France's raising of wine duties and thereby deprived Roanne of its principal foreign market.[60] These cases of hardship and failure aside, we must conclude that, on the whole, the effort to accommodate cotton and all other major textiles was successful. Most branches of France's highly variegated textile industry survived and even prospered in the late nineteenth and early twentieth centuries.

Last we come to commerce, finance, and transport. An examination of these interests in the late nineteenth century surely provides the acid test for the notion that the tariff reform of the 1890s contributed to the accommodation of all major economic interests in France. For, though the tariff policy of 1892 clearly helped most sectors of agriculture and industry, the benefits that accrued to commerce, finance, and transport are, at first glance, harder to discern. These interests, after all, represented the "free trade nexus." They had gained the most from trade liberalization in the 1860s, had worked hardest for the extension of free trade policies in the 1870s, and ostensibly had the most to lose from the increased protection of agriculture and industry in the 1890s. In point of fact, however, these interests did not suffer measurably from the new tariff system, as is apparent, first, in the fate of French railroads. The directors of these railroads had been strong champions of tariff liberalization in the 1850s because, to get started, the railroads were thought to need the traffic provided by trans-European commerce and by the importation of English and Belgian industrial products into France. Indeed, this was probably true through the 1870s. But by the eighties and nineties the situation was changing. The expansion of the French rail network increased the proportion of domestically produced goods—agricultural and industrial—in the railroads' total cargo. Consequently, railroad companies began to see the logic of protection-

60. Marcel Goninet, *Histoire de Roanne et de sa région*, 2 vols. (Roanne, 1975), II, 225.

ist arguments as, for example, when the AIF pointed out that the substitution of domestically produced iron for imported iron in French consumption would raise the traffic on French railroads by a factor of ten (because the French metallurgists had to move ten tons of raw materials—iron ore, coal and coke, pig iron—for every ton of iron or steel they produced and marketed).[61] Therefore, by the 1890s, the railroads were no longer the staunch opponents of protection they had been thirty years before. Nor were they hurt (but were perhaps even helped) by the selective return to protection of 1892—a return that left the transit trade unaffected by increases in duties on goods for domestic consumption and that allowed the lucrative importation of foreign coal and other industrial raw materials to continue and to increase. After declining during the depression of the mid-eighties, the total traffic on French railroads advanced 20 percent between 1888 and 1894, up to 12 billion kilometer-tons, and grew another 33 percent in the ensuing decade, up to 16 billion kilometer-tons in 1903.[62]

Similarly, the tariff reform of the 1890s did not threaten the mercantile interests of Paris, Lyons, and the ports as much as might be expected. Many merchant capitalists were able to adapt quickly to the new order because of the liquidity of their assets. For example, Gustave Roy, who had made his fortune by importing and exporting cotton goods and had long supported free trade as an aid to that commerce, saw the handwriting on the wall in 1891. Even as his brother-in-law, Georges Berger, fought to preserve the liberal trade regime in parliament, Roy was setting up his sons in the weaving of cotton at Rouen to take advantage of the expected rise in French duties on imported cloth. In the years that followed, Roy Frères increasingly abandoned the business of importing English yarn into France and exporting high-quality cottons to Europe and America and instead concentrated on producing shoddy cottons for the Indochinese market and other protected colonial markets.[63] As the autonomy of the

61. Rapport du comité, December 12, 1883, p. 25, AN 27 AS 1.
62. Dominique Renouard, *Les transports des marchandises par fer, route, et eau depuis 1850* (Paris, 1960), p. 37.
63. Roy dossier, AN F[12] 5262.

French national and colonial market became an established fact, other Parisian and Lyonnais capitalists followed suit and abandoned international commerce for domestic manufacturing. Still others shifted their capital from trade to land, securities, railroad shares, and especially foreign industrial stocks and government bonds. Yet most probably remained in some aspect of the import-export business—and continued to prosper—because "the return to protection" did not reduce the volume of French foreign commerce but only altered its composition. That is, higher tariffs did reduce the importation of foodstuffs and some manufactures after 1892, but the rising importation of raw materials more than compensated for this loss. After a momentary slump in the early 1890s, total French imports rose and, coupled with the continuing rise of French exports, provided favorable circumstances for those whose business was moving goods in and out of France.[64] Thus, despite the restriction of a protectionist regime, most merchants and merchant bankers in France survived and prospered. Exactly how they did so is perhaps best seen in the development of the major French ports in the 1890s and beyond.

French seaports had to adjust to a new pattern of trade after 1892, but the volume of their trade did not suffer in the process.

64. While the value of cereal imports dropped from an annual average of 467 million francs in 1877–1886 to 214 million in 1887–1896 and the value of livestock imports fell from 170 million francs a year before 1885 to 38 million francs a year after 1900, the average annual value of industrial raw materials imports (in millions of francs) advanced as follows:

	1877–1886	1887–1896	1897–1906
Coal	158	178	274
Flax	68	59	73
Cotton	196	187	266
Wool	324	334	433
Oil Seeds	153	178	192

French special commerce—expressed in decennal averages in millions of francs—advanced as follows:

	1877–1886	1887–1896	1897–1906
Imports	4,460	4,106	4,612
Exports	3,307	3,407	4,246
Total	7,767	7,513	8,858

Source: Levasseur, *Histoire du commerce*, ii, 731–777, 820.

On the contrary, over the long run from 1875 to 1907, the traffic through French ports rose 17 percent, a rate of increase second only to Great Britain's.[65] France's largest ports—Marseilles, Le Havre, Bordeaux—all participated in this growth, although each was affected somewhat by the changes in tariff policy and the resultant changes in commerce.[66] Le Havre, for instance, continued to rely on imports and the transit trade. In the case of the latter, which was carried on through bonded warehouses immune to domestic customs, the tariff reform was much less crucial than railroad rates. Indeed, the lowering of freight costs on the routes to central Europe, in order to make Le Havre competitive with Antwerp and Hamburg, was the chief problem facing this segment of the city's commerce in the 1890s, as in the 1870s. On the other hand, increases in certain duties in 1892 altered, though did not cripple, the structure of Le Havre's import trade. In the 1890s the traffic in English textiles and hardware dropped off, and the once lucrative commerce in American foodstuffs disappeared, but the rising influx of American oil and cotton, British coal, Brazilian coffee, and African products like copper, rubber, and cocoa more than took up the slack.[67] Moreover, Le Havre continued to thrive on the transatlantic passenger traffic. Throughout the 1880s Le Havre served as the major embarkation point for the waves of emigrants bound to America from Germany and central Europe. In the early 1890s the passenger traffic slowed as the steamers outgrew Le Havre's facilities, but the completion of new facilities in 1895—and periodic enlargements of the port thereafter—revived and maintained its strong position in the transatlantic service.[68] Finally, Le Havre grew as a regional trade

65. Ibid., p. 717.
66. According to the *Annuaire statistique*, 6 (1883), 375; 15, 556–557, the tonnage of foreign commerce in the three largest ports increased as follows:

	1881	*1893*
Marseilles	3,444,197	4,151,968
Le Havre	2,112,866	2,355,116
Bordeaux	1,643,338	1,925,496

67. Deposition of the Le Havre Chamber of Commerce, AN F[12] 6916; Levasseur, *Histoire du commerce*, ii, 697–699.
68. Marthe Barbance, *Histoire de la Compagnie générale transatlantique* (Paris, 1955), pp. 155–163; J. Fleury, "Le Havre et la Seine maritime," *Revue des deux*

center for western Europe in the nineties despite chronically
inadequate rail services. In particular, the opening of the Tancar-
ville canal in 1887, skirting the unnavigable Seine estuary,
brought a dramatic increase in the river traffic between Le Havre
and Rouen. As Rouen emerged after 1899 as the chief entrepôt for
grain and coal bound for Paris, Le Havre prospered as a center for
transshipment.[69] In short, Le Havre enjoyed steady growth and
general prosperity despite the increased import duties in France.
To be sure, it had not become—and never would become—
Europe's principal Atlantic port, as Jules Siegfried and others
had hoped in the 1870s, but this was not the fault of French tariff
policy alone. Even under complete free trade, unfavorable geogra-
phic location, poor railroad facilities, and other factors would
probably have kept it from achieving that status.

France's largest port, Marseilles, seemed to be affected by the
tariff of 1892 even less than Le Havre. In the 1890s Marseilles
continued to develop along the lines laid down in previous
decades. It remained the port of departure for the chemicals and
textiles of the Rhône, the Loire, and even the Vosges, and a port
of entry for wine, raw silk and cotton, and colonial products such
as Algerian iron ore. Various transformation industries utilizing
imported raw materials continued to grow also. The chief of
these, flour milling and semolina manufacture, prospered despite
prohibitive grain duties because the Méline tariff extended the
temporary admission of foreign wheat. Indeed, as wheat imports
for all of France fell precipitously after 1885, those for Marseilles
rose from 1,700,000 hectoliters in 1879 to 2,000,000 in 1889.[70]
Likewise, with the continued free importation of oil seeds, the
soap industry expanded after 1892. Marseilles's only real disap-
pointment in the 1880s and 1890s was its inability to compete
with Genoa in the transit trade between western Europe and the
Orient via the Suez Canal. Here again the tariff was a minor
consideration, the main problem being poor rail connections

mondes, May 1, 1895, pp. 189–206; Jules Charles-Roux, "La grande navigation et
les ports français," Revue des deux mondes, March 15, 1907, pp. 432–447.

69. Levainville, Rouen, p. 173.

70. Deposition of the Marseilles Chamber of Commerce, AN F¹² 6916; Levasseur, Histoire du commerce, II, 706–709.

between Marseilles and its hinterland. In sum, Marseilles maintained a steady, respectable rate of growth in the 1890s which suffered only by comparison with the growth rates of Genoa, Hamburg, and Antwerp.[71]

Similarly, the trend toward protection had little effect on the development of Bordeaux, France's third largest port and a traditional stronghold of the free trade party. Bordeaux stagnated from 1880 to 1895, even though tariff policy remained liberal through most of those years, because it continued to lack harbor facilities suitable for the new steamers and because the phylloxera epidemic reduced the wine production of the Gironde, the traditional staple of its export commerce. Bordeaux expanded in the late nineties in part because exports revived when wine output returned to the level of 1875 and the timber industry of the neighboring Landes boomed (Bordeaux exported 475,000 tons of Landes timber in 1900, versus 50,000 tons thirty years earlier). More important, Bordeaux grew because of the development of its imports, despite the Méline tariff, and because of the appearance, for the first time, of the types of manufacturing and processing industries Marseilles already possessed. Specifically, the continuing low duty on English coal made its importation on a large scale practical for Bordeaux in the 1890s. This trade amounted to 1,800,000 tons annually (versus 200,000 in the 1870s) and accounted for three-fifths of Bordeaux's imports by 1914. This heavier volume of trade, in turn, stimulated efforts to modernize the port—the channel was deepened and larger wharves were built—and led to the construction of an industrial zone at La Bastide on the right bank of the Gironde where Kuhlmann and Saint-Gobain installed chemical works, Schneider built shipyards, and canning and food processing plants arose, such as Maurel and Prom's Grande Huilerie Bordelaise, a peanut oil refinery.[72] Because these new industries depended largely on raw materials that were not protected, they were little affected by the

71. Marseilles grew 22 percent between 1880 and 1890, while Genoa grew 146 percent, Hamburg 145 percent, and Antwerp 182 percent (Jules Charles-Roux, "La jonction du Rhône à Marseille et l'utilisation de l'étang de Berre," *Revue des deux mondes,* February 1, 1893, p. 610).

72. Louis Desgraves and Georges Dupeux, *Bordeaux au XIXe siècle* (Bordeaux, 1969), pp. 375–396.

protectionism of the Méline tariff. Indeed, as Bordeaux industrialized and diversified, its dependence on the wine trade decreased and so did the local preoccupation with export commerce. Thus, if the tariff reforms of 1882–1892 represented a theoretical defeat for the commercial interests of Bordeaux and the other ports, they did not generally spell economic disaster. All ports survived and expanded under the new regime—as did the other commercial centers, Paris and Lyons—and thus, in the end, all could live with it.

It should now be apparent that the tariff policy of the 1890s, in conjunction with other elements of French economic policy, did indeed effect the accommodation and reconciliation of all major economic interests in France. Moreover, the success of that accommodation should be equally apparent from the way in which all interests—agricultural, industrial, or commercial, free trade or protectionist—grew and prospered, or at least survived, in the 1890s and early 1900s. If further testimony to the success of this accommmodation is needed, it can surely be found in the decline of the tariff as a political issue after 1892 and in the simultaneous waning of conflict between free traders and protectionists. To be sure, the issue of tariff reform was raised from time to time after 1892—as in 1909–1910[73]—but it never again galvanized the interests as it had between 1860 and 1892. Similarly, free traders (or at least "economic liberals") still formed ad hoc committees to debate the tariff from time to time, as they did in 1890–1891, but, once having dissolved their association in 1882, they never again organized on a national scale. Ironically, the fate of the protectionists was not significantly different. Although they maintained and even expanded their national organization (converting it into the AIAF, the Association de l'industrie et de l'agriculture française, in 1893), this group increasingly devoted its attention to issues other than the tariff.[74] Moreover, its very size

73. On the tariff of 1910, see Raymond Poidevin, "Protectionnisme et relations internationales: L'exemple du tarif douanier français de 1910," *Revue historique,* 245 (1971), 47–62.

74. By 1887 the AIF's list of demands included, besides tariff protection, reform of the consultative committee on railroads, suppression of preferential freight rates for long-haul shippers, reservation of state contracts for French firms,

and the diversity of its composition made it less and less an agency of combat and more and more a ceremonial body dedicated to defending the status quo. Therefore, never again did it play the aggressive role in economic policy making that, as the AIF, it had played between 1878 and 1892.

The decline of the free trade and protectionist parties as important political pressure groups and the demise of the tariff as a major political issue meant that all major economic interests were satisified with the composite, compromise tariff policy of the 1890s. It also meant that, after thirty years of controversy, consensus had at last replaced conflict in French economic politics. The emergence of such a consensus, in turn, played a vital role in the political and economic dramas that dominated the French scene at the close of the nineteenth century.

---

expansion of consular services overseas, reform of the Conseil supérieur du commerce, and colonial expansion (*Voeux*, February 2, 1887, AN F^{12} 4841).

The free traders were similarly broadening their interests, and increasingly their priorities were converging with those of the protectionists on matters beyond the tariff. Indicative of this change, Léon Say drew up an agenda of economic reforms in 1883 in which he ranked tariff liberalization behind balancing of the national budget and railroad reform and only slightly ahead of overseas colonization (Léon Say, *La politique des intérêts* [Paris, 1883]).

Conclusion

If most of the businessmen and politicians who participated in the parliamentary battles over tariff policy in 1878–1882 and 1890–1892 perceived the long-term effects of tariff reform only dimly, those effects are considerably easier to perceive today. We can now see that, in the economic realm, the Méline tariff and the broad accommodation of interests associated with it helped to stabilize and solidify the capitalist system of enterprise in France after the shocks of the "Great Depression" of 1876–1896 and thereby established the framework for French economic development in the twentieth century. Similarly, we can see that, in the political realm, the tariff settlement produced a new level of political solidarity within the grande bourgeoisie and helped to create the bourgeois-peasant alliance that assured the survival of a socially conservative, bourgeois-dominated Republic from the 1890s down to the debacle of 1940. It also produced an even longer lasting legacy in that the tradition of interest accommodation, inherited from the nineteenth century, has enabled France in the postwar period to avoid (by and large) the divisive and often bloody political confrontations that punctuated its earlier history.

The process of economic stabilization, solidification, and equilibration to which tariff reform contributed had two aspects.

First, it involved, after years of high attrition and rapid turnover in the ranks of French businesses and businessmen, the emergence of a set of firms and a set of entrepreneurs and managers which, once established, continued to dominate the French economy well into the twentieth century. Indeed, one need only scan Jacques Boudet's compendium on French business[1] to realize that, except in branches of industry created after 1900 on the basis of new technology, the dominant firms of the mid-twentieth century were already entrenched by 1900, that the families in command of French industry and commerce at mid-century had, in most cases, risen to that position by the beginning of the century, and that, consequently, the French enterprise system knew a level of stability after 1900 that was unknown in the nineteenth century.

This turn of events owed something to the natural, "Darwinian" process whereby superior (that is, more efficient) firms destroyed and/or absorbed inferior firms during the depression years and then, during the upturn of the nineties, expanded and entrenched themselves to a degree that made future domestic challenges to their position all but impossible. Yet stabilization involved more than just the triumph of the strong over the weak. It also involved conscious efforts by all surviving firms to reduce competition within their ranks and thus to secure the position of all among them. Such efforts were manifested most clearly in the cartelization movement that, although not as extensive in France as in Germany, was nevertheless a crucial feature of French business development in the fin de siècle and a crucial factor in the stabilization of certain industries. As we have already noted, cartelization occurred in the linen and cotton industries around 1900. It occurred in coal the following year, when the colliers of the Nord and the Pas-de-Calais formed the Entente des Houillères. Most important, cartelization had come to iron and steel in 1887, well before coal and textiles, when the Comité des forges, under the leadership of Martelet of Denain-Anzin, divided the domestic market among its members, set up a uniform system of product classification and pricing, and established production quotas.[2] Simultaneous with the creation of cartels, there were

1. *Le monde des affaires en France de 1830 à nos jours* (Paris, 1952).
2. Comité des forges de France, *La sidérurgie française, 1864–1914* (Paris, n.d.),

efforts on other levels to mitigate strife and foster solidarity among firms and businessmen at the turn of the century, including the formation of producer syndicates, the strengthening of the chambers of commerce (each became an assembly of syndicate presidents), and the founding of the National Assembly of Chamber of Commerce Presidents.

By providing a favorable environment for this cartelization and organization, the tariff reform of the 1890s entered into the stabilization of the French business system. In some cases the new tariff provided the increment in protection needed to save domestic producers from foreign competition and to allow them to divide the domestic market among themselves (especially in some branches of textiles and metallurgy). In other cases it did not increase protection but did at least resolve issues that had stood in the way of full cooperation among industrialists. It was no accident, for example, that the reorganization and strenthening of the Comité des Forges in 1887 coincided with the resolution of the long-standing controversy over temporary admissions of pig iron or that, with the tariff settled in 1892, the Comité became increasingly effective in managing metallurgical production and marketing in France in the 1890s.

While thus contributing to the "organization of capitalism," tariff reform was also contributing to the second major facet of economic stabilization—the equilibration of agriculture, industry, and commerce and the formation of a consensus among the leaders of all sectors on the need to maintain a balanced, mixed economy in France. Specifically, the tariff policy of the 1890s struck a balance between agriculture and industry by giving agriculture sufficient protection to survive foreign competition while simultaneously limiting the impact of that protection on industry (the protection of agriculture may have hurt industry in that higher food prices meant higher labor costs, but maintenance of duty-free access to foreign raw materials compensated industry to some extent). Moreover, after a thirty-year period in which commercial, financial, and transport interests had been given preferment by the government and had consequently dominated the national economy, the compromise tariff of the

---

p. 447. On the cartelization of coal, see Marcel Gillet, *Les charbonnages du nord de la France au XIXe siècle* (Paris, 1973), pp. 220–300.

1890s restored a balance between "travail national" on the one hand and the commerce-finance-transport nexus on the other. At the same time, the larger accommodation of which tariff reform was a part reduced tensions among the different sectors of the economy and helped to create a mood of mutual tolerance, even mutual support, among them. Once established, this new sense of solidarity in French business exhibited surprising staying power. Neither the rapid industrial growth before World War I, with the attendant rise of new industries and new entrepreneurs, nor the stresses and strains of the war itself undercut the half-conscious, half-unconscious agreement, laid down in the 1890s, to protect all *positions acquises* and to manage and even limit economic development for the benefit and security of all established interests. Consequently, beyond the boom of 1896–1914 came an extended period of economic lethargy and business conservatism which, despite the criticisms and calls for change emanating from some quarters in the 1920s and 1930s, would not be overcome until after World War II.[3]

The "organization of capitalism" and the entrenchment of certain enterprises and entrepreneurs had political counterparts in the solidification of the parliamentary Republic and in the consolidation of political power in the hands of the bourgeois dynasties in the 1890s. Moreover, as in the case of the economic consolidation of the capitalist system, this political consolidation of the capitalist system depended on some extent on the accommodation of interests in the realm of tariff policy that was effected in the last decade of the century.

By 1879 the grande bourgeoisie had fought off a challenge from the Left by the lower middle classes and workers of Paris (the Commune), as well as challenges from the Right by monarchist "notables" (the "Moral Order" and Seize Mai regimes) and had

3. On the contemporaneous perceptions of economic lethargy and the demands for reform by French capitalists in the interwar period, see Richard F. Kuisel, *Ernest Mercier, French Technocrat* (Berkeley, 1967), pp. 45–88, and "Auguste Detoeuf, Conscience of French Industry, 1926–1947," *International Review of Social History*, 20 (1975), 149–174. Also Charles S. Maier, "Between Taylorism and Technocracy: European Ideologues and the Vision of Industrial Productivity in the 1920s," *Journal of Contemporary History*, 5 (1970), 27–61.

taken control of the Republic. Over the next decade, they ruled France either directly, through bourgeois dynasts like Léon Say, or indirectly, through their clients, the Opportunist Republicans, led by Jules Ferry and Charles de Freycinet. Indeed, so confident were they of their position in these years that they could indulge in intraclass struggles on various issues of economic policy and could countenance continued division among themselves on the tariff without fear of undermining their overall political supremacy. Even in the heyday of the Opportunist Republic, however, it was becoming clear that, in the era of universal male suffrage, the political supremacy of the capitalist bourgeoisie—or of any other class or party—was fragile and dependent on the support that class could muster among the rural and urban masses. And it was precisely that support that the Opportunists began to lose amid the political scandals and economic crises of the 1880s and early 1890s. Their position was challenged first in the parliamentary elections of 1885 and then more seriously by the rise of Boulanger and the Boulangists in 1887–1889. Escaping those threats, the bourgeois Republicans (who by then called themselves Progressistes) soon faced an even more ominous threat from a new generation of Radical politicians and from the Socialists, who made a successful debut in the municipal elections of 1892 and emerged as a national political force in the parliamentary elections of the following year. Just how ominous this threat was became apparent in the spring of 1896, when the first all-Radical ministry under Léon Bourgeois pushed an income tax bill through the Chamber with Socialist help.[4]

As bourgeois politicians were losing their hold on parliament, the capitalist bourgeoisie was facing the additional threat of worker revolt in the industrial towns beyond Paris. First announced by the strikes of the early 1880s, the growth and increasing militancy of the French labor movement came to dominate the bourgeois consciousness in the 1890s, especially in 1893 and 1899–1900, when workers staged massive strike waves in quest of higher wages, shorter hours, and better working conditions. Right or wrong, capitalists viewed this activity—especially when accom-

4. Final passage of the income tax was blocked, however, when the Senate—in a controversial maneuver—forced Bourgeois to resign by holding up credits for the Madagascar expedition.

panied by the specter of "confiscatory" income taxes—as nothing less than a frontal assault on capitalist property and thus as a dire threat to their social and economic position.

Amid this prolonged "crisis of bourgeois authority," the second round of tariff reform under the Third Republic took on a political significance that the first round in 1878–1882 had lacked. Of course it would be wrong to say that the accommodation of interests on the tariff in 1892 was designed solely to serve the political ends of the Republican bourgeoisie. We have already seen that that accommodation sprang primarily from the parliamentary give-and-take among economic interests preoccupied with the immediate economic situation. But it is not too much to suggest that Jules Roche—a rising journalist-politician closely linked to conservative bourgeois circles by the late 1880s (after starting his career as a Radical)—had an eye on the political situation when he proposed a compromise tariff bill in 1890, nor is it too much to suggest that Jules Méline likewise took politics into account when presiding over the legislation of the tariff in 1891–1892. Indeed, only by allowing for such political considerations can one explain why this longtime agent of the ultraprotectionist Vosges cotton industry suddenly tempered his protectionist zeal and played the part of the moderate compromiser in 1891. In any case, whatever the motives of Roche and Méline, and whether or not the tariff of 1892 was meant to serve political purposes, ultimately it did so.

First, by establishing or at least confirming agricultural protection, the Méline tariff saved the peasants from the foreign competition that threatened to destroy them and thereby transformed the peasants' perception and appreciation of the bourgeois Republic. Whereas in the 1870s the peasants had supported the Republic mainly as a passive barrier to any aristocratic-monarchist assault on the Revolutionary land settlement, in the 1890s (once the Republic had embraced agricultural protection) the peasants came to view it as the necessary guarantor of their social and economic position. As a result, after flirting with anti-Republican politicians in 1885 and 1889, the peasants threw their considerable voting strength back to the bourgeois Republicans (that is, the Progressistes) in 1893 and 1898. And they continued to vote for socially and economically conservative Republicans thereafter (that the peasant vote increasingly went to candidates calling themselves Radical-Socialists after 1900 does not contradict this generalization; it only points up how the new, rural-based Radical party shed its reform program and became a bulwark of social and economic conservatism after the overthrow of the Léon Bourgeois government in 1896).

If the Méline tariff reinforced the bourgeois-peasant alliance on which capitalist political power depended, it also offered ground on which the industrial and commercial wings of the capitalist bourgeoisie—at odds economically and sometimes politically since the mid-nineteenth century—could come together to defend the capitalist Republic against its opponents on the Left and the Right. Specifically, the traditionally free trade capitalists of Paris, Lyons, and the seaports—satisified that the new tariff accommodated their interests—dropped their opposition to protection in the mid-nineties, as was reflected in the changing editorial line of the *Journal des débats*. Then, through the Comité national républicain du commerce et de l'industrie and similar bodies, they joined with the industrial *patronat* to support the Méline cabinet's successful effort to block antibourgeois social and fiscal reforms (such as the income tax) in 1896–1898 and later to sustain Réné Waldeck-Rousseau's "government of Republican defense" in its equally successful effort to meet the "collectivist" challenge to bourgeois property in 1899–1902.[5]

Thus, thanks in large measure to the tariff reform of the 1890s and the accommodation of economic interests, the capitalist elite was able to preserve its political, economic, and social supremacy

5. Pierre Sorlin, *Waldeck-Rousseau* (Paris, 1966), pp. 354–364, 391–449, 461–480. The Waldeck-Rousseau government is best remembered for resolving the Dreyfus Affair in Dreyfus's favor and for launching the anticlerical policies that eventually led to the separation of church and state. But Sorlin shows that perhaps its key accomplishment was in associating the Radicals and even some Socialists with a conservative solution to the labor question. Waldeck-Rousseau recognized the workers' right to strike and even condoned the strike wave that followed his accession to office, apparently in the belief that workers agitating for specific wage and hour improvements offered no real threat to the capitalist order. But he stood firm against their more "revolutionary" demands for the establishment of a legal minimum wage and legal limits on working hours, as did all subsequent Radical and Moderate ministries. As a result, thoroughgoing labor legislation was not forthcoming in France until the Popular Front.

in France despite the discrediting of specific bourgeois politicians in the scandals of the fin de siècle and despite the growing alienation of the working class and the resultant growth of the socialist and syndicalist movements. Although it appeared to move to the Left at the turn of the century, the Third Republic remained after 1900 (at least until 1936) what it had been before 1900: a stronghold of bourgeois property and capitalist enterprise.

Finally, the tariff reform of the late nineteenth century left an additional legacy that transcended the Third Republic and has continued to influence French politics down to the present: the technique of interest accommodation. Having first developed in the economic politics of the nineteenth century, interest accommodation reappeared after World War I in the heroically un-heroic efforts to "recast" and perpetuate the bourgeois order recently described by Charles S. Maier.[6] It can also be seen after World War II in the Monnet Plan (the French style of voluntary, "exhortatory" economic planning which has developed since the forties is really not much different from the "planning" conducted in parliament in the 1880s and 1890s, except the emphasis now is more on stimulating growth than on defending vested interests). More recently, interest accommodation was manifested in the Fifth Republic's unabashed appeasement of the trade unions to overcome the threat posed by the "events of May" in 1968. Indeed, it is perhaps not too much to say that, since the early Third Republic, the accommodation of interests has become a permanent feature of the French political style, a permanent alternative to revolution as a method of economic and social reform, a permanent mechanism for maintaining order and stability in a changing world. Moreover, this development has not been limited to France but can be perceived in all liberal democracies, including the United States. For that reason, the close study of French tariff politics presented here, in addition to making the development of modern France more comprehensible, may also cast light on the fundamental political processes at work throughout the Western world in modern times.

6. Charles S. Maier, *Recasting Bourgeois Europe: Stabilization in France, Germany, and Italy in the Decade after World War I* (Princeton, 1975).

Appendix 1

Membership of the Protectionist and Free Trade Associations in 1878

A. Association de l'industrie française[1]

President: Alexandre Jullien, chairman of the board and director, Société des forges et fonderies de Terrenoire, la Voulte, et Bessèges

Vice-presidents:
Adolph Japy, Japy Frères, Beaucourt, hardware and clock-making
Arthur Joly de Bammeville, spinner and weaver, director of the Houillères de l'Aveyron
J.-B. Martelet, managing director, Forges de Denain et d'Anzin
J. Mignon, director, Société de constructions navales du Havre
Félix Moreaux, managing director, Compagnie de Fives-Lille
Arthur Petitdidier, Société d'armements maritimes

1. Names, titles, and other information are as listed in *L'industrie française,* March 21, 1878, pp. 89–90.

Charles Saint, Saint Frères, cloth manufacturers
Emile Vuillemin, chairman, Comité des houillères du Nord
et du Pas-de-Calais

Secretaries:
Sampson Jordan, director, Compagnie des hauts-fourneaux
de Marseille
Paul Schneider, director, Houillères de l'Aveyron
Emile Widmer, director of silk floss spinning mills at
Essones and Amilly

Treasurer: Troullier, David Troullier et Adhemar, Epinal
and Saint-Quentin

Members of the Action Committee:
Paul Aclocque, former deputy, managing director, Société
des forges de l'Ariège
Bichon, shipbuilder, Lormont-Bordeaux
Maurice Blin, cloth manufacturer at Elbeuf
Anselme-Henri Bocquet, jute spinner, Bocquet, Carmich-
ael, Dewailly et Cie, Ailly-sur-Somme
Amédée Burat, engineer, Compagnie des mines de Blanzy
Cabrol, spinner and weaver at Flers
Albert Courant, spinner at Le Havre
Paul-Ferdinand Delaville le Roulx, managing director,
Compagnie des mines de Grand'combe
Alfred Delesalle, spinner at Madeleine-lès-Lille
Alfred Dupont, former deputy, vice-chairman, Comité des
Houillères du Nord et du Pas-de-Calais
Augustin Farcot, machine builder, Saint-Ouen
Jules Favre, spinner at Epinal
Alphonse Fould, Dupont et Fould, forge masters at Pompey
(Meurthe-et-Moselle)
Gargan, president, Chambre syndicale des mécaniciens,
chaudronniers, et fondeurs de Paris
Alphonse Grimault, Mignon, Rouart, et Delinières, iron
pipe, Paris
Emile Japy, Japy-Marti-Roux, clockmakers
Charles Laederich, spinner at Epinal

Emile Magnier, Comptoir de l'industrie linière, Paris and Lille

François Marrel, Marrel Frères, forge masters at Rive-de-Gier

Alfred Ponnier, Vincent Ponnier et Cie, Senones (Vosges)

Honoré Reverchon, former deputy, director of the Compagnie des forges d'Audincourt

Henri Schneider, manager-director, Usines du Creusot

Sessevalle, director of the Société anonyme de Commentry-Fourchambault

Jean Vignal, chairman of the board, Société des Chargeurs réunis

Adhering Members:

Baron Oscar d'Adelsward, forge master, Hersanges (near Longwy)

Edouard Agache, spinner at Lille

Alexandre et Schwartz, spinners at Remiremont

Camentrion Aubé, cloth manufacturer at Rouen

Bedel, père et fils, forge masters and steelmakers, La Berardière, Saint-Etienne

Henri Bergasse, director, Compagnie des transports maritimes, Marseilles

Victor Bertel, manufacturer at Rouen

Boigeol Frères et Warnod, spinners at Giromagny (Haut-Rhin)

Alexis Boittelle, Compagnie des mines de Béthune

Bollaert, Compagnie des mines de Lens

Bolay et Morot, cotton sewing thread, Paris

Emile Bossière, shipowner, Le Havre

Bourlon de Sarty, chairman of the board, Compagnie des mines de fer de Camerata

Burton, director, Compagnie des mines, fonderies, et forges d'Alais

Emile Cail et Cie, machine builders, Paris

Cartier-Bresson, cotton thread, Paris

Chalmeton, director, Compagnie houillère de Bessèges

Vosges Chamber of Commerce, Epinal

Paul Champy, manufacturer at Gisors
Emile Charrière et Cie, ironmakers, Allevard (Isère)
Nicholas Claude, senator, spinner, and weaver, Saulxures
(Vosges)
Cocquel, manufacturer at Amiens
Edouard Davillier, manufacturer at Gisors
Delamarre-Deboutteville, spinner at Rouen
Gustave Denis, spinner and weaver at Fontaine-Daniel
(Mayenne)
Louis Deschamps, spinner at Petit-Quevilly-lès-Rouen
Desgênetais Frères, spinners at Bolbec
Ernest Desouches et Cie, silk floss spinners at Graville-
Saint-Maurice (Seine-Inférieure)
Dietsch Frères, weavers at Saint-Dié
Dumond de Montclez, chairman of the board, Compagnie
des usines à zinc du Midi
Duret et fils, spinners at Brionne (Eure)
Alfred Fauquet-Lemaitre, spinner and weaver at Bolbec
Ernest Feray, senator and manufacturer at Essonnes
Arthur Feray, cotton and flax spinner at Essonnes
Léon Feray, machine builder and spinner at Essonnes
Flobert, hardware manufacturer, Maison Flobert et Cadillac
Jacques Galliard et Cie, spinners and weavers at Barentin
Gallet Frères, spinners and weavers at Flers
Germain-Duforestel, spinner at Condé-sur-Noireau
Hoffet, director, Houillères de Ronchamps (Haute-Saône)
Jacob Holtzer et Cie, steelmakers at Unieux (Loire)
Jules Hurel, representative of Le Creusot at Paris
Paul Jamin, forge master at Eurville
Joseph Labbé, forge master at Gorcy (Meurthe-et-Moselle)
Aristide Lair, spinner at Condé-sur-Noireau
La Rochette et Cie, forge masters at Givors
Lasson, Salmon, et Cie, forge masters at Abainville (Meuse)
Camille Laurens, engineer, Compagnie houillère de Saint-
Eloy (Puy-de-Dôme)
J.-J. Laveissière et fils, metallurgical manufacturing, Paris
Laurent Frères et Beaux-frères, hardware and locks,
Plancher-lès-Mines (Haute-Loire)

Julien Le Blan, flax spinner at Lille

Paul Le Blan, flax spinner at Lille

Eugène Le Maistre, spinner and weaver at Bolbec

Georges Lemaitre-Lavotte, manufacturer at Bolbec

Lemaitre-Westphalen, spinner at Lillebonne

Lement, Veil, et Cie, spinners at Blamont (Meurthe-et-Moselle)

Lescure, director, Compagnie des fonderies et forges de l'Horme (Saint-Chamond)

Levainville, director, Compagnie des mines de Compagnac

Henri Loyer, spinner at Lille

Lucas, Société cotonnière de Saint-Etienne du Rouvray

Commines de Marsilly, general manager, Compagnie des mines d'Anzin

Alfred-Camille Martellière, managing director, Société des forges de Montataire

Masurier, shipowner and director, Société des Chargeurs réunis

Masurel fils, cotton spinner at Roubaix

C.-F. Mathieu, former deputy, chief engineer, Usines du Creusot

Constant Mathieu, director, Compagnie des mines de houille de Courrières, Douai

Mercier et Meyer, spinners at Ourscamps (Oise)

Theodore Meynier, chairman of the board, Société des mines de Brassac

Adrien de Montgolfier, senator, general manager, Compagnie des hauts-fourneaux, forges, et aciéries de la Marine

Morel et Winkler, spinners at Epinal

Louis Motte-Bossut, spinner at Roubaix

Meunier et Prevost, spinners at Albert (Somme)

Adolphe Noblot, spinner at Héricourt (Haute-Saône)

Oeschger, metallurgical manufacturer, Biache-Saint-Vaast (Pas-de-Calais)

Parron, director, Compagnie des mines de Mokta-el-Hadid

Augustin Pouyer-Quertier, senator, cotton spinner at Rouen

Alfred Rénouard, flax spinner at Lille

Xavier Rogé, managing director, Usines de Pont-à-Mousson

Saint-Gobain, Chauny, et Cirey, glass and chemicals

Scheurer et Sahler, spinners at Audincourt (Doubs)

Seitz et Cie, spinners at Granges (Vosges)

Ernest Siegfried, spinner at Le Havre

Jules Thivenet, fabric maker at Mâcon

Augustin Thouroude, merchant at Rouen

Touron-Lemaire et fils et Mairesse, spinners at Saint-Quentin

Vendroux, Clement, Verlingue et Cie, Saint-Pierre-lès-Calais

Verdié et Cie, iron and steelmaking, Firminy (Loire)

François Viellard-Migeon, senator, forge master at Morvillars (Haut-Rhin)

Richard Waddington, deputy, Seine-Inférieure

Walterflaugue, managing director, Société des usines de Gouille (near Besançon)

B. Association pour la défense de la liberté commerciale et industrielle et pour le développement des traités de commerce[2]

President: Adolphe d'Eichthal, member, Conseil supérieur de l'agriculture et du commerce

Vice-presidents:

Jean-Simon Dauphinot, president, Chamber of Commerce of Reims

Oscar Galline, president, Chamber of Commerce of Lyons

Claudius Gerontet, president, Chamber of Commerce of Saint-Etienne

Gosselin, president, Chamber of Commerce of Boulogne

Alphonse Grandval, president, Chamber of Commerce of Marseilles

---

2. Names and other information are as listed in the memorandum of the director of the Bureau of Commerce to the minister of commerce, December 30, 1878, AN F¹² 6385.

Louis-Adolphe Houette, president, Chamber of Commerce
of Paris
Armand Lalande, president, Chamber of Commerce of
Bordeaux
Thivel-Duvillars, president, Chamber of Commerce of Ta-
rare
Henri Fould, vice-president, Chambre syndicale du com-
merce d'exportation
Joseph Garnier, senator, Alpes-Maritimes
Léon Hiélard, president, Union centrale des chambres syn-
dicales
Gustave Roy, Chamber of Commerce of Paris

Members:
E.-J. Albert, merchant, Paris
A. Appert, industrialist, Paris
A. Armandy, silk spinner
A. Bonnet, Chamber of Commerce of Bordeaux
Eugène Brélay, cloth merchant, Paris
Pierre Bertrand-Milcent, cloth merchant, Cambrai
E. Blandin, Epernay
Emile Baillière, Chamber of Commerce of Paris
Alexandre Clapier, former deputy, Marseilles
Victor Crespin, Chamber of Commerce of Calais
Francisque David, merchant, Saint-Etienne
P. Devol, Chamber of Commerce of Calais
Duval brothers (probably Fernand and Edgar Raoul-Duval)
Léon Fould
Baron Auguste de Fourment, wool spinner and deputy,
Somme
Gaston Grandgeorge, spinner and weaver of combed wool
Jules Hayem, industrialist, Paris
Léon Legrand, spinner and weaver of combed wool
P. Leroy-Beaulieu
Lilienthal, Chamber of Commerce of Lyons
J. Levois, Chamber of Commerce of Paris
Frédéric Levy, president, Comité central des chambres syn-
dicales

Edouard Lecouteux, general secretary, Société générale des agriculteurs

Lechat, mayor of Nantes

Emile Menier, deputy, Seine-et-Marne

A. Loussel, merchant

Mulaton, Chamber of Commerce of Lyons

Camille Marcilhacy, Chamber of Commerce of Paris

E. Maurel, president, tribunal of commerce, Bordeaux

Mancouet, cotton manufacturer

Frédéric Passy

Natalis Rondot, Chamber of Commerce of Lyons

Maurice Rouvier, deputy, Bouches-du-Rhône

Auguste Sévène, Chamber of Commerce of Lyons

Tezenas du Montcel, Chamber of Commerce of Saint-Etienne

Pierre Tirard, deputy, Seine

Appendix 2

Selected French Import Duties, 1860–1900 (expressed in francs per 100 kilograms except where indicated)

I. *Livestock and Foodstuffs*

II. *Coal, Iron, and Steel*

III. *Machinery and other Metallurgical Manufactures*

IV. *Textiles*

I. Livestock and foodstuffs	Maximum duties (the general tariff)			Minimum duties (the conventional tariff to 1892)		
	pre-1881	1881	1892	1860–1882	1882	1892
Horses	31.20*	30.00*	30.00*	‡	‡	‡
Oxen	3.74*	15.00*	10.00	3.60*	‡	‡
Cows	1.25*	8.00*	10.00	‡	‡	‡
Sheep	0.31*	2.00*	15.50	‡	‡	‡
Hogs	0.31*	3.00*	8.00	0.30*	‡	‡
Poultry	exempt	20.00	20.00	exempt	5.00	‡
Fresh beef	0.62	3.00	25.00	exempt	3.00	‡
Wheat grain	0.62	0.60	5.00	0.60	‡	‡
Wheat flour	1.25	1.20	8.00–12.00	1.20	‡	‡
Semolina and pasta	6.24	6.00	10.00	3.00	3.00	8.00
Table wine (*vin ordinaire*)	5.20†	4.50†	1.20† per degree of alcohol to 10.90°; above 11°, 1.20† alcohol tax on each degree above 11°.	3.50†	2.00†	0.70† per degree of alcohol to 10.90°; above 11°, 0.70† alcohol tax on each degree above 11°.

*Per head.
†Per hectoliter.
‡Item not included in conventional tariff; general tariff applicable.

II. Coal, iron, and Steel	Maximum duties (the general tariff)			Minimum duties (the conventional tariff to 1892)		
	pre-1881	1881	1892	1860–1882	1882	1892
Coal and coke	0.125	0.12	0.12	0.12	0.12	0.12
Pig iron (*fonte brute*)	4.99	2.00	2.00	2.00	1.50	1.50
Bar iron (rails included)	{ 12.48 / 17.47	6.00	6.00	6.00	5.00	5.00
Sheet iron (unstamped)						
more than 1mm thick	24.96	7.50	7.50	7.50	7.00	7.00
1mm or less	24.96	10.00	10.00	10.00	9.00	9.00
Iron wire						
more than 2mm in dia.	37.44	6.00	8.00	6.00	6.00	7.00
1–2mm in diameter	37.44	6.00	11.00	6.00	6.00	10.00
.5–1mm in diameter	37.44	10.00	13.00	10.00	10.00	12.00
less than .5mm	37.44	10.00	22.00	10.00	10.00	20.00
Tinplate	49.92	13.00	{ 14.00§ / 15.00	13.00	12.00	{ 12.00§ / 13.00
Steel rails	37.44	6.00	7.00	9.00	6.00	6.00
Steel bars (ingots)	37.44	9.00	6.00	9.00	9.00	5.00
Sheet steel (hot-rolled, unstamped)						
more than 1mm thick	{ 62.40	9.00	7.50	{ 11.25	9.00	7.00
.06mm–1mm	62.40	9.00	8.00	11.25	9.00	7.50
less than .06mm	93.60	15.00	11.00	15.00	15.00	10.00

§Lower figure for tinplate more than .06mm thick.

III. Machinery and other metallurgical manufactures	Maximum duties (the general tariff)			Minimum duties (the conventional tariff to 1892)		
	pre-1881	1881	1892	1860–1882	1882	1892
Steam engines:						
stationary	31.20	6.00	18.00–	6.00	6.00	12.00–
marine	43.68	12.00	30.00‖	12.00	12.00	20.00‖
locomotive	49.92	10.00	20.00–24.00‖	10.00	9.00	15.00–18.00‖
Boilers:						
cylindrical	37.44	8.00#	12.00	8.00#	8.00#	9.00
tubular	37.44	12.00#	18.00	12.00#	12.00#	14.00
Spinning machines	49.92	10.00	18.00	10.00	5.00	12.00
Weaving machines	18.72	6.00	12.00	6.00	5.00	8.00
Machine tools and unspecified machinery	24.96–81.12‖	6.00–15.00**	15.00	6.00–15.00**	6.00–15.00**	10.00
Steel springs for vehicles	187.20	10.00	18.00	10.00	10.00	12.00
Detached pieces (axles, wheels, etc.)						
in forged iron	74.88–124.80‖	6.00	20.00–	6.00–10.00	6.00–9.00	12.00–
in forged steel	187.20	20.00	50.00‖	10.00–20.00	10.00–20.00	35.00‖
Vehicles:						
coaches (above 125 kg)	prohibited	50.00	60.00	*10% ad valorem*	50.00	50.00
velocipedes	prohibited	120.00	250.00		120.00	220.00
railroad freight cars	prohibited	9.00	11.00	9.00	9.00	9.00

‖ Duty varies according to weight.
Steel boilers taxed at 25 F/100 kg.
** Duty varies according to iron content.

IV. Textiles	Maximum duties (the general tariff)			Minimum duties (the conventional tariff to 1892)		
	pre-1881	1881	1892	1860–1882	1882	1892
Yarns††						
Flax and hemp: simple, unfinished	47.42–205.92	16.00–200.00	21.00–130.00	15.00–100.00	13.00–100.00	16.00–100.00
Jute: unfinished, up to 6,000m per kg.	74.88	6.25–12.50	7.50–12.50	5.00–10.00	5.00–10.00	6.75–11.00
Cotton: simple, unfinished	prohibited	18.50–372.00	19.50–403.00	15.00–300.00	15.00–300.00	15.00–310.00
middle gauge, no. 28	prohibited	25.00	36.50	20.00	20.00	28.00
Cotton: 2 or 3 strand twist, unfinished	prohibited	24.05–483.60	26.52–548.00	19.50–390.00	18.00–360.00	19.50–403.00
Combed wool: simple, bleached or unfinished	prohibited	31.00–124.00	43.00–124.00	25.00–100.00	20.00–80.00	28.00–80.00
Carded wool: simple, bleached or unfinished	prohibited	18.50–56.00	18.50–56.00	25.00–100.00	12.00–36.00	15.00–45.00
Silk floss: simple	78.00–124.80	93.00–149.00	95.00–150.00	75.00–120.00	75.00–120.00	75.00–120.00
Fabrics‡‡						
Linen cloth, unfinished	74.88–582.82	28.00–460.00	31.20–520.00	28.00–300.00	22.00–300.00	24.00–400.00
Damask table linen, unfinished	399.86–699.38	93.00–530.00	121.00–689.00	16% *ad valorem*	75.00–345.00	93.00–530.00

††Multiple numbers indicate range from heaviest to finest gauges.
‡‡Multiple numbers indicate range from sparsest to densest weaves.

Textiles (continued)	Maximum duties (the general tariff)			Minimum duties (the conventional tariff to 1892)		
	pre-1881	1881	1892	1860–1882	1882	1892
Jute cloth, unfinished 6–8 strands per 5 mm²	96.10–160.99	30.00	30.00	24.00	24.00	20.00
Cotton velours, unfinished: velvet / moleskins	prohibited / prohibited	143.00 / 100.00	} 150.00–250.00	85.00 / 60.00	115.00 / 80.00	} 116.00–190.00
Cotton tulle	prohibited	496.00–700.00	650.00–900.00	496.00–700.00	400.00–562.00	500.00–680.00
Cotton: embroidered muslin, unfinished	prohibited	360.00	400.00	10% ad valorem	180.00	320.00
Cotton-silk ribbon	prohibited	372.00	490.00	15% ad valorem	300.00	372.00
Pure woolen broadcloth, 400–550 grams per m²	prohibited	186.00	230.00	10% ad valorem	123.00	180.00
Wool-cotton blends, 400–550 grams per m²	prohibited	99.00	99.00	10% ad valorem	65.00	75.00
Pure silk and silk floss cloth, foulard, tulle, crepe, etc.	288.00–1747.20	exempt	600.00	exempt	exempt	400.00
Pure silk ribbon and velours	998.40	620.00	620.00	500.00	500.00	500.00

SOURCES: Jules Clère, ed., *Les tarifs de douane: Tableaux comparatifs* (Paris, 1880); *Bulletin de statistique et de législation comparée*, 11 (1882–1), 502–554; 31 (1892–1), 12–34, 187–217, 281–302; Eugene O. Golob, *The Méline Tariff* (New York, 1944), p. 174A.

Bibliographical Note

The notes accompanying each chapter indicate the specific documentation on which this study rests. To recapitulate that information in a lengthy bibliography would be redundant. A brief, general discussion of the sources, however, will provide some sense of the overall nature and dimensions of the material I have used and an orientation for future work on French tariff politics.

The late nineteenth century—the period just before the advent of the telephone launched the apparently irreversible decline of written communication—has left us a mass of documentary evidence on economic policy making and interest politics in France. This includes various kinds of official documents, periodical literature, memoirs and other published works, and a huge body of unpublished materials located in archives in Paris and elsewhere. In this study, I have concentrated on three categories of primary sources: unpublished papers in the Archives Nationales and the French Diplomatic Archives (Quai d'Orsay); published government records and statistics; and certain other published sources, including newspapers, journals, and the works of persons involved in tariff reform.

Archival Materials. Several collections were consulted at the Archives Nationales. The papers of the Association de l'industrie française (series 27 AS) provided little on the early phases of the association's activities (1878–1882), but included its annual reports and membership lists for the later years. The legislative archives (series C) included the manuscript minutes of the closed deliberations of the Chamber Tariff Commission in 1878–1881 and 1890–1892 (C 3223–3224 and C 5464–5465, respectively). The largest and most valuable collection consulted at the Archives Nationales was the F^{12} series, the papers of the Ministry of Commerce and Agriculture (to 1882) and of the Ministry of Commerce (after 1882). Scattered through this series are numerous files dealing with various aspects of French commercial policy in the late nineteenth century. The F^{12} series also includes such materials as the dossiers of businessmen receiving the Legion of Honor, which are invaluable for understanding the economic interests involved in the making of commercial policy. The following is a partial list of the files or groups of files in F^{12} explored, utilized, or, as the French say, "despoiled" (dépouiller) in the course of my research:

2573–2584. Requests by manufacturers for temporary admissions, 1860–1876.

4476A–4550. Industrial conditions by departments (prefects' quarterly reports), 1825–1888.

5080–5300, 8540–8750. Legion of Honor accorded to merchants, industrialists, etc. Individual dossiers, 1815–1940.

6191–6198. Trade treaties: diverse materials.

6367, 6418, 6916–6917. Conseil superieur du commerce, inquiry on tariff and trade treaties, 1890.

6416. Ratification of trade treaties, 1882. Papers of the Senate and Chamber committees.

6848–6915. Correspondence on customs duties by product.

6951–6957. Temporary admissions system, 1826–1903.

8851–9046. Economic negotiations with foreign countries by country.

At the archives of the Ministry of Foreign Affairs, the "Négociations commerciales" series was consulted concerning the trade negotiations with England, Belgium, Italy, and Switzerland from the 1870s to the 1890s. Special attention was given to the files on the trade treaties of 1882, which supplement the documents published in the "yellow books" on each treaty.

Government Publications. Less bulky than the archival sources—and perhaps more useful for that reason—were the various official publications bearing on economic matters and the making of tariff policy. These include parliamentary papers—debates, committee reports, the texts of bills, and the like—found in the *Journal officiel de la République française*; the *procès-verbaux* of administrative inquiries conducted by the Conseil supérieur du commerce; and the transcripts of parliamentary inquiries such as those of the Senate in 1877–1878 and of the Chamber Tariff Commission in 1878–1879. Also valuable were the Foreign Ministry's yellow books on the trade negotiations of 1881–1882, mentioned above. The texts of tariff laws and the schedule of duties were found in the Ministry of Finance's *Bulletin de statistique et de législation comparée.* Three statistical publications were indispensable for data on French trade, prices, and industrial production: *Annuaire statistique de la France,* especially volumes 1–20 (1878–1900); *Tableau décennal du commerce de la France avec ses colonies et les puissances étrangères*, vol. 1 (1867–1876), vol. 2 (1877–1886), and vol. 3 (1887–1896); and *Annales du commerce extérieur. France. Faits commerciaux.* The last of these consisted of two series: the reports of the Commission permanente des valeurs de douanes, which included its *valeurs arbitrées* (average prices of items in the tariff schedule computed annually), and the *Exposé comparatif* (French trade figures broken down by commodity, by country, etc.).

Other Published Primary Sources. A major source in this category was the proceedings of chambers of commerce. Almost all French chambers of commerce published their reports, minutes, and the like in some form in the late nineteenth century. The best collection of these is found in the library of the Paris Chamber of Commerce. A less complete collection is found in the Bibliothèque Nationale and a still smaller collection in the Library of Congress. For this study, various proceedings of the chambers of Paris, Rouen, Marseilles, Bordeaux, and the Vosges were consulted.

Another major source for the history of French tariff politics is newspapers and periodicals. In the original research on this subject, I read extensively in the French daily and weekly press, and the present study reflects that legacy in its occasional references to the *Journal des débats, La République française, Le Temps, L'Echo du Nord,* and other newspapers. The most important sources in this category for the present work were the official or quasi-official organs of the free traders and protectionists: the *Journal des économistes* and *L'économiste français* on the free trade side and *L'industrie française* and its successor, *Le travail national,* on the protectionist side. Also important was the organ of the Société des agriculteurs, the *Journal d'agriculture pratique.*

Beyond the periodical literature, the published works of the businessmen and politicians involved in economic politics were often very useful. These included the memoirs of duc Albert de Broglie, Camille de Meaux, and Gustave Roy, and the polemical tracts of Isaac Pereire, Léon Say, Augustin Pouyer-Quertier, Francisque David, Jules Siegfried, and many others.

Secondary Sources. The emphasis on primary sources should not obscure the debt I owe to the work of other historians. Indeed, it would have been difficult, if not impossible, to describe French economic conditions and the operations of French enterprises as fully as I have without the materials published in French economic and business history in the past quarter century. Again, the notes indicate the full range of these sources, but special mention is due the works of Claude Fohlen and Jean Lambert-Dansette on the textile industry and those of Bertrand Gille, Marcel Gillet, and François Crouzet on mining, metallurgy, and heavy industry. Of particular value was the data assembled in Jean Bouvier et al., *Le mouvement du profit en France au XIXe siècle: Matériaux et études* (Paris, 1965); Marcel Gillet, *Les charbonnages du nord de la France au XIXe siècle* (Paris, 1973); and T. J. Markovitch, "L'industrie française de 1789 à 1964," *Cahiers de l'I.S.E.A.,* ser. AF, 6 (1966). Finally, lest we forget that much of historical scholarship involves simply the rediscovery of what previous scholars knew of their own age, I must note three compendia that remain indispensable for the study of the economic and political life of late nineteenth-century France: Emile Levasseur, *Questions ouvrières et industrielles sous le Troisième République* (Paris, 1907), and *Histoire du commerce de la France*, 2 vols. (Paris, 1911–1912); and Adolphe Robert et al., *Dictionnaire des parlementaires français*, 5 vols. (Paris, 1891).

Index

Library of Congress Cataloging in Publication Data

Smith, Michael Stephen, 1944–
Tariff reform in France, 1860–1900.

Bibliography: p.
Includes index.
1. Tariff—France—History.   I. Title.
HF2095.S54   382.7'0944   79-25272
ISBN   0-8014-1257-9